12.99

RECLAIMING TRUTH
Contribution to a Critique of
Cultural Relativism

LEG┌

For my mother

Christopher Norris

RECLAIMING TRUTH

Contribution to a Critique of Cultural Relativism

Lawrence & Wishart
LONDON

Lawrence & Wishart Limited
99A Wallis Road
London E9 5LN

First published 1996
Copyright © Christopher Norris, 1996

ISBN 0-85315-815-0

Photoset in North Wales by
Derek Doyle & Associates, Mold, Clwyd.
Printed and bound in Great Britain by
Redwood Books Ltd, Trowbridge.

CONTENTS

v

ACKNOWLEDGMENTS

This book owes much to my friends, colleagues and postgraduate students in Cardiff, whatever their (often) vigorous differences of view on this or that topic of debate. There is no need to go into detail here since they will doubtless recollect the talking-points readily enough. I am particularly grateful to Robin Attfield and Andrew Belsey, whose hard work as successive heads of the Philosophy Section at Cardiff made it possible to teach, think, read and write to some purpose despite the sundry vexations of present-day British academic life. I also spent a rewarding six weeks at the School of Criticism and Theory (Dartmouth College, Summer 1994) where some of these ideas were tested and refined through discussion with my seminar participants and fellow faculty-members.

There are – as ever – some large debts of gratitude to various people who have commented on work-in-progress, cast a critical eye over early drafts, or invited me to speak at seminars and conferences which helped to clarify my thinking on crucial points. Thanks especially – for these and other reasons – to Roman Alvarez, Gideon Calder, Clive Cazeaux, Sally Davison (for numerous improvements of detail and structure), Ed Dascher, Gary Day, Heather Deegan, John Doherty, Joao Duarte, Michael Durrant, Andrew Edgar, Geoff Harpham, Malcolm Hayward, Terence Hawkes, Carol Jones, Kathy Kerr, Christa Knellwolf (for her ever-ready help and advice), Helena Kozakiewicz, Martin Kreiswirth, Thomas Krogh, Ernesto Laclau, Joe Margolis, Siri Meyer, Miroslav Milović, Stephen Moller, Radmila Nastic, Paul Norcross, Bert Olivier, Marianna Papastephanou, Penny Pether, Danièle Procida, David Roden, Obrad Savic, Peter Sedgwick, Maria-Helena Serodio, Diana Shaffer, Shiva Srinivasan, Morten Stroksnes, Alessandra Tanesini, Carmen Africa Vidal, and Barry Wilkins. Also – for the nth plus 1 occasion – to my wife Alison and my daughters, Clare and Jenny.

Parts of this book have appeared previously in journals or edited volumes. These include the *Yearbook of Research in English and American Literature* (Chapter One), *The Monist Library of Philosophy,* (Chapter Two), *Paragraph* (Chapter Three), *New Left Review* (Chapter Four), *Southern Humanities Review* (Chapter Five), and *The Cambridge Review* (Chapter Six). I am grateful to the editors and publishers concerned for their permission to reprint this material.

INTRODUCTION

These essays were written over a four-year period (1990-94) and offer a range of perspectives – for the most part highly critical – on developments in critical and cultural theory during that time. They express the conviction that developments 'in theory' (for example those around post-structuralism, postmodernism and deconstruction) have a relevance beyond their specialised appeal to a small section of the academic or higher-education community. That is to say, these developments both reflect and exert some impact – in however 'mediated' a fashion – on debates in the wider cultural and socio-political spheres.

We have now witnessed some seventeen years of corrupt, unprincipled and socially divisive Conservative rule, during which period the main opposition has been extra-parliamentary, and largely carried on by activists and pressure-groups dependent on alternative forms of critical analysis and debate. As I write – in June 1995 – there is hardly a day that goes by without some fresh news of government lies and cover-ups, systematic fraud in high places, judicial connivance at false convictions, under-the-counter (government-sponsored) arms deals with brutal and sometimes hostile regimes, insider-trading by those with a hotline to the relevant Treasury sources, and ex-cabinet ministers making huge profits from share options on privatised industries which they themselves – with admirable foresight – made sure to sell off at a large discount while in office. 'Private affluence and public squalor': never has Galbraith's diagnosis been more apt.

To any political theorist viewing these events from a certain distance it might well seem that the British system was undergoing a full-scale legitimation crisis, a terminal breakdown in the structures and values of democratic accountability. (For more on this topic see my discussion of Habermas and Chomsky in Chapter One.) And so indeed it is – a veritable crisis – if judged by the standards that still officially prevail in parliamentary rhetoric and the organs of 'legitimate' (mainstream journalistic) opinion. But things go on pretty much as before with each new scandal duly reported, discussed for some days or weeks, and then let drop for mere lack of interest or through a hard-bitten cynical belief that all politicians are much the same – give or take a few party slogans – and hence that old horses are not worth flogging once their headline-value depreciates. What we have, in fact, is not so much a crisis as a system of perpetual crisis-management, a kind of metastable condition where nothing – no evidence of lies, fraud, corruption, illicit profiteering, and the like – is sufficient to bring the Government down or even raise the question of ministers resigning when caught out in some flagrant abuse of office.

The post-1979 period (closing date presently unknown) will stand as a permanent reminder of how far democracy can be undermined and the values of truth and social justice perverted by an ideologically-driven crusade which adopts a rhetoric of high-toned 'principle' while honouring only the profit-motive and party-political interests. At present it seems to me that we *do* have a legitimation-crisis in this country if one accepts the postulate – basic to any democracy meriting the name – that no government can legitimately rule beyond a certain point of proven incompetence, mendacity, and corruption. But it is equally a sign of our depressed political times that such issues have scarcely been raised in the media or even (parliamentary knockabout aside) by Her Majesty's Loyal Opposition.

Whether cultural and critical theorists have managed to do much better is one question that I hope will be provoked by the essays collected in this book. For it is (or should be) a cause of some concern among left intellectuals that so much recent theorising – especially when conducted under the aegis of postmodernism – does more to promote than to counter the drift toward an ethos of cynical acquiescence in the wholesale levelling of value-distinctions between truth and falsehood, principles and dogma, or democratic institutions and the spurious rhetoric of privatised consumer-based 'freedom' and 'choice'. If these essays are dedicated to any single proposition it is to the claim (*contra* Stanley Fish) that theory has consequences, both positive and negative. On the positive side theory can offer grounds – reasoned and principled grounds – for rejecting much of what presently passes as commonsense or realist political wisdom; it can show that such wisdom is not only ideologically constructed, but also expressive of particular socio-economic and political interests, advanced under the cover of a spurious populist appeal to the 'values' of acquisitive individualism. On the negative side – as with Baudrillard and other purveyors of postmodern fashion – theory can work to promote a generalised scepticism with regard to issues of truth and justice, an outlook whose effect (if not always its avowed purpose) is to render such arguments pointless or absurd.

By way of introduction it is worth signalling a few of my reasons for thus taking issue with the 'politics of theory' as currently construed in various quarters of advanced (e.g. postmodernist or post-structuralist) debate. Chapter One – 'On the Discrimination of Discourse Theories' – puts this case most squarely by asking what results from the linguistic turn that has taken hold across numerous disciplines in the wake of Saussure's much-vaunted 'revolution' in the field of structural linguistics. Its chief effect, as I argue, has been to promote an outlook of fargone epistemological scepticism, joined to the cultural-relativist doctrine that questions of truth and falsehood (or right and wrong) are always internal to some specific language-game or localised 'form of life', and must therefore be judged only in accordance with their own immanent criteria. From which it follows that any dissenting judgment on reasoned or principled grounds – above all, any form of 'enlightened' *Ideologiekritik* – will necessarily involve some presumptive appeal to dogmatic (quasi-universal) standards of justice and truth.

Such ideas have gained ground all the more rapidly through their happening to fit with certain widespread trends in recent continental and post-analytical philosophy. Among them – to continue in this summary style – are the notion of the 'hermeneutic circle' elaborated by Heidegger, Gadamer, Ricoeur and others; Foucauldian or postmodernist assaults on the 'transcendental subject' as merely the relic of an outworn Enlightenment ethos, a mirage thrown up by the humanist imaginary through its delusions of ethico-epistemological grandeur; the strain of neo-pragmatist (or 'strong textualist') thinking popularized by Richard Rorty; Clifford Geertz's idea of 'thick description' as a means of somehow bridging radical differences of culture and language without invoking our own (ethnocentric) discourse of theory, reason or method; and – most influential of all – the Wittgensteinian recourse to 'ordinary language' (along with its associated cultural 'forms of life') as a solvent of manifold deep-laid problems and perplexities. Then again there is the thesis of 'ontological relativity', advanced by the philosopher W.V. Quine, and often taken to support the post-structuralist case that truth-claims of whatever kind – including those of the natural sciences – can only be construed in relation to this or that discourse, paradigm, conceptual scheme, or whatever. From here it is a short enough distance to various currently fashionable forms of holistic or anti-foundationalist argument; and then, at the end of the road these thinkers are travelling, to that strain of all-purpose 'against-theory' argument (premised on the non-availability of reasons or justifying grounds) which has nowadays become the argumentative stock-in-trade of rhetoricians like Stanley Fish.

Given all this it is hardly surprising – though in my view a cause for some concern – that literary and cultural theorists feel themselves emboldened to make large claims about the textual or discursive consitution of history, reality, and scientific truth, along with all the standards, protocols, or validity-conditions that have hitherto characterized those disciplines. In Fish's view this is nothing to worry about since theorizing is anyway a strictly inconsequential activity. At most it provides just an added measure of rhetorical or suasive back-up for beliefs and convictions that can make no sense unless they are already shared by a large enough section of our own 'interpretive community'. So if theories catch on then it is purely a matter of their persuasive or 'performative' aspect, their success in playing by the current (academic, professional, or cultural) rules of the game. And if they don't thus succeed – according to Fish – then there is nothing about them (no argument 'in theory') that could possibly count as a justification for changing our in-place habits of belief. Quite simply, rhetoric goes 'all the way down', to the point where any notion of principled dissent becomes just another form of pious self-deception on the part of certain (no doubt 'sincere') individuals – whether liberal, radical, Marxist, feminist, post-colonial, or whatever – whose 'marginality', so far from placing them at a disadvantage, in fact provides their strongest claim on the allegiance of other, like-minded dissident types. So if nothing succeeds like success, on Fish's view, then equally it is the case that theory always fails by its own professed standards of truth, rigour, critical insight, demystifying power, and so forth.

Of course there is a sense in which theory-talk does have 'consequences', that is to say, in so far as it secures a respectful hearing among people of a kindred (pro-theoretical) persuasion who are thus predisposed to take it seriously. To give it up and adopt Fish's deflationary line would not, he admits, be a sensible strategy for anyone with career ambitions in that particular interpretive community. No more would lawyers (or theorists of liberal jurisprudence) be well-advised to drop their talk of 'principles',

'justice', 'equity', 'due process' and the like, just because they have
been convinced (say by reading Stanley Fish) that such talk was beside
the point. For these 'positive' theorists (like their 'negative',
demystifying counterparts) can scarcely be expected to change their
tune so long as it provides them with a guaranteed *entrée* to the high
ground of peer-group or professional esteem. In which case – as Fish
mock-ruefully concedes – his own arguments 'against theory' can have
no consequences, positive or negative, aside from the somewhat
pyrrhic satisfaction of not falling prey to 'theory-hope' in its more
naive or self-deluding forms. Thus the utmost of Fish's expectation (or
so he would have us believe) is perhaps to get the odd postcard saying
'you're right' while otherwise everyone – or anyone whose views
count for anything – will go on talking and thinking exactly as before.

On the contrary, I would argue: theory has very real consequences,
not least in the ethico-political sphere, as indeed do these arguments –
understandably welcome to the jaded exponents of an 'end-of-
ideology' or 'end-of-history' creed – which reduce all questions of
truth or justice to the dead level of consensus belief. Chapters One and
Five are perhaps best read in tandem, the first as a mainly philosophical
critique of the linguistic (or textualist) turn and its exclusion of
alternative, more adequate resources, and the latter as reflecting on the
way that such fashionable ideas both mirror and promote the 'New
Times' ethos of inert consensus politics. That deconstruction is not a
part of this wider postmodernist drift – that it belongs much more
(despite Derrida's carefully-phrased caveats) to the tradition of
Enlightenment critique – is the main burden of my argument in
Chapters Two and Six. Elsewhere (in 'Spinoza, Marx, Althusser') I
discuss the drastically foreshortened perspective on intellectual history
that has produced, among other things, the notion – *de rigueur* in
post-structuralist circles – that Althusserian Marxism is hopelessly
outdated, tied as it was to that moment of high theoretical ambition
that marked the brief tenure of classic structuralist theory. What drops
out of sight on this reading is the entire philosophical context of
Althusser's work, or at any rate those crucial parts of it – for instance,
his deployment of Spinoza *contra* Hegel – which look like a parade of
mere name-antiquities to chroniclers of post-'68 French cultural
fashion. It is precisely through this lack of a wider, more informed
perspective – along with its parochial fixation on developments within
and around the belated discovery of Saussure – that 'theory' has
become such an ideological shuttlecock, such a feather in the wind of

short-term faddish group allegiance.

A more attentive reading of Althusser should also raise doubts about the current (mainly postmodernist) fashion of exporting literary-critical ideas into other, more-or-less contiguous disciplines (e.g. philosophy, historiography, and jurisprudence). Very often this move goes along with a levelling of the genre-distinction between those disciplines, such that history is treated as just another kind of narrative fiction (Hayden White), philosophy as a 'kind of writing' (Richard Rorty), or law as a wholly rhetorical activity where interpretation goes 'all the way down' (Stanley Fish). In each case this is taken as proof that no purpose can be served by appealing to validity conditions, truth-claims, ideas of right reason, principles of justice, etc, since such talk is finally just a product of suasive definition or communal belief. I contend that this amounts to a species of highly disabling relativist doctrine which – if followed through consistently – would prevent any kind of critical engagement within or between those disciplines. Moreover, I argue that these thinkers are operating with a narrowed and impoverished notion of rhetoric, one that treats language only in terms of its suasive or performative force, and which ignores that other, critical dimension (what Paul de Man calls the 'epistemology of tropes') where rhetoric may be seen to resist or deconstruct its own more questionable workings.

Chapter Four raises similar issues with regard to philosophy of science. It is aimed against the kinds of ultra-relativist doctrine that have lately been advanced by neopragmatists, postmodernists, 'strong' sociologists of knowlege, and others who seek to cast down the idols of scientific truth and method. These ideas all converge on the central thesis: that what counts as 'truth' or 'reality' at any given time is always relative to (or 'constructed in') some particular language-game, 'form of life', or culture-specific context of meanings and values. This is often taken – especially in the social sciences – as an *a priori* argument for excluding any appeal to validity-conditions beyond those which play some significant role in the language-game or life-form concerned. Such thinking finds warrant in Wittgenstein's famously obscure dictum that 'the limits of my language are the limits of my world'. This idea pointed forward from the early *Tractatus* – where it figures as a quasi-mystical acknowledgment of that which lies beyond the furthest bounds of propositional logic or descriptive metaphysics – to the later *Philosophical Investigations*, where it becomes the basis for a doctrine of full-fledged linguistic and cultural relativism. Similar notions are to be found in Thomas Kuhn's influential theory of paradigm-shifts, meaning-variance, and the discontinuity between normal and abnormal (or revolutionary) phases of science; in Paul Feyerabend's far-out ('epistemological-anarchist') variation on these themes; in Lyotard's raising of the narrative 'differend' or language-game incommensurability to a high point of radical postmodernist doctrine; in Foucault's ultra-nominalist approach to questions of meaning, reference, knowledge, and truth; and in various attempts – as with the strong programme in sociology of knowledge – to collapse the distinction between 'context of discovery' and 'context of justification'. What these all have in common is a failure – or downright refusal – to conceive that science can actually make progress in attaining a more adequate (causal-explanatory) grasp of real-world occurrent objects, processes and events.

Such scepticism – I argue – has lately been a cause of great confusion, not only as concerns epistemological (and ontological) issues but also, most notably in Feyerabend's case, with regard to those urgent ethical and socio-political questions that arise from the pursuit of scientific knowledge in various contexts of enquiry. For there is – to put it simply – not much point in criticizing *specific aspects* of science for their (real or supposed) unethical or anti-social consequences if this criticism is based on nothing more than a mixture of reactive prejudice, irrationalist dogma, Heideggerian 'depth-ontological' talk, and a received linguistic-conventionalist belief that all truth-claims (in science and philosophy alike) come down to just so many operative fictions, metaphors, or Rortian 'final vocabularies'. These ideas – common coin among postmodernist thinkers like Lyotard – serve to obscure the nature of science as a disciplined, constructive, truth-seeking enterprise. Moreover they block the way to an informed ethical or socio-political criticism of that enterprise which is not (so to speak) routinely underwhelmed by the evidence of real and continuing scientific progress in various fields of enquiry. For on the relativist account – whether in philosophy of science, in epistemology, historiography, political theory, or ethics – there could exist no basis for such criticism, no grounds of adequate factual or evaluative judgment.

It is this predicament that Lyotard blithely takes on board when he speaks of the 'postmodern condition' as that which necessitates 'judging without criteria', thereby opening thought to the maximum range of narrative differends, 'phrases in dispute', or diverse (strictly incommensurable) language-games. Hence also his fondness for those speculative aspects of the new physics – indeterminacy, complementarity, chaos-theory, quantum nonlocality and the like – enlisted in support of his thesis that science has now moved on into a postmodern epoch where 'constative' questions of truth and falsehood give way to a purely 'performative' or pragmatic reckoning. In Chapter Four I discuss some of the confusions that have characterised recent ideas about science among literary theorists, cultural historians, and proponents of the so-called 'strong' programme in sociology of knowledge. More constructively I put the case for a causal-realist approach to these issues inspired largely by the work of thinkers such as Wesley Salmon and Roy Bhaskar. This approach takes due account of depth-ontological advances in our knowledge of the physical world, though here, I should add, in a decidedly non-Heideggerian sense of the terms 'deep' and 'ontology', one which makes no concessions to the current anti-realist trend in philosophy of science. That is to say, it postulates a range of explanatory factors – causal attributes, dispositional properties, microphysical (molecular or subatomic) structures, etc – rather than offering a vastly generalized (hence altogether vacuous) diagnosis of 'technology' or 'Western metaphysics' as the deep-laid source of all our latterday discontents. At the same time it avoids the converse and equally disabling positivist assumption that such advances belong to a realm quite apart from the sphere of ethical value-enquiry or informed social criticism.

It seems to me that thinkers like Feyerabend, Rorty, and Lyotard are led into all manner of epistemological and normative confusion by this notion of science as an overweening 'discourse' which can best be cut down to size by treating it as just one language-game among others, devoid of any genuine cognitive or truth-telling warrant. Let me therefore close these prefatory remarks by re-framing the above schematic outline as a series of questions that the reader may find it helpful to keep in mind. What is (was?) the 'Enlightenment' tradition, or – as Habermas resonantly phrases it – the unfinished project of modernity? What is the relation between concept and metaphor (or reason and rhetoric) in the texts of philosophy? How should we understand Quine's doctrine of 'ontological relativity' in connection with similar ideas put forward by thinkers of a post-structuralist or postmodernist persuasion? Can truth-claims be reduced, as Foucault would have it, to transient effects of the epistemic will-to-power within discourse, or again (following Rorty) to so many preferential

language-games or 'final vocabularies?' What remains of the subject –
the Kantian reasoning, willing and judging subject – in the wake of its
supposed dissolution into the field of shifting discursive modalities or
multiple decentred 'subject-positions'? Is deconstruction indeed – as
some would claim – just a rather more specialized 'philosophical'
variant of theses propounded by postmodernist gurus like Lyotard?
Or is it not rather (as I argue here) a sustained analytic engagement
with issues that postmodernism has scarcely begun to address? Above
all: what resources can criticism muster in the face of this currently
widespread drift toward an ultra-relativist orthodoxy which in turn
lends support – whether wittingly or not – to forms of acquiescent
consensus ideology?

These questions may be seen to cut right across the boundary-lines
traditionally drawn between epistemology, ethics, politics, and
aesthetics or literary theory. To this extent my approach is
interdisciplinary and – to adopt the current parlance – 'intertextual'.
But I am also much concerned to specify the ways in which particular
disciplines of thought involve certain protocols of reading or method
that cannot be abandoned without giving up any claim to critical
validity. So far as possible I avoid assuming any previous specialized
knowledge, on the reader's part, of issues in recent analytic philosophy
or of developments in the 'other' (Continental) tradition. My hope is
to direct their interest towards a range of perhaps unfamiliar texts, and
also to encourage reflection on these matters from a standpoint largely
unbeholden to the current 'advanced' theoretical wisdom.

Note: I have not provided references for this Introduction since the
texts alluded to – for example, Althusser, Derrida, Foucault,
Habermas, Quine, Rorty – all receive adequate documentation
elsewhere in the book.

1

ON THE DISCRIMINATION OF DISCOURSE-THEORIES: THE 'LINGUISTIC TURN' IN PHILOSOPHICAL PERSPECTIVE

I INTRODUCTION

In its broadest, least technical sense *discourse* means simply 'talk' or 'conversation', sometimes with the hint of a didactic purpose (thus 'sermon', 'treatise' or 'lengthy address to some particular topic'). This latter development seems rather at odds with the word's etymology, going back to the Latin verb *discurrere*: 'to run about', 'range widely', 'wander off course', etc. And indeed there is something of the same ambiguity – or tendency to pull in opposite directions – when the word is taken up (as it has been often of late) into the usage of various specialized disciplines. I shall therefore look at some of the issues it raises for philosophy, linguistics, and the human sciences at large.

The allusion in my title is to A.O. Lovejoy's 1924 essay 'On the Discrimination of Romanticisms', his plea for a clearer, more nuanced sense of cultural perspective in the deployment of such ill-defined generic or period concepts.[1] As an intellectual historian and pioneering figure in the field of comparative literature, Lovejoy had obvious professional reasons for adopting this propaedeutic line. But there is a subtext to his essay, an undertow of cultural anxiety, which has perhaps become more legible now with the subsequent unfolding of historical events. Like Auerbach, Curtius and other comparatists of the interwar period, he is concerned not only with matters of scholarly scruple but also with the need to exercise those skills in the service of improved historical understanding, and – beyond that – in the interests of preserving a humane and civilized public sphere where such issues can be raised aside from all the pressures of partisan cultural strife.

Thus, for Lovejoy, it is important to distinguish, within the term 'Romanticism', those currents of enlightenment and counter-enlightenment thinking whose legacy is still very much with us, and whose complex relationship – across and within national boundaries – has exerted such a strong (even fateful) influence on the course of recent history. So there is more at stake in Lovejoy's work than an arcane dispute as to the meaning of that word in various contexts of cultural and socio-historical enquiry.

In this chapter I argue that the term 'discourse' is likewise a source of much confusion; moreover, that the current 'linguistic turn' across various disciplines has given rise to just the kinds of deep-laid bewilderment – the loss of important historical, philosophical and ethical distinctions – that Lovejoy deplores in 'Romanticism' and its cognates. To begin with, I shall follow his lead by offering a brief (and necessarily schematic) account of how the word has taken on such a range of disparate senses. I shall then broaden the discussion to include those various theoretical contexts of debate where it has figured, most often, as a flag-word for the more extreme present-day forms of ontological, epistemic, or cultural-linguistic relativism. And finally – to offset this negative line of argument – I shall discuss a number of thinkers (Chomsky, Habermas and Derrida chief among them) whose work provides a range of alternative resources for re-thinking the linguistic turn in relation to the truth-claims and values of enlightenment critique.

II BENVENISTE, LACAN, HABERMAS

The linguist Emile Benveniste was among the most influential thinkers about issues of language and subjectivity. On his account 'discourse' has to do with those aspects of language that can only be interpreted with reference to the speaker, to his or her spatio-temporal location, or to other such variables which serve to specify the localized context of utterance.[2] It thus lays claim to a distinctive and well-defined area of study, one that includes the personal pronouns (especially 'I' and 'you'), deictics of place ('here', 'there', etc.) and temporal markers ('now', 'today', 'next week') in the absence of which the utterance in question would lack determinate sense. Structural linguistics – following Saussure – treats language (*la langue*) as a trans-individual network or economy of signifying elements, conceived in ideal abstraction from the individual speech-act. Benveniste on the contrary sets out to analyse the various subject-positions ('enunciative modalities') that constitute the realm of discourse, *parole*, or language in its social-communicative aspect. But what he shares with Saussure's post-structuralist disciples is the working premise that subjectivity is constructed in and through language, since quite simply there is nothing (no possible appeal to the Kantian transcendental subject, to *a priori* concepts, self-evident truths, primordial intuitions, facts of experience or whatever) that would offer a secure vantage-point beyond the play of discursive representations. Clearly there are large philosophical implications bound up with this idea of language (or discourse) as the absolute horizon of intelligibility for thought and knowledge in general.

This is also what sets Benveniste's work apart from J.L. Austin's otherwise similar concern with the kinds of performative or speech-act modality exhibited by various instances of everyday discourse.[3] It may well be the case – as argued by post-structuralists like Shoshana Felman – that Austin's account of how we 'do things with words' is itself subject to all manner of performative slips, 'misfires', and returns of the linguistic-unconscious repressed.[4] But these anomalies require a good deal of ingenious coaxing from the style of down-to-earth, commonsense talk that goes along with Austin's suasive appeal to the wisdom enshrined in 'ordinary language'. Benveniste writes out of a very different intellectual culture, one that has traditionally laid most stress on the Cartesian virtues of system, method, and lucid self-knowledge. All the more provocative, therefore, is the way that his work seems to open a cleft – a moment of slippage or displacement – between the self-possessed subject posited by Descartes' *cogito, ergo sum* and the subject as construed in discourse-theoretical terms, that is to say, a pronominal 'shifter' caught up in the endless passage from signifier to signifier. Such at least is the reading of Benveniste promoted by post-structuralists eager to dissolve all the certitudes (or 'foundationalist' truth-claims) of philosophy from Descartes to the present. For on this account it is the merest of illusions – albeit an illusion deeply bound up with the entire project of 'Western metaphysics' – to imagine that thinking could ever attain the kind of punctual, transparent, self-present grasp envisaged by 'logocentric' reason. In Benveniste's terms the error can be diagnosed as a failure to distinguish between two levels of discourse, those pertaining respectively to the 'subject of the enounced' and the 'subject of enunciation'. Thus when Descartes offers the *cogito* as an indubitable ground of knowledge – a last refuge against all the threats of epistemological doubt – he can do so only by performing what amounts to a rhetorical sleight-of-hand, an utterance that seeks to collapse this distinction between the 'I' who thinks and the 'I' that is constituted as the subject-object of its own reflection. In which case, post-structuralists would argue, the Cartesian project necessarily miscarries since it generates linguistic aporias beyond its power to contain or control. And the same applies to those subsequent philosophies – from Kant to Husserl – which invoke some version of the transcendental subject as locus and arbiter of truth.

'Moi, j'est un autre' – Rimbaud's remark has become a watchword of recent post-structuralist theory. What Freud described as the split (*Spaltung*) between various levels of conscious, unconscious and preconscious mental functioning is now conceived as a kind of perpetual slippage from signifier to signifier, a process of *dérèglement* (Rimbaud again) whose effect is to deprive the first-person pronoun of its purely 'imaginary' self-sufficient plenitude. Hence the recent spate of speculative work – mostly by literary theorists – on the margin between philosophy and psychoanalysis, the latter having taken its own post-structuralist turn through the teachings of Jacques Lacan. To this way of thinking – 'French Freud' in colloquial parlance – there is no means of access to the unconscious save through the discourse between analyst and patient, a discourse whose transferential character is marked by all manner of linguistic swerves, substitutions, and displacements.[5] Moreover, we can best read Freud by attending to those symptomatic moments in his work where the 'agency of the letter' (or the deviant 'logic' of the signifier) emerges to disrupt and complicate his own project. If the unconscious is 'structured like a language', as Lacan claims, then the insights of linguistics – especially those derived from the work of structuralist thinkers like Saussure and Jakobson – are simply indispensable for any reading that would respect the exigencies of the Freudian text and not fall prey to various kinds of naive or mystified account. This may involve some degree of terminological latitude, as when Lacan suggests that terms like 'condensation' and 'displacement' were adopted by Freud (*faute de mieux*) from the mechanistic discourse current in his time, but that now – after Jakobson – we should render the one as 'metaphor' and the other as 'metonymy', thus restoring the unconscious to its proper dimension as a field of tropological drives and exchanges. Metaphor then becomes that aspect of the dreamwork – or the process of secondary revision – whereby one signifier substitutes for another, or where numerous meanings condense into a single ('overdetermined') image or symptom. And metonymy stands in not only for 'displacement' – the endless passage from signifier to signifier – but also for *desire* in so far as it involves a kind of structural non-fulfilment, an ineluctable lack which he equates with the Saussurian 'bar' between signifier and signified.[6] For desire is distinguished from straightforward (instinctual or physical) need by its entanglement in precisely those structures of discourse – of transference and deferred meaning – which prevent it from ever coinciding with its object in a moment of achieved equilibrium.

We are therefore hopelessly mistaken if we hold psychoanalysis accountable to standards of enlightened truth-seeking thought. It is the sheer *opacity* of the Freudian text – its resistance to any kind of lucid expository treatment – which Lacan views as the purveyor of truth, albeit a 'truth' that can scarcely be expressed in conceptual or rational-discursive terms. This is also (though some would consider it a charitable reading) why Lacan's own texts go out of their way to create syntactic and stylistic obstacles for anyone who looks to them in hope of discovering an easy route of access to the Freudian corpus. On the contrary: such access is everywhere denied by a style that raises difficulty into a high point of principle, or which (less kindly) takes bafflement as a guard against the requirements of plain good sense. Again it is Descartes who figures most often as the thinker who first set philosophy out on its delusory quest for 'clear and distinct ideas'. But psychoanalysis has travelled the same path, Lacan argues, in so far as it has embraced the imaginary ideal of a pure, unimpeded self-knowledge, an end-point to the therapeutic process when all such resistances would fall away and the subject accede to a full understanding of its own (hitherto repressed or sublimated) motives and desires. It is against this heresy – which he associates chiefly with American ego-psychology – that Lacan directs both his fiercest polemics and his practice of a style that makes no concessions to the Cartesian 'tyranny of lucidity'.

In support of this position he offers a new reading of Freud's famous sentence 'Wo *Es* war, soll *Ich* werden' (normally translated: 'Where *Id* was, there shall *Ego* be'). On the standard account – backed up by Freud's analogy with the draining of the Zuider See – this is taken to mean that psychoanalysis performs a similar task of reclamation, delving down (as it were) into the 'deep' unconscious and restoring its content to the daylight realm of consciously available memories, thoughts, and experiences. But as Lacan reads it the sentence bears a precisely opposite meaning, i.e. that consciousness can never attain that wished-for state of theoretical mastery, since it must always find itself subject to forces (or effects of linguistic displacement) quite beyond its conceptual grasp. Hence his rewriting of Descartes' formula in a version that insists on the absolute *impossibility* of closing this gap between the ego-ideal (a product of 'imaginary' misrecognition), and the order of discourse – or signifying chain – which constantly subverts that specular self-image. 'It is not', Lacan says, 'a question of knowing whether I speak of myself in a way that conforms to what I am, but rather of knowing whether I am the same as that of which I speak'. And again, 'What one ought to say is: I am not wherever I am the plaything of my thought; I think of what I am where I do not think to think'. (' "*Cogito ergo sum*" *ubi cogito, ibi non sum*'.)[7] Psychoanalysis could scarcely go further in its quarrel with the truth-claims of philosophy, or (some would say) in its perverse desire to discredit those claims by treating them as symptoms of philosophy's epistemic will-to-power over language, the unconscious, and whatever falls outside its own *de jure* privileged domain. It is not surprising, therefore, that Lacan's work has received little notice from philosophers except those few (mostly French or French-influenced) thinkers who have themselves embraced some version of the current linguistic/post-structuralist turn.[8] For if Lacan is right – whatever that could mean – then philosophy has always been the unwitting dupe of a language that everywhere exceeds and baffles its powers of conceptual grasp.

Some philosophers – Jürgen Habermas among them – have rejected not only this Lacanian reading of Freud but the entire post-structuralist project of which it forms a prominent part. In his early book *Knowledge and Human Interests* (1968) Habermas set out to defend psychoanalysis against the charge of 'irrationalism' that has so often been levelled against it.[9] Freud is on the contrary a thinker who belongs very firmly to the Enlightenment tradition, or in the company of those – from Kant to Husserl – who have sought to sustain the 'philosophic discourse of modernity' in face of various threats from sceptics and opponents like Nietzsche. At this time Habermas had not yet adopted his stance of overt antagonism toward post-structuralism and allied strains of counter-enlightenment thought. But it is clear enough already that he interprets Freud's cardinal maxim – 'Where *Id* was, there shall *Ego* be' – in a sense diametrically opposed to Lacan's cryptic rendition. On this account the phrase is best construed as a version of the Kantian motto *Sapere aude!* ('Have the courage to think for yourself!'); that is to say, as an appeal to the values of reason and emancipatory knowledge in the private as well as the public-political sphere. Thus for Habermas the task of psychoanalysis is to bring the subject to a conscious (reflective) awareness of those repressed or sublimated memories, motives and desires that would otherwise stand in its way. In so far as Freud's theories can claim any kind of intellectual validity or therapeutic power they must be seen as deriving from that same tradition of enlightened *Ideologiekritik*, a tradition whose resources Habermas equates with the interests of a genuine participant democracy premised on the values of open dialogical exchange.

Nothing could be further from Lacan's response to the question that Freud famously posed in the title of his late essay 'Analysis Terminable or Interminable?'. From a Lacanian standpoint there is simply no end to the detours of the unconscious signifier, the way that language – or the discourse of desire – is forever caught up in a metonymic chain whereby truth becomes purely a figment of the Imaginary, a function whose value cannot be assigned except in relation to this or that transient subject-position, like the purloined letter in the story by Edgar Allan Poe which Lacan took as a kind of allegorical *mise-en-scène* for the psychoanalytic encounter.[10] Such are the complexities of transference and counter-transference – the two-way exchange of symbolic roles between patient and analyst – that nobody can occupy the privileged position envisaged by the ego-psychologists and other perverters of the Freudian truth. Like Descartes (as Lacan reads him) they are the victims of a specular misrecognition whose effect is precisely to bolster the ego's deluded quest to make reason master in its own house. Small wonder that Habermas, in his recent writings, has targeted this whole post-structuralist discourse as a species of latter-day Nietzschean irrationalism allied to a deeply conservative turn against the truth-claims of enlightened critique.[11] To which the Lacanians respond – predictably enough – by deploring his attachment to an outworn discourse of reason, enlightenment, and truth, a discourse (so it is argued) whose liberal rhetoric conceals a tyrannizing will-to-power over language, desire, and whatever eludes its self-assured rational grasp.[12]

It is hard to imagine any possible *rapprochement* between those (like

Habermas) who would uphold the values of critical-emancipatory thought and those others (postmodernists and post-structuralists among them) who regard such values as possessing no more than an illusory or long-since obsolete appeal within the philosophic discourse of modernity. And this despite the fact – very evident in his recent writings – that Habermas has himself travelled a long way toward acknowledging the force of certain anti-foundationalist arguments, thus abandoning at least some areas of the Kantian high ground staked out in *Knowledge and Human Interests*. What this shift of focus amounts to is a version of the currently widespread 'linguistic turn', the invocation of language as an ultimate horizon of intelligibility, or the denial that we can ever attain any knowledge save that vouchsafed through discourses, language-games, signifying systems, structures of representation, etc. Habermas has taken full measure of these arguments, redefining his project in terms that derive from speech-act philosophy and the theory of communicative action, as distinct from those epistemological concerns that characterized his earlier work.[13] But he rejects the postmodern-pragmatist idea that discourse goes all the way down, that rhetoric (not reason) is what finally counts, since the only criterion for a valid or persuasive argument is the extent to which it happens to fit in with some existing language-game or cultural 'form of life'.[14] Such doctrines are philosophically bankrupt, he argues, expressing as they do a vote of no confidence in the capacity of thought to criticize false beliefs, to distinguish valid from invalid truth-claims, and to analyse the causes – as distinct from the reasons – that produce various kinds of prejudice, self-ignorance, or 'commonsense' dogmatism. Moreover, they are politically and ethically harmful in so far as they promote a conservative agenda of inert consensus-based values and attitudes, an 'end-of-ideology' creed which equates truth with what is (currently and contingently) 'good in the way of belief'.

This is why Habermas describes his project as a 'universal pragmatics', one that makes room for a critique of those existing values from the standpoint of an 'ideal speech-situation', a regulative idea (in the Kantian sense) of what we can and should aspire to as participant members of a free and open democratic order. For it is clearly the case that any current (*de facto*) consensus may always be subject to a range of distorting pressures and influences, as for instance through the workings of state censorship, of press manipulation, media bias, educational underprivilege, inequalities of access to the relevant information-sources, etc. What Habermas therefore seeks to conserve

– and what sets him decidedly at odds with the current postmodern-pragmatist wisdom – is a critical sense of those factors that conspire to thwart or frustrate the shared aspiration to a public sphere of openly communicable reasons, motives, interests and values. Nor are these issues confined to the realm of abstruse philosophical debate. For it can readily happen – as with recent variations on the post-ideological/'New World Order' theme – that some existing currency of consensus-belief, for example in the virtues of 'liberal democracy', US-style, gets taken at face value without any question being raised as to the gulf that exists between rhetoric and reality, or the actual effects of US policy in the domestic and geo-political spheres.[15] Only by keeping such distinctions in view can philosophy live up to its social and ethical task, that is to say, its commitment to a critique of consensus values wherever these serve as a refuge or smokescreen for other, less humanly accountable interests.[16] To this extent – and despite his concessions to the anti-foundationalist case – Habermas still keeps faith with the discourse of enlightened or critical-emancipatory thought, a project whose central (Kantian) tenet is the exercise of reason against the more beguiling self-images and rhetorics of the age.

III FIGURES DRAWN IN SAND: FOUCAULT ON KANT

There are, as I have suggested, some large issues at stake in this ongoing conflict of interpretations over the term 'discourse' and its various modes of employment. For if it is indeed the case that reality and truth are wholly linguistic or discursive constructs then the way seems open to just the kind of blanket scepticism that has typified recent thinking in the more 'advanced' quarters of cultural theory. Nowhere is this doctrine pushed further – and the problems with it more tellingly revealed – than in Michel Foucault's lifelong attempt to practise a form of intellectual history that would finally dispense with all notions of 'truth' save that which treats it (in Nietzschean fashion) as a product of the epistemic will-to-power whose various discursive structures and modalities constitute the object of analysis. In *Les mots et les choses* (1966) this project is conceived as an 'archaeology' of knowledge, a digging-down through the sedimented layers of discourse to uncover the shifting paradigms – the diverse orders of representation – that have characterized 'truth' during various epochs of the Western (post-renaissance) natural and human sciences.[17] What is thereby revealed, according to Foucault, is an ensemble of signifying practices that regulates the economy of discourse at any given time, and which thus determines what shall count as a veridical proposition, a valid truth-claim or authorized statement. Such is the unthought axiomatics – the deep grammar of presupposition – which cuts across received disciplinary boundaries and brings to light the structural kinship that exists between (for instance) the emergent discourses of nineteenth-century anthropology, philosophy, historiography, linguistics, political economy, Darwinian evolutionary theory, and so forth. At this point 'a deep historicity entered the heart of things', displacing the earlier (synchronic or classificatory) paradigm, and installing 'man' – the Kantian subject – as a strange 'empirico-transcendental doublet', a creature of necessity in the natural realm but also, in the ethico-political sphere, the author and agent of his own freely-willed destiny. Foucault (like Lacan) sees nothing but grandiose delusion in this attempt to wrest a space for enlightenment values – for autonomy, critique, and practical reason – from the order of discursive representations wherein the humanist subject discovers its own imaginary lineaments. Hence his famous dictum that 'man' is just a momentary fold in the fabric of discourse, an 'invention of comparatively recent date', a 'figure drawn in sand at the ocean's edge, soon to be erased by the incoming tide'.[18] For it is Foucault's contention – echoed by numerous subscribers to the recent vogue for 'theoretical anti-humanism' – that with the advent of language (or discourse) as an ultimate horizon of intelligibility we are somehow compelled to relinquish all ideas of autonomous reflection, agency, or choice.

Nothing really changes, in this respect at least, when Foucault later drops the archaeological metaphor and adopts a more overtly Nietzschean rhetoric of 'genealogy' and 'power/knowledge'. Undoubtedly this change marked a turning-away from the ethos of detached, almost clinical rigour that had characterized his writing in *Les mots et les choses* and its methodological companion-volume '*L'Archéologie du savoir*' (1969). From now on Foucault would repudiate what he saw as the false ideal of scholarly objectivity, following Nietzsche in his call for an active, interventionist project of enquiry which acknowledged its own motivating interests and which set out to write a 'history of the present' – a strong-revisionist account

– rather than a 'monumental history' based on outmoded (positivist) notions of method and truth.[19] Similar changes were occurring elsewhere on the scene of avant-garde French cultural debate, as the period of high structuralist rigour gave way to a post-structuralist fascination with whatever seemed to elude, baffle or frustrate the best efforts of systematizing thought. Thus, for example, Roland Barthes announced an end to the old (and, as he now thought, deluded) 'scientific' quest for a narrative poetics that would do for literary criticism what Lévi-Strauss had done for structural anthropology, that is, provide a universal grammar of signifying functions which could be shown to underlie the surface multiplicity of myths, customs, and storytelling conventions. Having himself once subscribed to this heroic endeavour – in influential works like *Mythologies*, and his essay 'The Structural Analysis of Narrative' – Barthes now declared it a forlorn hope, a project that would always miscarry in so far as it ignored the plurality of meanings encountered in the reading of any given text.[20] Such was the poverty of structuralism, its refusal to acknowledge the irreducibility of writing (*écriture*) to any model or paradigm drawn from the stock of existing narrative grammars.

This shift in Barthes' position was clearly signalled in the title of his essay 'From Work to Text', suggesting as it does the obsolescence of the literary 'work' concept (turned back towards notions of organic unity, authorial control, self-contained narrative structure, etc) and gesturing toward an open-ended 'freeplay' of signification – an 'unlimited textuality' – which at last slips the bonds of that old, repressive hermeneutic regime. 'Change the Work Itself' was another such essay of chastened anti-methodological retrospect, lamenting the fact that his own techniques of structural demystification (as practised so brilliantly in *Mythologies*) could nowadays be deployed with perfect assurance by any student who had learned the required set of tricks.[21] Henceforth – for Barthes as for Foucault – it is a question of actively *transforming* myths and their naturalized (bourgeois-ideological) content by the practice of a writing that rejects all notions of latent truth or methodological rigour. And in *S/Z* (1970), his massively extended 'analysis' of Balzac's novella *Sarrasine*, Barthes shows just how far it is possible to go with this idea of the text – not the unitary 'work' – as a tissue of signifying codes and conventions, a field opened up for active intervention on the part of a reader no longer constrained by orthodox notions of interpretative truth. If the 'birth of the reader' is always at the cost of the 'death of the author', then Barthes is more than happy to pay this price, along with the abandonment of a structuralist paradigm whose claims now strike him – despite their erstwhile appeal – as a last refuge of that same old nostalgia for the long-lost stability of method and meaning.

Foucault pursued a parallel course in his passage from a broadly structuralist 'archaeology' of the human sciences to the Nietzschean 'geneaological' researches that occupied his thinking from the early 1970s onwards. But in his case the shift was more overtly politicized, aimed toward exposing the ubiquitous relation between knowledge and power, or the complicity that had always existed between 'truth' and its various (disciplinary and institutional) contexts of production. This called not so much for an explanatory *theory*, in the structuralist or demythologizing mode, as for a Nietzschean 'transvaluation of values', a *wirkliche Geschichte* ('practical-performative history') that would challenge the received (doxographic) account by undermining the very grounds – or discursive terrain – upon which these issues had hitherto been engaged. If Marxism had once gestured in this direction ('Philosophers have merely interpreted the world; our task is to change it!'), the radical force of such injunctions had now been lost by its constantly lapsing back into truth-based or epistemological talk of ideology, false consciousness, reality *versus* appearances, etc. And the same applied to any 'discourse' – structuralism included – whose aim was to establish its own veridical credentials by adopting a self-deceptive stance of noble disinterest beyond what Nietzsche had unerringly diagnosed as the agonistic field of power/knowledge differentials. This stance could be maintained only by ignoring the extent to which knowledge was *always* in the service of a covert, disavowed, but none the less imperious will-to-power over bodies and minds.

Such had indeed been Foucault's major premise in his series of copiously documented studies on the history of psychiatric medicine, of clinical regimes, penal institutions, and of human sexuality as an object of various disciplinary techniques, from ancient Greece and Rome, through the Christian confessional, to Freudian psychoanalysis.[22] This work is sufficiently well-known for me to offer only the briefest of summaries here. In each case, he argues, we tend to take the view that progress comes about through greater understanding, and that as attitudes become more tolerant – more 'liberal', 'progressive', or 'enlightened' – so power loses its coercive (or punitive) aspect and yields place to knowledge (to welfare provision, social services, psychiatric counselling etc) as a far more civilized means of addressing such problems. To Foucault's way of thinking, on the contrary, this 'progress' constitutes a massive extension and refinement of power/knowledge, a range of techniques whereby the forms of disciplinary surveillance and control reach down into every last detail of our social, political, libidinal, sexual, and affective life-world. Of course we have travelled a long way ('we' inhabitants of the present-day Western liberal democracies) from the gruesome scenes of judicial torture and public execution so graphically described in the opening pages of Foucault's *Discipline and Punish*. And we can likewise – if with rather less confidence – think ourselves decently remote from the kinds of coercive (self- and other-mutilating) discipline that once sought to police the boundaries of normative heterosexual conduct against the perceived threat of 'deviant' behaviour or 'perverse' acts and desires. All the same we are deluded, on Foucault's account, if we derive comfort from entertaining what he calls the 'repressive hypothesis', i.e. the notion that we have lately emerged from some dark (perhaps 'Victorian') age of sexual prejudice and ignorance into the daylight world of achieved self-knowledge and resulting liberal tolerance. For this ignores the extent to which our sexual desires have now become subject to an endless and compulsive putting-into-discourse, a process whose origins can indeed be traced back to the Graeco-Roman (especially the stoic) techniques of 'voluntary' discipline and self-formation, but which takes a more intensive confessional form with the passage to Christian and latterday secular modes of internalized restraint. And this is also the case – Foucault argues – with those clinical, psychiatric and penal regimes whose relinquishment of power in its overt, 'spectacular' form goes along with a whole specialized array of power/knowledge techniques, means by which the subject is persuaded 'voluntarily' to monitor the truth of his or her actions, thoughts and desires. So far from countering or alleviating the effects of power, such discourses provide it with numerous points of entry to regions of experience – of 'private' self-discipline – that were hitherto beyond its reach.

Hence Foucault's continued (and intensified) campaign to discredit the truth-claims of enlightenment critique, a discourse whose sole effect – as he saw it – was to legitimize this process under cover of a pseudo-emancipatory rhetoric premised on the false (imaginary) ideals of autonomy, self-knowledge, and truth. But the question then arises as to how Foucault can justify his talk of resistance, opposition, language as 'counter-praxis' and so forth, given his stance of thoroughgoing Nietzschean disdain for those values. For if indeed it is the case – as he purports to believe – that any such dissident stance is constructed in and through some existing language-game of instituted power/knowledge, then one might as well admit that resistance is coopted from the outset, reduced to just a move on the chequer-board of available discourses or subject-positions. There are many indications in the last essays and interviews – before his tragic early death in 1984 – that Foucault had come around to acknowledging this problem and re-thinking the relation between truth, ethics, and the values of enlightenment critique.[23] Among them is the fact that he returns so often to Kant as the founder of that philosophic discourse of modernity whose consequences we are still living through, and which cannot be treated – Foucault now thinks – as just another transient episode in the history of shifting power/knowledge formations. In fact these late writings are everywhere concerned with the three great questions of Kantian thought in its epistemological, ethical, and socio-political aspects ('What can we know?' 'What ought we to do?' and 'What may we reasonably hope for?')

It would nevertheless be wrong to offer these texts as evidence that Foucault underwent a dramatic conversion-process, a belated *rapprochement* with enlightenment values and truth-claims. Such a reading would have to ignore the many signs that Foucault is adapting Kant to his own purposes, that he still views with scepticism Kant's high claims for the transcendental subject as autonomous locus of reason, judgment and will, and moreover – following from this – that he redefines 'autonomy' in a sense more akin to the aesthetic self-fashioning of a poet like Baudelaire than the Kantian exercise of practical reason in the public (ethical and socio-political) sphere. This revisionist strategy appears most plainly in his essay 'What Is Enlightenment?', a piece that takes its bearings – and indeed its very title – from one of Kant's addresses to that theme, but which effectively skews the whole debate around so as to grant the aesthetic (or the project of 'autonomous' self-creation) absolute pride of place.[24] In which case – as Richard Rorty is quick to point out – he might as well push all the way with this idea, forget about old-fashioned grandiose topics like the 'political responsibility of the intellectuals', and acknowledge (in postmodern-liberal-pragmatist style) that, since language-games are all that we have, then the best thing to do is to produce new 'vocabularies', new images and metaphors of the self that

answer to our private needs and desires.[25] Such, after all, is the lesson
to be drawn from those various discourses, Foucault's among them,
that have left no room for the Cartesian *cogito*, for the Kantian
transcendental subject, or for the 'self' as anything more than a passing
assemblage out of the languages currently and contingently to hand.

So when Foucault returns to Kant it is still with the purpose – as
Rorty reads him – of putting those self-images back where they
belong, in the field of open-ended linguistic possibility, of 'private'
self-descriptions that overstep the mark if they claim any warrant, any
legislative power, in the wider (ethical or socio-political) sphere. On
the positive side this means that gifted individuals or 'strong
revisionists' like Foucault can offer a whole range of languages,
role-models, self-images, life-styles and so forth for emulation by
other, less gifted types. In negative terms it translates into the
cautionary message: that intellectuals can best be kept from doing
harm by ignoring (or debunking) their political pretensions, reading
them in the way we read the novelists or poets, and thus coaxing them
back into the fold of postmodern 'liberal ironists'. And if this invites
the charge of political bad faith – of private-aestheticist indulgence –
then Foucault has a ready line of response, according to Rorty. He can
always say: 'I stand with you as a fellow citizen, but as a philosopher I
stand off by myself, pursuing projects of self-invention which are none
of your concern'. And again: 'I am not about to offer philosophical
grounds for being on your side in public affairs, for my philosophical
project is a private one which provides neither motive nor justification
for my political actions'.[26]

That this reading has a certain *prima facie* plausibility – that it picks
up on one fairly prominent aspect of Foucault's late thought – is clear
enough in the way that Foucault contrives a passage, in 'What Is
Enlightenment?', from the Kantian (philosophical) discourse of
modernity to 'modernism' in its literary-aesthetic usage. And there are
other passages, notably in a 1983 interview with Dreyfus and
Rabinow, where he likewise seems to think of ethical conduct as
primarily a matter of aesthetic cultivation, of private self-fashioning in
a realm quite apart from the public-political realm. Thus: 'Why
couldn't everyone's life become a work of art? Why should the lamp or
the house be an art object, but not our life?'[27] Nietzsche and
Baudelaire would seem to be his tutelary spirits, along with the ancient
stoic philosophers whose meditation on the various techniques or
disciplines of self-fashioning are a constant point of reference in *The*

History of Sexuality. All of which tends to bear out Rorty's claim that Foucault had no use for any notion of the self – let alone for any variant of the Kantian 'transcendental subject' – except in so far as these ideas could be thoroughly historicized, treated as purely contingent products of this or that language-game, cultural 'form of life', etc. On this view the only significant difference between early ('archaeological') and late ('genealogical') Foucault is the shift from a critical-diagnostic standpoint that contents itself with simply dispelling transcendental illusions to a Nietzschean stance which – more usefully, to Rorty's way of thinking – offers a whole range of alternative 'vocabularies' (or modes of self-description) to put in their place.

Nor, presumably, would Rorty see any reason to modify this position in light of Foucault's later writings on Kant. For he could always point out that when Foucault finds a use for that old vocabulary – for terms like 'critique', 'truth', 'reason', 'autonomy', 'self-knowledge' and so forth – they reappear as items in a different language-game, a discourse devoid of any Kantian (quasi-transcendental) grounds or truth-claims, and wholly redefined in accordance with Foucault's historicist and private-aestheticist values. Take the following passage from 'What Is Enlightenment?', one of many that Rorty could plausibly cite in support of his case. 'This critique will be genealogical', Foucault specifies,

> in the sense that it will not deduce from the form of what we are what it is impossible for us to do and to know; but it will separate out, from the contingency that has made us what we are, the possibility of no longer being, doing, or thinking what we are, do, or think. It is not seeking to make possible a metaphysics that has finally become a science; it is seeking to give new impetus, as far and wide as possible, to the undefined work of freedom.[28]

Undeniably this reads very much like a further piece of argument in the sceptical vein of *Les mots et les choses*, a disarticulation of the Kantian faculties – knowledge, will, and judgment – which treats them as artefacts of a certain period-specific discourse, that same 'analytic of finitude' which gave rise to man (the transcendental subject) as delusive figment of his own Imaginary. To this extent Rorty can claim good warrant for his version of the late Foucault. But it is none the less a resolutely partial reading which ignores any details – or complicating factors – that go against the postmodern-pragmatist grain. For there is also much evidence, in those same late texts, that Foucault now perceived the disabling consequences of a nominalism pushed to the point where 'truth' became merely a reflex product of power/knowledge differentials, where 'critique' was just the name for some vaguely-defined project of aesthetic self-fashioning, and where the 'subject' survived only as a kind of rhetorical alibi, a place-filling predicate adopted for want of any ready alternative. At very least, he now thinks, 'Kant's reflection is a way of philosophizing that has not been without its importance or effectiveness during the last two centuries'.[29]

No doubt this could still be construed in a Rortian sense, that is, from a postmodern-pragmatist angle on enlightenment 'discourse' that would treat it as contingent upon values and assumptions specific to our own prehistory as creatures of a given cultural time and place. But elsewhere Foucault states the case more strongly, and in a language that scarcely conceals its Kantian provenance. Thus: '[t]he work of philosophical and historical reflection is put back into the field of the work of thought only on condition that one clearly grasps problematization not as an arrangement of representations but as a work of thought'.[30] And again: '[t]hought is freedom in relation to what one does, the motion by which one detaches oneself from it, establishes it as an object, and reflects on it as a problem'.[31] Such a 'work of thought' would be strictly inconceivable – just another species of transcendental illusion – if indeed it were the case, as Foucault had once argued, that thinking in its various modalities (cognitive understanding, practical reason, and judgment) was constituted through and through by pre-given discourses, signifying systems, or forms of representation. Still less could reflection achieve the kind of critical distance – the detachment from existing language-games or cultural mores – that Foucault here defines as the precondition for any ethics that merits the name.

I should not wish to over-state the extent of Foucault's turning-away from post-structuralist ideas and his coming-to-terms with the legacy of enlightenment critique. His scepticism still shows through in the statement that this is just a 'certain manner of philosophizing', a discourse whose continuing pertinence for 'us' has to do with 'the analysis of ourselves as beings who are historically determined, to a certain extent, by the Enlightenment'.[32] It is also clearly marked in Foucault's persistent will to aestheticise ethics, or to redefine 'autonomy' in terms of private-creative self-fashioning. Such a project concerns 'the kind of relationship you ought to have with yourself, *rapport à soi*, which I call ethics, and which determines how the individual is supposed to constitute himself [sic] as a moral subject of his own actions'.[33] Even so, it is hard to see how self-knowledge could ever come about in the absence of that capacity for critical thought – for what Foucault elsewhere, albeit rather vaguely, calls 'this sort of ethico-epistemologico-political question' – which alone enables the subject to establish the necessary distance from his/her pre-reflective impulses, volitions, or desires. This is why Foucault often sounds most authentically Kantian at just those moments when he seems most inclined to disavow – or at any rate to qualify – his attachment to the philosophic discourse of modernity. Thus: 'the thread that may connect us to the Enlightenment is not faithfulness to doctrinal elements, but rather the permanent reactivation of an attitude – that is, of a philosophical ethos that could be described as a permanent critique of our historical era'.[34] There is nothing in this sentence, minor differences of idiom apart, that could not have figured in Kant's original essay 'What is Enlightenment?'

It may be said that Foucault is here having it both ways, clinging to his view of enlightenment discourse as a product of its own, historically circumscribed place and time, while invoking a rhetoric of 'permanent critique' in order to endorse his own radical credentials and avoid the consensus-based pragmatist appeal to what is currently 'good in the way of belief'. But this ignores his main point: that if the Kantian question was that of 'knowing what limits knowledge has to renounce transgressing', then today this question has to assume a more 'positive' (emancipatory) form: 'in what is given to us as universal, necessary, obligatory, what place is occupied by whatever is singular, contingent, and the product of arbitrary constraints?'.[35] Which is, after all, much akin to the relationship that Kant envisaged between issues in the realm of cognitive enquiry (where intuitions must be 'brought under' adequate concepts, and reason thus prevented from running wild in the empyrean of pure speculative thought), and questions of an ethical or socio-political character (where reason justifiably transcends such constraints in the interests of promoting freedom, autonomy, and the exercise of uncoerced critical judgment). That is to say, it is still a version of the Kantian argument from 'conditions of possibility', despite Foucault's desire to historicize Kant by rejecting any premature (uncritical) appeal to those conditions as universally given. Thus: 'the study of [modes of] problematisation (that is, of what is neither an anthropological constant nor a chronological variation) is the way to analyse questions of general import in their historically unique form'.

No doubt Foucault gives a different inflection to Kant's way of distinguishing the 'universal' and the 'necessary', on the one hand, from the 'singular', 'contingent' and 'arbitrary' on the other. That is to say, he still sides with Nietzsche *contra* Kant at least to the extent of opposing 'universal' values in the name of those 'singular' events, occurrences, or moments of 'transgressive' desire that resist assimilation to the normalizing discourse of instituted power/ knowledge. But the question remains: what can such 'resistance' amount to if conceived (as Foucault often tends to suggest) on a purely reactive, quasi-mechanistic model of equal and opposite forces, such that power-interests will always generate corresponding knowledge-effects, and these in turn give rise to some counter-discourse – a resultant of differential forces – whose effectiveness resides entirely in its relation to those same ubiquitous power/knowledge interests? It is as if Foucault had grafted a Hobbesian image of the 'state of nature', the unending war of each against all, onto a Newtonian metaphor of discourse as a force-field of reciprocal (but also self-cancelling) motions and energies. Such ideas are pre- rather than post-Kantian, their effect being simply to revoke Kant's critical philosophy by assimilating issues of will, judgment, moral conscience or practical reason to the order of causal-determinist explanation proper to the natural sciences. And the turn toward 'discourse' as a limiting term of analysis – whether in its structuralist, its post-structuralist, or its Nietzschean-genealogical guise – does nothing to alleviate this dead-end predicament. For its effect, as Foucault obliquely acknowledges, is merely to substitute the prison-house of language (or of subject-positions assigned therein) for the constraints of material or physical causality. Nor does it help to take the line adopted by some of Foucault's post-structuralist exponents, namely that of arguing that 'discourses' are multiple or overdetermined, with the subject as an ongoing 'site of struggle' within and between them. For this amounts to a modified (language-based) version of the same crypto-Hobbesian thesis, the idea of a conflictual process that is somehow carried on in the absence of anything – reasons, values, principles, or justifying grounds – which could make sense of that process in humanly intelligible terms. Here, as with Lacan, the argument leads to a point where the subject is so completely 'decentred' – so much a plaything of linguistic structures beyond its utmost powers of reflective grasp – that it becomes simply a product of discursive definition, a word (like 'force' in Newtonian physics) lacking any real explanatory power but employed to balance the equations.

In *Les mots et les choses* and other writings of his early ('archaeological') phase this issue was effectively shelved – or kept out of sight – by Foucault's stance of high-structuralist disdain for that whole tradition of subject-centred epistemology and ethics that ran, on this Heideggerian account, from Descartes, through Kant, to Sartre and the avatars of humanist existentialism. Lévi-Strauss had set the terms of this dispute in his well-known polemical exchange with Sartre, asserting the claims of a structural-synchronic methodology over those of a 'totalizing' (dialectical) approach that sought to understand historical events through ascriptions of agency, collective purpose, class-consciousness, intersubjective *praxis*, etc.[36] So it was that the structuralist paradigm – Saussurian linguistics and its various offshoots – came to capture the high ground of cultural debate for Foucault and other arbiters of the post-1960 Francophone 'sciences of man'. To the extent that the subject figured at all in this discourse of theoretical anti-humanism it appeared as nothing more than an effect of language, an epiphenomenal disturbance in the otherwise seamless order of signs. But as Foucault moved into his activist phase – his involvement with various groups campaigning for radical reforms in psychiatric medicine, the penal system, treatment of sexual minorities, 'deviant' sub-cultures, etc – so this position came to strike him (I suggest) on the one hand as an avoidance of deep-laid philosophical problems, and on the other as a pretext for opting out of more urgent ethico-political concerns. Not that Foucault ever went so far as to repudiate the whole post-structuralist 'problematic' and kindred variations on the linguistic turn in its latest counter-enlightenment form. But his doubts are clear enough in those late essays and interviews, texts that bear witness to a profound reorientation of his thinking with regard to questions of truth, self-knowledge, and the ethical 'work of thought'.

IV THE ETHICS OF DISCOURSE: CHOMSKY *CONTRA* POST-STRUCTURALISM

Meanwhile, and (as it might seem) altogether elsewhere, discourse-theorists and Anglo-American philosophers of language have found themselves confronting related issues in their own disciplinary context.

I shall need to conduct a rather snapshot survey of the field – and pass over some otherwise salient differences of view – in order to establish this relation.

In the lexicon of systemic linguistics (influenced by the work of M.A.K. Halliday) 'discourse' is a term standardly applied to any instance or aspect of language belonging to a level of complexity higher than the individual sentence.[37] It thus falls outside the scope of grammatical analysis and involves considerations of context, implicature, relevance, presupposition, ontological commitment, etc. And it can also be said to lead beyond linguistics in so far as that discipline is primarily concerned to assign a determinate (syntactic or semantic) description to some given corpus of sentences. For any adequate theory of discourse – if such a theory could ever be attained – would need to do more than account for our 'competence' as speakers and recipients of a vast (potentially infinite) range of well-formed linguistic utterances. It would have to encompass: (1) every detail of our relevant (context-specific) knowledge of the world; (2) the various conventions, interpretive frameworks or conceptual schemes whereby to represent this knowledge; (3) a modal (or 'possible worlds') component enabling the theory to distinguish actual from fictive, hypothetical or other such counterpart realms; and (4) some means of making explicit – of rendering in formal explanatory terms – what mostly subsists at the level of tacit understanding. Umberto Eco makes the point most succinctly by remarking that such a theory would approximate the condition of an ideal encyclopaedia, rather than an ideal dictionary.[38] That is to say, its scope would necessarily be coextensive with the sum total of human knowledge, experience, beliefs, dispositions and so forth. Nothing less seems required if the study of discourse is to make good its methodological claims. Like semiotics – in many respects the same programme under a different name – discourse-theory seems committed to the principle *nihil humani mihi alienum puto*.

Some philosophers (Hubert Dreyfus among them) have argued that this project must always fail for reasons intrinsic to the very nature of language and thought.[39] Nowadays the issue is most often raised in the context of other closely-related projects like Artificial Intelligence (AI), machine translation, and computer-simulated language acquisition. The counter-argument, briefly summarized, is that human intelligence simply doesn't operate in the manner envisaged by discourse-theorists, or by those in the AI research community who would reduce it to so many discrete chunks of information, such as might then form the basis of a (no doubt immensely complex) computer programme. This idea gains a certain plausibility from our knowledge of the brain's neuro-physiological structure, i.e. from the fact that synapses function in accordance with a digital (or on-off) binary logic. But it is wrong – just a species of category-mistake – to assume that this logic can be carried across into the realm of human perception, knowledge and experience, a realm characterized (as Dreyfus argues) by certain irreducibly intentional aspects. Thus if the mind indeed functions, in AI parlance, as an information-processing mechanism, it does so *not* through an arduous sequence of bit-by-bit 'digital' sorting, but through something in the nature of an 'analogue' appeal to aspects of experience – qualitative aspects – which cannot be captured by even the most sophisticated software programme. Of course this line of argument has numerous parallels in the history of debate between those who uphold some version of what is now called 'central state materialism' and those who assert the distinctive character of mental attributes or predicates. But it has been polarized anew – and received some sharper formulations – as a result of the claims now jointly advanced by discourse-theory, cognitive psychology, and computer-simulated language acquisition.[40]

Here again, I would argue, we are witnessing a re-run of some long-familiar debates, notably the free-will/determinism issue and its equivalent in linguistic terms, i.e. how to account for the open-ended creativity of language (Saussure's *parole*) while acknowledging the various systemic constraints that characterize language in its structural-synchronic aspect (*la langue*), and which alone make communication possible. It was Chomsky who posed this question most squarely, rejecting the structuralist approach on account of its merely descriptive (not explanatory) scope, its lack of theoretical refinement, its failure to integrate syntax with semantics at the level of sentence-meaning, and – above all – its treatment of language as a pre-given network or structural economy of signifying codes and conventions.[41] For this model effectively precludes any concern with the question of linguistic 'competence', i.e. the transformational-generative process whereby a finite stock of phonological, syntactic and semantic elements gives rise to a (potentially infinite) repertoire of well-formed grammatical sentences. There was, of course, a good deal of specialized debate around issues of relative priority, with Chomsky moving from his early position (where syntax was assigned the determinant role) to his subsequent view that the theory must incorporate a generative-semantic component. These technicalities need not concern us here, save to point out that they always have a larger (philosophical) dimension, an aspect which Chomsky was later to address in works like *Language and Responsibility*.[42] For if linguistics cannot rest content (as he argues) with pursuing a merely structural-descriptive approach – if it has to take account of issues in cognitive psychology, theory of knowledge and philosophy of mind – then by the same token it must often raise questions concerning the scope and limits of human reason, the possibility of knowing what we mean and meaning what we say, or of speaking and acting responsibly in matters of shared moral concern. In short, there is a close (if highly complex) relation between Chomsky's work in theoretical linguistics and his public stance as a dissident intellectual, criticizing US domestic and foreign policy in the interests of creating a wider sphere of informed participant debate.[43]

However, one may question whether these interests are best served by Chomsky's commitment to a rationalist tradition descending – as he argues in *Cartesian Linguistics* – from Descartes and the Port Royal school of grammarian-logicians.[44] For on this account the thinking or speaking subject stands in as nothing more than an abstract convenience, a nominal entity or product of reflexive definition (*cogito, ergo sum*), lacking any attributes through which it might relate to the realm of humanly-intelligible motives, reasons, knowledge-constitutive interests, and so forth. That is to say, it becomes just a discursive subject-position in exactly the sense defined (and deconstructed) by those present-day sceptics – Lacan among them – for whom Descartes figures as the ultimate progenitor of all such humanist illusions. Since Chomsky nails his colours so firmly to the Cartesian mast it may seem otiose to criticize his thinking on Kantian grounds. But the criticism has some point if one considers the problems that Chomsky faced, firstly in explaining the precise order of relationship between syntactic structures and issues of semantic interpretation, and secondly in showing how a realm of human freedom and ethico-political responsibility could exist despite the constraints embodied in a strong universalist theory of innate linguistic competence. What drops out of sight in this Cartesian (or narrowly rationalist) perspective is the whole range of factors – epistemic, situational, evaluative – that bear upon language in its contexts of everyday usage, and that cannot be accounted for by any such model.

Thus the subject becomes the 'ghost in the machine' of transformational-generative grammar, brought into being by the need to postulate some notional source, some locus of linguistic 'creativity' or 'freedom' to set against an otherwise implacably determinist order of language, thought, and representation. And at this point all the unresolved (strictly insoluble) problems of Cartesian dualism crowd back upon Chomsky's linguistics, among them the antinomies of mind and nature, subject and object, language as a domain of infinitely varied speech-acts and language as the set of finite (rule-bound) derivations that somehow underlie this open multiplicity.

Not that such problems are in any way peculiar to Chomskian linguistics. Indeed it may be said that they arise of necessity – like Kant's antinomies of pure reason – whenever thought touches on speculative issues like the origin of language, the relationship of genesis and structure, or (after Saussure) the issue of priority between *langue* and *parole*. But in Chomsky's work they are posed with particular emphasis, partly on account of his deep-laid attachment to this mentalist (or dualist) paradigm, and partly because they are always bound up with questions of an ethico-political import. It is only fair to recall Chomsky's own quite explicit reservations in this regard, that is to say, his various cautions against the idea that there exists a direct or consequential relation between specialized work in a discipline like linguistics or cognitive psychology, and matters of political conscience or principle. If radical empiricists like Hume and Russell could arrive at such different (roughly speaking, 'conservative' and 'left-liberal') positions, then equally it is the case that a rationalist philosophy of mind might well be taken as lending support to an ethics or a politics far removed from Chomsky's stance of activist dissident critique. Clearly there is a risk of simplification – of conflating disparate realms – in any attempt to extrapolate directly from the one to the other domain. After all, it is the aim of transformational-generative grammar to provide a working model of linguistic competence at a level of abstract generality far removed from localized differences of culture, psychology, subjective experience, idiolectal variations and so forth. In which case it could only be a category-mistake – an illicit passage from the universal to the particular – if one sought to derive any normative social or political values from Chomsky's 'revolution' in linguistic thought.

So much by way of cautionary prologue. All the same it would be just as naive (or perhaps a strategy of evasion) to ignore the many passages in Chomsky's work where he does suggest that some such relationship exists. For there is clearly a sense in which Chomsky's ideas about language go along with his philosophy of mind and his conviction that 'democracy' involves something more than an attitude of passive, uncritical compliance with existing (consensus-based) values and beliefs. One can trace this connection right back to his celebrated early review of B.F. Skinner's book *Linguistic Behavior*, where Chomsky decisively refuted the idea that language-acquisition (or speaker competence) could ever be explained in terms deriving from the behaviourist model of stimulus-response psychology.[45] Hence also his objection to the structuralist paradigm: that it treated language as a given (pre-constituted) field of signifying relations, such as to exclude – or to declare off bounds for its own descriptive purposes – any dealing with the speaker's innate capacity for producing and interpreting well-formed grammatical sentences. This capacity could not be explained, Chomsky argued, by any theory (whether behaviorist or structuralist) that took no account of the cognitive processes involved in thus producing such a range of meaningful expressions from the finite stock of phonological, syntactic and semantic ground-rules. Linguists who ignored this manifest truth about language – its witness to the sheer resourcefulness of human cognitive and expressive powers – were thereby espousing not only a false (demonstrably inadequate) set of methodological premises but also a drastically reductive view of subjectivity, agency and thought.

It is at this point that the argument assumes a normative or ethico-political dimension. For when Chomsky speaks out as a critical intellectual – opposing US military adventures, abuses of power, corporate corruption, cover-up campaigns, media collusion, support for right-wing dictatorships, subversion of democratically-elected governments, etc – then he does so from a standpoint of reasoned and principled dissent that implicitly draws upon his other, more specialized researches. Nor is this simply a matter of public prestige, of his having accrued a certain measure of 'cultural capital' (in Bourdieu's socio-diagnostic sense of that phrase) which gains him an audience – or publicity profile – denied to less eminent persons. For there is often, in these writings, a tacit appeal to the *sensus communis* of enlightened participant debate, the public sphere of free and open critical enquiry which Chomsky sees as most aptly prefigured in the Cartesian-rationalist tradition. At least it may be said – despite his express caveats – that one's view of the prospects for achieving such advancement in the socio-political realm is likely to be influenced (for or against) by one's thinking on these other, more 'technical' issues in the philosophy of language and mind. It is here that Chomsky takes issue most sharply with behaviorism, structuralism and allied schools of thought. Whatever their manifest differences of approach, these theorists start out from a shared major premise: namely, that language can best be treated as in some sense a predetermined repertoire, a stimulus-response mechanisms (or a structural economy of differential terms) whose functioning neither requires nor admits considerations of speakerly competence. And his review of Skinner is already alert to the wider implications that may easily be read into any such reductive or mechanistic treatment of mind, language and human cognitive capacities. For it is no great distance, on this view, from Skinner's extreme version of the empiricist doctrine *nihil in intellectu quod non prius in sensu* to the notion that behaviour (or 'social attitudes') can always be modified by proper application of the requisite positive or negative reinforcements.

Quite apart from such dire Orwellian prognoses there is also a sense in which these ideas about language give rise – or lend spurious 'philosophical' support – to an outlook of inertly consensus-based thinking in the socio-political sphere. That is to say, they fall in with the attitude (espoused by many conservative thinkers from Burke to Oakeshott) that the interests of society are best served by a decent respect for established values, a willingness to repose on the wisdom of the ages as embodied in existing institutions, and – coupled with this – a healthy disregard for any reasoned counter-argument or principled critique of such values. It scarcely needs saying that Chomsky adopts an antithetical stance on each of these questions. And he does so not only as a matter of alternative persuasion, of beliefs arrived at through private conviction or membership of some different (dissenting) interpretive community. Rather, he presents it as a case borne out on the one hand by the massively-documented *evidence* of US war-crimes, disinformation, public-opinion management and so forth, and on the other by the always implicit appeal to standards of truth and right reason which in turn find warrant – albeit indirectly – in his own more specialized areas of research. To put it very simply: one's view of such matters will always at some point have to do with one's estimate of the human capacity for criticising false (unfounded, irrational or taken-for-granted) beliefs, and hence for resisting various forms of ideological recruitment. It will turn, that is to say, on the

answer one gives to certain seemingly quite abstract and 'philosophical' questions. These latter will include (for instance) the nature of our
cognitive processes, the degree of their dependence on pre-given
stimuli (or in-place habits of thought), and conversely – as Chomsky
would argue – the extent to which our powers of language-acquisition,
of interpretive competence or intellectual grasp go beyond the
explanatory scope of any such crude behaviorist account. And the
same would apply to structuralist (or post-structuralist) conceptions of
language in so far as they treat all appeals to the subject – to the
speaking, thinking, willing or judging subject – as merely a species of
'transcendental' illusion, best honoured (as in Foucault's famous
valedictory pages) with the passing tribute of a sigh. Such claims have a
more than methodological significance, as likewise do Chomsky's
countervailing arguments for the continued validity of a rationalist
paradigm in linguistics and (implicitly) the human sciences at large.

Merely to review some of the titles of his books over the past two
decades – titles like *Language and Responsibility* or *Linguistics and
Politics* – is evidence enough that Chomsky still holds to a version of
this strong-consequentialist thesis, i.e. that issues in the philosophy of
language or mind have a definite (if far from straightforward) bearing
on issues of ethics and politics. The point could be made in negative
form by remarking how the same equation holds in reverse for a
conservative thinker such as Oakeshott. Thus one of his books
(*Rationalism in Politics*) conveys by its title precisely the opposite set
of principles with regard to the sanctity of custom, the virtues of a
settled (consensus-based) order of civic and communal life, and the
dangers consequent upon elevating reason to the role of supreme
arbiter in questions of moral and political conscience.[47] Of course this
issue has long been at the heart of post-enlightenment debate on the
scope and limits of critical-emancipatory thought. Moreover, it has
always figured prominently at times of intensified ideological strife –
post-revolutionary epochs or periods of global instability like the
present – when philosophers found themselves impelled to adopt a
more overt political stance. What places Edmund Burke (or the later
Coleridge) at odds with the truth-claims and values of enlightened
critique is also what divides an Oakeshott (or a Roger Scruton) from
contemporary versions of the Kantian appeal to 'ideas of reason' as
arrived at through the *sensus communis* of open participant debate.[48]
And it is often – if tacitly – the main point at issue in Chomsky's
quarrel with schools of linguistic thought (behaviorist or structuralist)

27

which offer no credible account of speaker-competence, which treat the mind as a passive receptacle for pre-given stimuli or structures of sound and sense, and which thus ignore all the striking evidence of how far the human capacity to produce and intepret well-formed grammatical sentences exceeds the utmost explanatory powers of any such reductive model. On the one hand these theories manifestly fail since they beg a whole series of crucial questions – issues of language-acquisition, cognitive psychology, the relation between 'deep' and 'surface' grammatical features, between syntax and semantics, structure and genesis, etc – which cannot be simply shunted aside by an act of *de jure* methodological exclusion. On the other they promote a philosophy of mind (more exactly: a desire to purge linguistics of all such Cartesian 'mentalist' residues) which very easily translates into an attitude of low regard for the subject – the speaking and thinking subject – and its knowledge-constitutive interests.

From here it is a short step, as I have argued, to that current (chiefly post-structuralist) strain of theoretical anti-humanism whose *soi-disant* 'radical' credentials are oddly compromised by its affinity with various latter-day forms of conservative or counter-enlightenment thought. These issues are just as live nowadays – on the left and among the new generation of right-wing 'end-of-ideology' ideologues – as they were during that earlier period of post-revolutionary disenchantment when thinkers like Coleridge scrambled to vacate the exposed high ground of Kantian critical philosophy. That is to say, the debate still turns upon questions of a jointly epistemic and ethico-political nature, questions concerning the scope and limits of cognitive understanding, practical reason, and judgement in its various (determinate or reflective) modes. Of course it needs stressing that Kant, like Chomsky, sees the dangers that arise if one confuses these orders of thought, as by seeking to derive ethical prescriptions (or maxims of practical reason) from arguments concerning the scope and limits of theoretical understanding or cognitive enquiry. Indeed, a major part of Kant's purpose in the three *Critiques* is to prevent such errors by assigning each faculty its own legitimate sphere of jurisdiction, beyond which it cannot (or should not) venture on pain of running into all kinds of deep-laid conceptual bewilderment. Hence the 'antinomies of pure reason', those vexing aporias – like the issue of freewill *versus* determinism – that thinking inevitably encounters when it ignores the distinction between determinate judgements (i.e. those belonging to the realm of phenomenal or cognitive experience, where intuitions must always be brought under adequate concepts) and judgments of a reflective or ethico-political character (where no such rule can possibly apply, since here the appeal is always to 'ideas of reason' which are subject to no such validating standard).[49] One must therefore proceed with great caution in claiming to derive an ethics (or a politics) of the kind that Chomsky would endorse from any putative basis in a rationalist theory of mind, knowledge, or language-acquisition. For such arguments ignore Kant's cardinal distinction between phenomenal and noumenal orders of judgment, i.e. those pertaining to the exercise of thought in its cognitive-conceptual mode and those that have to do with our acts of freely-willed (autonomous) decision or judgment. At which point the old Cartesian antinomies resurface to much the same troublesome effect, confronting us with the choice between a speculative ethics devoid of all human (real-world) consequence and a determinist outlook that assimilates *every* kind of thinking – practical reason included – to the realm of phenomenal necessity.

V IDEAS OF COMMUNITY: KANT, WITTGENSTEIN, LYOTARD

Thus it is hardly surprising that Chomsky (like Kant) should reject any straightforward analogical appeal from the evidence of linguistic universals – *a priori* structures of logico-grammatical competence – to questions of ethics, politics, social responsibility, etc. But he also sees very clearly (again like Kant) that these boundaries cannot be held in place by a rigid compartmentalization of the faculties that would, for example, prevent issues in the realm of epistemology or theoretical understanding from affecting our view of how moral agents are placed with regard to the dictates of practical reason in particular contexts of historical, social or situated human choice. That is to say, there must always come a point in the exercise of autonomous (enlightened) reflective judgment where its maxims on the one hand take account of various worldly, circumstantial or factual considerations, and on the other involve some ultimate appeal to the conditions of possibility – epistemic conditions – for arriving at a knowledge of the relevant facts whereby to orient practical reason in its quest for the right choice of maxim. No doubt Kant goes some lengthy (even tortuous) ways around in articulating the various orders of relation between judgment in its determinate and reflective modes, or again, between the interests of cognitive enquiry and the interests of practical reason as represented by the *sensus communis* of enlightened participant debate.[50] But it is also the case – as Onora O'Neill argues in her fine recent book *Constructions of Reason* – that these two kinds of knowledge-constitutive interest are closely bound up at every stage of Kant's critical philosophy, and furthermore that we shall misconstrue his project if we fail to perceive this overall governing design.[51] Hence the main purpose of O'Neill's book: to show 'how and why the account of reason's authority is articulated in political metaphors and how this determines the form of his vindication of reason'.

Of course there are those (among them Wittgensteinians, pragmatists and liberal-communitarians) who criticise Kant for his alleged 'formalism' in ethics, his resort to abstract or generalised precepts – like the Categorical Imperative – which offer little help in our everyday, practical, decision-making lives.[53] Hegel was the first to voice this criticism, rejecting what he saw as the empty rigours of Kantian moral law in favour of an ethics of *Sittlichkeit*, a sense of those various specific (if sometimes conflicting) obligations – civic, familial, professional, etc – that define what it means to be a member of this or that cultural community.[54] And the charge is taken up by present-day philosophers (notably Bernard Williams and Michael Walzer) who likewise recommend that we abandon the quest for absolute values, transcendent moral principles, or Kantian regulative maxims.[55] For such talk will come to seem simply pointless, they urge, once we learn the lesson of recent (anti-foundationalist) arguments in philosophy and the human sciences: namely, that practices of ethical judgment are justified only by the role they play within a given 'language-game', a shared community of beliefs and values, or (in late-Wittgensteinian parlance) a certain cultural 'form of life'. Beyond that there can be no criteria, no justifying principles or philosophic 'grounds' whereby to support one's case. But, as O'Neill remarks, such arguments very easily lean over into the kind of inert consensus-based thinking – or the pragmatist appeal to what is (currently and contingently) 'good in the way of belief' – that ends by denying the very possibility of reasoned or principled dissent.

Of course, as these writers concede, it may often be useful – rhetorically effective – to adopt a high-toned language of 'reason' and 'principle' in contexts (like that of our present-day Western liberal democracies) where such talk still wins a respectful hearing among fellow citizens or members of the same interpretive community. Nevertheless one is mistaken – like all those deluded 'enlightenment' types from Kant to Habermas, Chomsky, Rawls and company – if one thinks thereby to criticize or challenge the currency of in-place belief. For on this account – as argued by neo-pragmatists like Richard Rorty and Stanley Fish – one will *either* gain credence by appealing to some existent (no matter how marginal or specialized) interest-group, *or* one's case will inevitably fall on deaf ears for want of any common language, any shared beliefs or agreed-upon sense of what counts – rhetorically speaking – as an adequate address to the issues at hand.[56] If rhetoric indeed goes 'all the way down' (in Fish's oft-repeated phrase) then the same can be said of consensus values in so far as they define the very scope and limits – the horizon of intelligibility – for any discourse that seeks a participant role in the ongoing 'cultural conversation'. There are no further grounds, no reasons or principles save those that possess some degree of suasive efficacy, some measure of appeal among those bred up on a decent respect for such talk.

From here it is but a short step to fashionable variants on the 'end of ideology' or 'end of history' theme – lately revived by Francis Fukuyama – which see no room for significant differences of view on issues of truth, justice and right in a world where US-style liberal democracy has finally won out, and where dissent comes only from diehard ideologues who have yet to catch up with these latest rules of the conversational game.[57] No doubt there are pragmatists and communitarians – Walzer included – who would wish to have no truck with this particular form of preemptive rhetorical consensus-bending. But it is hard to see what critical resources they could muster against it, given their likewise dismissive attitude toward any line of argument premised on the values of truth, reason, enlightenment, principle, or *Ideologiekritik*. For this excludes the possibility that conflicts may develop not only within or between the various beliefs, values and ethical codes current in some given interpretive community, but also – as Kant sought to demonstrate – between a broad-based consensus that would claim to encompass all such localized differences of view and the dictates of principle (or grounds for conscientious dissent) arrived at through an exercise of autonomous critical judgment. Such would be the case, for instance, of a lone protestor against racial discrimination in a society that was otherwise wholly given over to the rhetoric, the practices and taken-for-granted beliefs of white supremacist doctrine. (Consider the example of Twain's Huck Finn, declaring that he would rather go to hell than turn in his friend the runaway slave, despite the sheer weight of antebellum consensus ideology – religious, social, and moral – that enjoined the opposite course of action.) Or again, it would provide the only means of justification for a conscientious objector who held out against the rhetoric of total mobilization in a country embarked upon an unjust war in the name of natonal salvation, manifest destiny, a 'New World Order', or whatever. With instances like these it makes little sense to invoke communitarian principles or resort to some version of the argument from 'forms of life' by way of characterizing the issues involved. What they show is the capacity of moral agents to adopt a position squarely opposed to the current self-images of the age, and to do so, moreover, through an independent process of critical reflection that cannot be justified in terms of any presently existing language-game, interpretive community, or ethical belief-system. It is at this point that talk of 'reason' and 'principle' goes beyond the mere appeal to a suasive rhetoric or a sense of what counts as good-faith argument with members of the relevant interest-group.

Such extreme cases may be rare – hardly to be met with outside the realm of fiction or philosophic thought-experiments – but they none the less capture something of importance as regards the relation between belief, ideology and Kantian practical reason. For they indicate what is wrong with the notion advanced by communitarian thinkers like Peter Winch, those who argue – often with reference to Wittgenstein – that 'a decision can only be made within the context of a meaningful way of life'.[58] Of course this is true in the obvious (and trivial) sense that moral agents, social critics or advocates of principle will always make appeal to *some* set of values that has been (or might be) acknowledged as 'meaningful' by *some* (existing or conceivable) community of belief. But it becomes more dubious – indeed morally disabling – if pushed to a point where decisions or judgments must be viewed as strictly meaningless unless they make sense by criteria internal to the practice, the language-game or cultural 'form of life' in question. This is why, as O'Neill shrewdly remarks, 'even those Wittgensteinian writers who reject relativist readings of Wittgenstein do not offer an account of moral practice and decision that goes beyond the practice-based conception of ethical decision offered by relativist writers'.[59] They are unable to do so precisely on account of this internalist perspective on ethical issues that identifies the criteria for meaningful debate with the range of language-games currently on offer, and which thus sees little use for talk of 'reason' or 'principle' unless such talk forms a part of some existing moral or political vocabulary.

No doubt there is a difference of emphasis or tone between, on the one hand, liberal-communitarians like Walzer who would reject any charge of relativism by appealing to the virtues (the substantive moral and socio-political benefits) of a liberal-pluralist ethos, and on the other hand neo-pragmatists like Rorty and Fish who would view such claims as just another 'discourse' (or suasive rhetoric) thrown up by the ongoing cultural conversation. But the difference will appear less decisive if one asks, with O'Neill, what reasons the former can provide for not pushing right through with this idea that issues of truth, justice and right in the end come down to what is presently viewed as 'good in the way of belief'. Nothing more, it seems, than a decided preference for 'our' liberal institutions and their associated moral vocabulary, a preference that lacks not only any means of argued or principled justification but also – more seriously – any ethical resources whereby to criticise the various abuses, the manipulative rhetorics and forms of distorted consensus appeal that can pass themselves off under cover of a language-game (and a notional 'form of life') equated with just those liberal-democratic values. In short, they might as well go all the way with Rorty and Fish, abandon the attempt to head off relativist (or neo-pragmatist) versions of the argument, and accept that – for all practical purposes – truth, right reason and social justice are synonymous with consensus belief.

O'Neill helps to pinpoint the fallacy here when she distinguishes Kant's idea of the *sensus communis* from other (e.g. Wittgensteinian) variants of the communitarian case.

> Whereas 'common sense' is used to refer to understandings that are actually shared, in an actual community or more widely, the *sensus communis* consists of those principles or maxims that constrain understandings, indeed practices of communication, that can be shared in any *possible* community ... They articulate the self-discipline of thinking that will be required if there is to be communication among a plurality whose members are not antecedently coordinated.[60]

There are three main points to be made about this passage, all of them with a bearing on my own line of argument. One is O'Neill's contention that Kant is *not* a 'foundationalist' either in epistemology or in ethics, if by this we mean a thinker whose ultimate appeal is to the subject construed as an absolute, transcendent, indubitable source of knowledge and truth. On the contrary, she argues: such readings of

Kant ignore the many passages – in the first *Critique* and elsewhere – where he identifies this as the typical rationalist error, the mistake of supposing (like Descartes) that reason has only to reflect upon its own innate or self-evident attributes in order to ward off the demon of sceptical doubt and erect an edifice of *a priori* knowledge immune to any further such assaults. For it is Kant's conviction – usefully summarized in the above passage from O'Neill – that reason has always to *justify* its claims through a process of open critical debate, or (to adopt his own favoured kinds of metaphor) in the 'parliament' or 'tribunal' of the faculties, each with the freedom to press its own case with due deference to the communal (truth-seeking) interest. Nor are these 'faculties' conceived in wholly intra-subjective terms, that is to say, as belonging to the isolated, autonomous individual in the exercise of his/her unaided cognitive or reasoning powers. For this is O'Neill's second main point: that 'autonomy' in the Kantian sense of that term also involves an appeal to the *sensus communis*, the realm of shared (inter-subjective) truth-claims, values and judgments which alone provides an adequate forum for settling any issues of priority or boundary-disputes. Hence Kant's otherwise puzzling distinction between reason in its 'private' and 'public' modes of employment, the former having to do with one's commitments as a matter of (e.g.) professional, civic or guild obligation, while the latter concerns one's ethical duty as prescribed by maxims of practical reason which transcend any such limiting perspective. But again, we mistake Kant's position if we construe it in typecast 'foundationalist' terms, that is to say, as an autarchic or somehow self-authorizing voice of conscience that derives its precepts from the subject as sovereign disposer of reason, morality and truth. What drops out of sight in this reading of Kant is the role he assigns to communal debate – to the process of uncoerced democratic argument – in establishing the terms and conditions on which enquiry is able to proceed.

From which it follows (O'Neill's third point) that there is no making sense of Kantian ethics *or* Kantian epistemology unless we take account of those regulative ideas that comprise his socio-political philosophy, among them the various themes addressed in so-called 'marginal' writings like 'What Is Enlightenment?', 'What Is Orientation in Thinking?', 'The Conflict of the Faculties', and 'On Perpetual Peace'.[61] For it is here – in what might be called his Fourth Critique or 'Critique of Political Reason' – that Kant works out the speculative basis for an ethics founded on the values of human reciprocity, dialogue, and open participant debate. Thus:

> the reason why Kant is drawn to explicate the authority of reason in political metaphors is surely that he sees the problems of cognitive and political order as arising in one and the same context. In either case we have a plurality of agents or voices (perhaps potential agents or voices) and no transcendent or preestablished authority ... Reason and justice are two aspects to the solution of the problems that arise when an uncoordinated plurality of agents is to share a possible world. Hence political imagery can illuminate the nature of cognitive order and disorientation, just as the vocabulary of reason can be used to characterise social and political order and disorientation. Kant frequently characterises dogmatism (rationalism) as a failure of discursive order, hence as anarchy; just as he characterizes dogmatism (rationalism) as a form of despotism, a triumph of unjust discursive order.[62]

This is not the place for a lengthy exposition of Kant's critical philosophy. My point is more simply that it raises issues in epistemology and ethics – and also for disciplines like linguistics and cognitive psychology – which are largely ignored by proponents of the present-day anti-foundationalist orthodoxy. What these thinkers seem to have in mind when they attack the 'subject-centred' discourse of Enlightenment is not so much Kant (or if so, a very partial and distorted reading of Kant) but rather that strain of 'dogmatic' or 'despotic' rationalism that Kant criticised in Descartes and other precursors. Hence the current notion – current at least among Foucauldians, Lacanians, post-structuralists, postmodernists, neo-pragmatists and a good many liberal-communitarians – that the only alternative to that old foundationalist paradigm is an ethics that renounces all Kantian talk of autonomy, principle, critique, maxims of practical reason etc, and which seeks no criteria for moral judgment beyond those supplied by some existing language-game, discourse, or cultural form of life.

From here – I suggest – it is no great distance to those other, more extreme forms of postmodern scepticism espoused by theorists like Jean-François Lyotard. On this view the only maxim worth preserving is that which enjoins us to multiply the range of 'first-order natural pragmatic narratives', to avoid ever judging between them (since each disposes of its own immanent criteria), and thus to maximize the heterogeneity – the strictly incommensurable character – of those various 'phrase-regimes' (whether cognitive or evaluative) that solicit our belief in any given case.[63] For, as Lyotard sees it, we commit an injustice – an abuse of the narrative 'differend' – if we think to adjudicate the issue from a standpoint that one or other party (or both) would reject as non-binding, perhaps even 'meaningless' by their own criteria. What this amounts to, in short, is a version of the Wittgensteinian (language-games) argument joined to a post-structuralist doctrine of the 'arbitrary' sign, of truth as a product of linguistic or discursive convention, and of the subject (the knowing, willing or judging subject) as likewise nothing more than a transitory figment of the obsolete humanist imaginary. I shall have more to say about Lyotard, since his work claims philosophical (indeed Kantian) warrant for what is perhaps the furthest point yet reached in this postmodern rush to abandon every tenet of enlightenment thought.

Such ideas have gained credence mainly as a result of their targeting a naive (and thus easily deconstructed) notion of the subject-presumed-to know, a notion that derives more from Descartes than Kant, and which scarcely survives an attentive reading of the relevant passages in Descartes. After all, as Christina Howells acutely remarks,

> Descartes envisages the body as origin of the passions, emotions, and sentiments that go toward the constitution of the *vrai homme* (true man). If mind as thinking substance is radically distinct from human emotions, passions, and so on, then the Cartesian subject may be seen as potentially divided in a more far-reaching sense than the mind-body dualism would initially suggest. In any case, what is certain is Descartes' ambivalence with respect to the location of the subject, whether it lies in the 'soul' alone or in an intimate fusion of body and soul.[64]

One may suspect that many post-structuralists have simply not read Descartes – or if so, that they have read him with very fixed preconceptions – when one finds them routinely deconstructing that mythical entity, the Cartesian subject as unitary source of truth, self-knowledge, and will. And it requires no very subtle or sagacious reading of Kant to remark what is there as a matter of explicit statement in the first *Critique*: namely, that these antinomies are such as to prevent consciousness from every coinciding with itself in a punctual moment of achieved self-knowledge or lucid reflective grasp. Thus, according to Kant,

[w]e do not have and cannot have any knowledge whatsoever of any such subject. Consciousness is, indeed, that which alone makes all representations to be thoughts; and in it therefore, as the transcendental subject, all our perceptions must be found, but beyond this logical meaning of the 'I' we have no knowledge of the subject in itself, which as substratum underlies this 'I' as it does all thoughts.[65]

Howells' point is that post-structuralism has defined its own agenda – its genealogies of power/knowledge, its rejection of 'Enlightenment' truth-claims and values, its dismantling of 'the subject' in whatever (Cartesian or Kantian) guise – in reactive opposition to a highly partial and dubious reading of intellectual history. The result (as can be seen most plainly in Foucault's case) was an avoidance of questions which then returned to haunt the discourse of post-structuralist theory, creating all manner of unresolved tensions and aporias. For if one thing is clear from recent shifts in 'advanced' Francophile thought it is the fact that announcements of the 'death of the subject' were (to say the least) somewhat premature.[66] What has given rise to this widespread resurgence of interest is a dawning recognition – however belated – of the various philosophical dead-ends (not to mention the ethico-political consequences) that thinking inevitably encounters when it assimilates reason, subjectivity and truth to the structures of linguistic or discursive representation.

Thus when Foucault speaks of Kant in the essays and interviews of his final decade it is with a view to reopening this question of the subject, now conceived – albeit problematically – in terms of moral agency as a kind of aesthetic self-fashioning (*rapport-à-soi*), a choice of life-style voluntarily adopted in relation to one's own authentic wishes and desires. No doubt this is a curious reading, one that shifts over, in the course of his essay 'What Is Enlightenment?', from Kant to Baudelaire as tutelary figure, or from the philosophic discourse of modernity to modernism as a cultural, literary ethos. It is also much akin to those skewed postmodernist readings of Kant – Lyotard's among them – that take the third *Critique* as their privileged point of departure, and which moreover focus on the Kantian sublime as the trope of ultimate 'heterogeneity', the name for whatever exceeds or baffles the powers of determinate judgment.[67] Hence the current high vogue for talk of the sublime among postmodern theorists and culture-critics who are able to exploit its paradoxical implications – 'presenting the unpresentable', and so forth – as a salutary check to the overweening discourse of enlightenment rationality and truth.[68] For it is at this point, according to Lyotard, that the cognitive 'phrase-regime' comes up against its limits, that sensuous intuitions can no longer be 'brought under' adequate concepts (as required in the domain of theoretical understanding), and that practical reason thus finds itself obliged to judge henceforth 'without criteria', or in the absence of determinate (factual, evidential or procedural) grounds of argument.

Of course this reading is not without warrant in the Kantian text. It picks up on the analogy that Kant himself draws between aesthetic judgement in its sublime ('suprasensible') aspect and the dictates of morality – or practical reason – as issuing from a likewise suprasensible realm (the ethical 'kingdom of ends') beyond all merely self-interested motives, all private desires, contingencies of circumstance, calculations of means-end (utilitarian) benefit, etc. To this extent Lyotard is a faithful exponent of the relevant passages in Kant, as can also be said – again up to a point – of Foucault's markedly aestheticist reading in the essay 'What Is Enlightenment?'. But they both go beyond any reputable standards of scholarly or critical accountability when they raise the sublime (or, in Foucault's case, the idea of aesthetic self-fashioning) to a kind of counter-enlightenment watchword, a pretext for rejecting any reasoned appeal to the *sensus communis* of truth-seeking interests in the ethical and socio-political sphere. And they do so, I have argued, mainly as a result of their confusion with regard to the 'transcendental subject' of Kantian thought, their tendency to view it (in quasi-Cartesian terms) as a wholly self-sufficient, self-acting, self-originating – and hence wholly imaginary – ground of reason and truth.

It is this misapprehension – well documented by Howells in the above-cited essay – which has lately given rise to the more extreme forms of anti-foundationalist thought. They include – on a quick and by no means exhaustive count – the Foucauldian idea of 'discourse' (or representation) as the limit-point of intelligibility for ethics, philosophy, historical enquiry and the human sciences at large; Lyotard's postmodernist notion of phrase-regimes (or narrative pragmatics), coupled with his heterodox reading of the Kantian sublime; post-structuralist talk of the 'arbitrary' sign, of floating signifiers, texts without authors or referents, the subject as a species of transcendental illusion, an epiphenomenal side-effect of language, etc; and lastly – more moderate in its claims but tending in the same direction – the liberal-communitarian case for language-games (or cultural 'forms of life') as the only meaningful context for adjudicating issues of truth, justice and right. In each case there is a failure to conceive how the subject could *both* exercise a power of autonomous, reasoned, principled decision *and* at the same time refer that decision to the wider community of knowledge-constitutive interests, of truth-claims, ethical judgments and evaluative priorities arrived at through the process of open participant debate. And there is also, following from this, a contraction of the Kantian 'public sphere' to the point where it exists only as so many 'discourses' of power/ knowledge, oppressive institutions (penal, psychiatric, sexual, pedagogical and so forth) to which the subject relates *either* by internalizing their disciplines – and thus being constituted through and through as a passive bearer of those same structures-in-dominance – *or* by pursuing various projects of aesthetic (private-individualist) self-creation. This is Foucault's last line of defence against his own, drastically reductive conception of truth, knowledge and human interests. And it is closely related to Lyotard's idea of 'judging without criteria', his treatment of the sublime – in isolation from the other modalities of judgment – as that which somehow debars all recourse to shared (intersubjective) standards of reasoned or principled debate.

I call this a skewed reading because it ignores so much that is of crucial importance to Kant's doctrine of the faculties in order to promote its own postmodern or counter-enlightenment agenda. For Kant, we should recall, these sublime intimations went along with an equal and countervailing stress on the beautiful as a realm of likewise 'suprasensible' experience which none the less held out the promise of agreement – of harmonious reconciliation – when referred to the 'tribunal' of the faculties in concert, or their image as projected in a possible community of informed evaluative taste. Here also there is a speculative link between aesthetics and ethics, though one that affords far more in the way of effective socio-political orientation. Such is Kant's idea of the *sensus communis*, the measure of potential (as opposed to existing or *de facto*) agreement attainable in matters of shared human concern. It is the difference (to repeat) between consensus-based doctrines for which truth is just a matter of received or doxastic belief, and arguments which hold to some regulative notion of truth at the end of enquiry, some means of criticising a false or distorted consensus through the appeal to Kantian 'ideas of reason' (or Habermas's 'ideal speech-situation'). But Lyotard will have none of

39

this, believing as he does that such notions belong to an outworn ('enlightenment') meta-narrative of reason, progress and truth which has long been overtaken – rendered obsolete – by the melancholy record of historical events to date. (Of course this begs the question of how he could possibly make such a judgment, given Lyotard's professed outlook of extreme cognitive scepticism, his rejection of truth-claims in whatever historical or factual-documentary guise, and his idea that evaluative statements pertain to a wholly different [heterogeneous] order of discourse.) So it is that the sublime, on this postmodern reading, comes to stand as an index of the gulf that exists between ethics and other modalities of reason, or the sheer impossibility that judgments be referred to any tribunal save that of their own, self-sealed and self-authenticating warrant.

Thus Lyotard: 'If you asked me why I am on that side, I think that I would answer that I do not have an answer to the question "why?", and that this is of the order of ... transcendence'. And again: 'When I say "transcendence", it means I do not know who is sending me the prescription in question'.[69] Perhaps he enters this caveat lest the word be understood in a religious (Kierkegaardian) sense, i.e. as claiming access to a realm of authentic revelation vouchsafed solely to those in possession of the requisite spiritual grace. As Lyotard would have it his account is nothing more than a faithful rendition of the Kantian precept: that ethics (practical reason) belongs to a realm quite apart from all contingent, circumstantial, or self-interested motives, and must therefore be viewed as necessarily 'transcending' the phrase-regime of cognitive judgment. But it should none the less be clear to any open-eyed reader of Kant – that is, any reader not yet given over to the current postmodernist line – that this constitutes a massively slanted interpretation, one that promotes the idea of 'sublime' heterogeneity at the cost of ignoring those numerous passages where the maxims and principles of practical reason are indeed brought to bear upon issues of real-world, situated agency and choice. Moreover, this applies even to the Categorical Imperative, regarded by many of Kant's critics – from Hegel to the liberal-communitarians – as belonging to a realm of abstract universality austerely remote from the kinds of problem encountered in the conduct of our everyday lives. For it is only on a pragmatist (consensus-based) theory of what counts as 'meaningful' moral debate that one is driven to deny the relevance of such principles, whether as endorsing or as calling into question one's acculturated habits of conduct and belief. Otherwise it will seem nothing less than self-evident that reflective individuals may sometimes find themselves torn between the values specific to their own time and place and a sense of those humanitarian obligations that transcend such a limiting perspective. But 'transcendence' in this latter, more authentically Kantian usage of the term has nothing in common with Lyotard's idea of a sublime modality of judgment, receiving its 'prescription' from God knows where and refusing to offer the least semblance of reasoned or principled justification. What such arguments amount to – just as clearly in Foucault's case – is a wholesale aestheticisation of ethical discourse which redefines 'autonomy' in private-individualist terms, and which blocks the appeal to any wider community of intersubjective understanding.

Not that the relationship between precept and practice is always a straightforward matter, such as might obtain if there existed algorithmic decision-procedures for deriving specific moral guidance from the stock of generalized ethical rules. Thus Kant often comments, in O'Neill's words, on 'the opacity of the human heart and the difficulty of self-knowledge', as well as on the fact that 'merely asking an agent what his or her maxim is in a given situation may not settle the issue'.[70] Indeed, it is quite in keeping with Kant's sense of the problems and perplexities involved that 'these limits to human self-knowledge constitute the fundamental context of human action'.[71] But to raise them – like Lyotard – into a creed of out-and-out ethical decisionism founded on the incommensurability-thesis is a reading that finds no warrant in the Kantian text. For as O'Neill very pertinently remarks, '[t]he underlying intentions that guide our more specific intentions are not in principle undiscoverable … Even when not consciously formulated they can often be inferred with some assurance, if not certainty, as the principles and policies that our more specific intentions express and implement'.[72] But this requires what Lyotard, by his postmodernist lights, is unable (or unwilling) to allow: the existence of a rational *sensus communis*, a public sphere of avowable intentions (along with their associated reasons, values, and knowledge-constitutive interests) which alone provides an adequate forum of debate for deciding such issues.

O'Neill makes the point as follows in a passage that precisely inverts Lyotard's postmodernist order of priorities, as well as laying out Kant's critical philosophy (in particular the relation between epistemology and ethics) in clear-headed summary form.

Human beings can receive a manifold of intuitions, subject to the structural constraints of the forms of intuition. They can synthesize this manifold using empirical concepts in accordance with the categories of the understanding. However, they can deploy the categories in complete acts of judgment only if they adopt and follow certain Ideas of reason or maxims to organize that judging ... [Thus] the complex capacities that we call sensibility and understanding are not usable without 'Ideas of reason', that is, without the adoption of maxims to regulate the use of these capacities in thinking and acting. An account of human knowledge will be systematically indeterminate unless these maxims are identified and vindicated.[73]

For Lyotard, conversely, it is a high point of principle that human knowledge is indeed 'systematically indeterminate', that judgment must always proceed 'without criteria' (or in the absence of any possible validating grounds), and that this applies not only in the realm of evaluative (ethical or aesthetic) judgment but also – by analogy – to truth-claims advanced in the domain of cognitive understanding. In one respect at least there is a degree of convergence between his and O'Neill's readings of Kant. That is to say, they both treat Kant's political essays as forming an integral part of his critical philosophy, and not – in the mainstream interpretive tradition – as mere outworks or appendages. But the resemblance has an end as soon as one asks what lessons may be drawn from this enlarged perspective on the Kantian corpus as a whole. For Lyotard, it means starting out from the sublime as that which paradoxically claims to 'present the unpresentable', and which thus – at the furthest point of radical 'heterogeneity' – reminds us of the absolute gulf that exists between 'Ideas of reason' (progress, democracy, perpetual peace, etc) and any concept of historical truth as a matter of *adequate and justified* representation, i.e., as a jointly epistemic and ethico-political mode of enquiry. In other words the sublime serves Lyotard as a kind of all-purpose deconstructive lever whose effect is to produce a generalized disturbance, a disarticulation of the faculties which not only sunders cognitive from evaluative judgments, but also opens a rift between the orders of sensuous intuition and conceptual understanding, or again, between reason in its speculative, practical, and epistemo-critical aspects.

But there are other possibilities that are not closed off – merely pushed out of sight – by this whole postmodernist line of approach.

42

What O'Neill demonstrates (though she never mentions him by name) is the sheer wrong-headedness of Lyotard's reading, its obsessive latching on to themes – like that of the Kantian sublime – which assume such prominence in postmodern discourse only through a wilful ('strong-revisionist') desire to undermine the grounds of rational consensus. For otherwise commentary can always pursue the more fruitful (constructive or truth-seeking) path which leads, via the beautiful and its cognate 'Ideas of reason' to a better understanding of how thought may proceed in its various cooperative (not conflictual or 'heterogeneous') modes of employment. Postmodernists like Lyotard set their face against any such reading since it involves the appeal – the reasoned and principled appeal – to a *sensus communis* of enlightened judgment whose guiding maxims are so sharply at odds with their own cynical wisdom. And the same applies to post-structuralism, neopragmatism and other such variants of the 'linguistic turn' pushed to the point where reason, subjectivity and truth become just products of discursive definition, ideas that we can well do without (so it is urged) once delivered from that old enlightenment ethos. But as Foucault at length came to realise – and as appears all too plainly in the nihilist babble of postmodern gurus like Baudrillard – this often goes along with a wholesale regression to that stage of uncritical (pre-enlightenment) thought when truth was indeed what counted as such according to the dictates of consensus belief.

VI DESCARTES OR KANT? THE SUBJECT IN QUESTION

I would therefore endorse Joseph Graham's case, in his recent book *Onomatopoetics*: that post-structuralism has engendered all kinds of conceptual confusion through its adherence to a narrowly Saussurean paradigm of language and representation, and its failure to engage with other, more sophisticated work in this area.[74] His view finds support from a good many shrewd and knowledgeable commentators, among them Thomas Pavel (in *The Feud of Language*) who mounts a sustained critique of post-structuralist theory from a jointly philosophical, linguistic and socio-political standpoint.[75] More generally, there is a sense of surprise when linguists on occasion get together with literary theorists and find that these latter have erected a handful of Saussurean precepts – the 'arbitrary' nature of the sign, the inscrutability of reference, the idea of language as a system of differences 'without positive terms' – into a high point of method and principle, a doctrinaire creed with ambitions far beyond Saussure's more modest (heuristic) attempt to establish a working basis for the study of language in its synchronic aspect. They are apt to look askance at post-structuralism for two main reasons. Firstly, it ignores so much of what has happened in subsequent linguistic debate, from Chomsky's transformational-generative theory of syntax (along with its semantic refinements and extension into the realm of cognitive psychology) to those later developments in discourse-theory – often influenced by work in artificial intelligence or machine translation – which claim to supersede both the structuralist and the Chomskian paradigm. Secondly, it gets things wrong even on its own elective home-ground by treating Saussure as the fount of all linguistic wisdom, as a wholesale ideologue of the arbitrary sign and suchlike 'radical' notions, derived from a resolutely partial reading that ignores his specific disciplinary concerns.

Hence the post-structuralist attitude of blithe indifference with regard to questions that cannot be ignored without producing a veritable 'return of the repressed' in the form of insoluble antinomies, blind-spots or aporias. Chief among these are: (1) the epistemological question of how linguistics (or philosophy of language) relates to issues in the realm of meaning, knowledge, and truth; (2) the question of the subject, or of *intentionality* as a simply ineliminable attribute of language, despite all the current (epiphenomenalist) talk of subject-positions, enunciative modalities, insertion into the symbolic order, etc; and (3) – following directly from this – the ethical question of what must be involved in our *taking responsibility* for the meaning, the operative truth-conditions, and the real-world consequences of our various speech-acts. As with Foucault, these are issues that return to vex post-structuralist theory, strive though it may to treat them as so many transcendental illusions or figments of the humanist Imaginary. For they are always within reach of the larger, more urgent question: what scope can exist for the exercise of practical reason – that complex conjunction of knowledge, will, and reflective judgment – if our actions (like our speech-acts) are ineluctably subject to an all-embracing order of causal, social, or structural-linguistic determinism? This is why I have argued that post-structuralist theory, so far from superseding the philosophic discourse of modernity, in fact shows signs of lapsing back into a pre-modern (pre-enlightenment) ethos of uncritical consensus-belief.

Not that one can find any ready answer to these questions by substituting Chomsky for Saussure, or appealing to the Chomskian (transformational-generative) paradigm as a bridge between linguistics and the rationalist tradition in epistemology and philosophy of mind. For here again there are problems – philosophical problems – when it comes to reconciling the two major claims of this theory, i.e. that language is a rule-bound (finite) repertoire of syntactic forms which can none the less generate a vast (potentially infinite) range of well-formed utterances, and which moreover bears witness – for just this reason – to the human capacity for wresting freedom from the realm of pre-given structural constraints. Of course these problems only arise if one seeks to extrapolate from the specialized domain of syntactic theory to questions of a wider (cognitive or ethico-political) import. Otherwise the relevant answers have to do with recursive functions, generative paradigms, relations between 'deep' and 'surface' structure and so forth, topics which are dealt with (properly enough) by application of various explanatory models derived from logic, mathematics, and set-theory. But of course this does nothing to resolve the freewill/determinism issue, which indeed appears all the more sharply in light of Chomsky's rigorous theoretical demands. That is to say, there is a basic conflict of principles – an *aporia* in the strictest sense of that term – between the idea of language as a rule-governed system amenable to rigorous (transformational-generative) treatment, and the idea of language as a locus of human autonomy, freedom, and creative potential.

Hence, as I have suggested, Chomsky's unwillingness to specify the relation between language, ethics and politics beyond the most generalised statements of principle. No doubt there is a fallacy – an illicit passage from the descriptive to the normative sphere – involved in any reading that would move on directly from a rationalist theory of mind, speaker-competence or language-acquisition to an argument for (e.g.) left-liberal or other such progressive political values. For on Chomsky's account these are *necessary and universal* features of language, a set of constraints – productive and enabling constraints – that transcend all localized differences of time, place and cultural context, as well as all idiosyncratic variations of intelligence, mind-set, stylistic register and so forth. So one can understand Chomsky's very guarded response when asked by interviewers to amplify on the relation between language and politics, or to take a more explicitly *engagé* stance as regards this presumed alignment of interests. But he is clearly not prepared to let go of such analogies altogether, as appears in his early review of Skinner, in his critique of Saussurian (structuralist) linguistics, and in later works where the issue is presented very much in ethico-political terms, i.e. as a choice between theories of language that acknowledge or deny the constitutive role of innate human intelligence. And it is here precisely – in Chomsky's Cartesian-rationalist appeal to innate ideas – that one discovers the source of all his philosophic problems. For this appeal goes along with a notion of the subject as unitary, self-sufficient origin of language and thought, a generative matrix (or 'black box' in the current AI parlance) whose autonomous functioning renders it an object of rigorous theoretical enquiry.[76] Post-structuralism is a kind of flip-side variant of this same Cartesian position, starting out as it does by construing 'the subject' in narrowly rationalist terms, and then devising all manner of knock-down arguments to show how this 'imaginary' ego-ideal is just a product of linguistic (or ideological) misrecognition.

I have described some of these strategies already, among them Benveniste's account of the gap that opens up between the 'subject of the enounced' and the 'subject of the enunciation', Lacan's psychoanalytic thesis of the subject as constituted through and through by effects of linguistic (metaphorical or metonymic) displacement, and Foucault's demotion of the 'transcendental' subject as the merest of superinduced language-effects, a notion thrown up by the obsolete *epistēmē* of nineteenth-century thought. It is evident enough what these all have in common: a failure to acknowledge any possibility save the choice between Cartesian rationalism on the one hand and, on the other, a version of the 'linguistic turn' that views discourses (or structures of representation) as all that remains once the subject is deprived of its illusory 'foundational' role. Less obvious, perhaps, is Chomsky's entanglement in the same self-imposed philosophical dilemma, his espousal of a doctrine ('Cartesian linguistics') that drastically narrows the available options for a theory of language and mind. It is this impoverished notion of the subject – the bare forked creature of Cartesian dualism – that allows the post-structuralists (and also neo-pragmatists like Rorty) to score some easy rhetorical points at the expense of 'foundationalist' thinking in general, Kantian epistemology and ethics included. But in so doing they completely ignore all the salient differences between Descartes and Kant, in particular – as O'Neill so convincingly argues – the role played by Kantian 'Ideas of reason' as a source of regulative aims and s (li..e ...e *sensus communis* or truth at the end of enquiry) apply just as much to the project of cognitive (epistemological) /standing as to practical reason or issues in the realm of ethico-political debate. These ideas are regulative (*not* constitutive) in the sense that they exert a claim upon our interests as members of an enlightened truth-seeking collectivity, but that they cannot be validated by direct appeal to their own self-evident truth as a matter of empirical warrant, logical deduction, or *a priori* conceptual necessity. It is for lack of any such nuanced account of 'the subject' under its various aspects (e.g. the crucial Kantian distinction between 'determinate' and 'reflective' modes of judgment) that Chomsky finds himself able to offer only the most generalized thoughts with regard to topics like 'linguistics and politics' or 'language and responsibility'.

What this amounts to, in effect, is another version of the standard structuralist (and post-structuralist) fallacy, the confusion created when explanatory techniques from some specialized area of study are carried across into other realms of thought where they assume untoward (usually determinist) implications. Thus Chomsky is right to criticise structuralism for its treatment of *la langue* – of language in its structural-synchronic aspect – as the sole legitimate object of interest. For this has two main consequences: firstly, that *parole* (and the question of speaker-competence) is excluded from the purview of structural linguistics, and secondly that *langue* becomes a kind of conceptual prison-house, a theory of pre-given language structures which takes no account of the human capacity for producing any number of well-formed grammatical expressions. But, as we have seen, Chomsky's own project runs into similar problems when he attempts to offer a philosophically articulated account of how the constraints upon grammatical well-formedness (and hence upon the rational 'grammar' of thought) can be reconciled with a broadly enlightenment (or liberal-democratic) outlook that stresses the values of autonomy, critique, and ethical accountability. In short, Chosmky would have done much better in his quest for intellectual antecedents had he looked to Kant and the history of post-Kantian critical debate, rather than to Descartes, the Port-Royal grammarians, and other such exponents of a rationalist philosophy devoid of these jointly epistemic and ethical resources.

What emerges from this latest 'conflict of the faculties' is a displacement or evasion of central Kantian issues, a recourse *either* to determinist ideas of subjectivity as constituted in and by language, *or* –

the other horn of this dilemma – to a notion of the subject a source and guarantor of truth, transparently accessible to knc through the exercise of rational reflection. It is this myth of unmediated self-presence – the legacy of Cartesian thought – which easily shows up as the merest of specular delusions when exposed to the 'rigours' (such as they are) of Lacanian psychoanalysis, or the undeceiving methods so deftly applied by a discourse-theorist like Benveniste. The whole debate is thus skewed to make it apppear an issue of choice between, on the one hand, naive (subject-centred or 'foundationalist') epistemologies and, on the other, an approach that takes its bearings from language and finds no room for such obsolete items of faith. Post-structuralism offers numerous examples of this straw-man strategy at work, from Barthes's widely touted 'death of the author' – and Foucault's albeit more nuanced meditations on the theme – to various pronouncements of an end to the so-called 'metaphysics of presence', the demise of Western 'logocentrism', and other sub-Derridean *idées recues*.[77] What they all have in common is the reference to Descartes (not Kant) as their assumed point of departure, and the habit of discovering – each time afresh and with the same sense of scandalized revelation – that the subject thus conceived is a fictive construct, a 'plaything' of language, or a figure that dissolves, upon closer inspection, into the force-field of discursive (unconscious) drives and substitutions.

As I remarked above, such ideas appear 'radical' only in the context of a French intellectual tradition where authority is perceived as vested in the truth-claims – the inherited cultural capital – of a Cartesian quest for clear and distinct ideas, a conception of the self-possessed, unitary subject-presumed-to-know whose privileged status can then be dismantled pretty much to order by anyone possessed of the requisite techniques. Outside this tradition – as viewed (for instance) by Frankfurt School theorists or commentators with a good working knowledge of post-Kantian philosophical debate – such ideas are bound to seem just a frivolous distraction, a reactive (so far from a 'radical') posture adopted solely for polemical purposes.[78] What post-structuralism has to ignore – if it is to maintain the least semblance of credible argument – is the existence of alternative, more complex and resourceful theories of the subject, theories that avoid the Cartesian reduction (along with its unworkably dualist treatment of the mind/body or free-will/determinism issue), and which offer a far more articulate account of the relationship between pure and practical reason, or again, between cognitive understanding (its determinate powers and limits) and the exercise of moral will and reflective judgment. For one result of the current *Auseinandersetzung* between 'theory' in its French and German cultural contexts has been the failure of post-structuralism to address such questions at anything like an adequate level of informed philosophical grasp.

As it happens there is a little-known dialogue between Chomsky and Foucault – transcribed from a Dutch television interview – which brings these issues very clearly into focus, since it shows Chomsky defending his rationalist position in response to Foucault's ultra-sceptical claims concerning the power-politics of truth, the demise of enlightenment values, the obsolescence of ideas like 'the political responsibility of the intellectuals', and so forth.[79] What is most striking about this encounter is the sense of missed opportunity, of cross-purpose argument and – more than once – of downright mutual incomprehension. Thus when Chomsky argues for the intellectual's role as a voice of dissenting moral conscience, a voice that must sometimes be raised in protest against the currency of popular belief, Foucault hears only the arrogant tone of an old-style 'universal' intellectual, the presumption of one who trades on his cultural capital – his own (highly specialized) form of expertise – in order to tell other people what to think. And conversely, when Foucault attacks such self-aggrandizing notions in the name of a 'micropolitics' of power/knowledge, a local intervention in specific struggles over (e.g.) prison-reform, psychiatric practice, oppression of sexual minorities, etc, Chomsky sees this as an evasion of the issue with regard to the primary (truth-telling) role of the engaged critical intellectual. Here again, one has the impression that these thinkers are not so much engaged in productive debate as caught up in an exchange of typecast antagonist positions where 'the subject' is conceived on the one hand as the last (Cartesian) guarantee of autonomous reason and truth, and on the other as a merely fictive construct out of the various strategies of power/knowledge at play in any given situation. What is lacking – and what might have clarified (if not resolved) the issue between them – is an understanding of autonomy that goes beyond this sterile opposition of 'naive' (foundationalist) and downright dismissive (postmodern) attitudes on the question of the subject. And by far the most resourceful tradition of such thinking is that which descends from Kant and the philosophic discourse of enlightenment critique.

VII DISCOURSE, DIFFERENCE AND THE 'ENDS OF MAN': HUSSERL, LEVINAS, DERRIDA

Needless to say, Kant's doctrine of the faculties has given rise to many problems and boundary-disputes, with the result that some upholders of enlightenment thinking – Habermas among them – have shifted ground at least to the extent of embracing a 'universal pragmatics' (or a 'theory of communicative action') in response to current anti-foundationalist arguments.[80] But this is not so much a wholesale capitulation as a limited concession to the 'linguistic turn', one that maintains a commitment to the values of emancipatory thought, and which rejects any move to assimilate the subject – the knowing, willing, judging subject – to the force-field of contingent power/knowledge interests. Nor is it simply a matter of divergent national or cultural traditions, with the Francophile camp pretty much given over to post-structuralism, postmodernism and kindred ideas, while the German (Frankfurt-dominated) school keeps faith – at whatever critical remove – with the heritage of Kantian-enlightenment thought. For this ignores the extent to which some French thinkers (Ricoeur and Derrida among them) have engaged with that 'other' philosophical tradition through readings that continue to respect its epistemological and ethical imperatives, even while marking their distance from it in certain crucial respects. And this despite the widespread assumption – encouraged by polemicists on both sides – that the rift is so deep and goes so far back that there scarcely exists any prospect of constructive dialogue. As against this view the point needs stressing that Derrida has produced some of the finest, most cogent and *responsible* readings of Kant to be found in the recent literature, despite what will no doubt strike many commentators as a wilful disregard for mainstream (orthodox or academic) protocols of method.[81] For it is Derrida's contention – like Kant's before him – that we should take nothing on faith as regards the authority of established (consensus) wisdom, but should think and read always with a vigilant awareness of the problems, discrepancies, or anomalous details that are easily passed over by exegetes bent upon maintaining the orthodox line. And these problems have to do in large part with Kant's attempt, throughout the three *Critiques*, to establish a complex inter-articulated order of priorities and relationships between cognitive understanding, practical reason, and aesthetic judgment.

Undoubtedly Derrida does much to destabilise the structure of

Kantian thought, or to draw out those 'unthought axiomatics' that both govern Kant's project and render it susceptible to a deconstructive reading.[82] By the same token he also raises questions with regard to the subject in its various roles as guarantor of knowledge and truth, as locus of autonomous moral agency, and as arbiter of issues in the evaluative (aesthetic and ethico-political) sphere. In each case, as he shows, these boundary-distinctions prove difficult – indeed impossible – to maintain, so that Kant is obliged to have oblique resort to all manner of analogies, metaphorical ruses, and (so to speak) cross-faculty exchanges in order to save appearances. But this is not to say that deconstruction – like post-structuralism – simply jettisons the notion of 'the subject' as a piece of surplus metaphysical baggage, a specular image whose eclipse is now presaged by the advent of discourse as the absolute horizon of intelligibility. On the contrary: what Derrida often asserts – and the more so in face of this recent fashion for Heideggerian, Foucauldian and other such forms of anti-humanist dogma – is the necessity that the subject should indeed be conserved as a strictly *indispensable* point of reference, even while remarking the problems that arise for any straightforward (epistemological or ethical) appeal to the subject as a grounding presupposition of knowledge or practical reason.

This argument received its earliest (albeit rather negative) formulation in his 1968 essay 'The Ends of Man', one purpose of which was to question the intelligibility – and, beyond that, the ethical implications – of any discourse that proclaimed a radical break with the heritage of humanist or anthropocentric thought.[83] And the point is made with more affirmative emphasis in Derrida's recent writings, especially those that engage the vexed issue of Heidegger's politics – his endorsement of National Socialist ideology – in relation to his (avowedly) post-metaphysical, post-humanist, post-enlightenment return to the sources of 'authentic' Being and truth. 'I do not intend to criticise [this] humanist teleology', Derrida writes. For '[i]t is certainly more urgent to remember that despite all our refusals and avoidances of it, it has remained up till now ... the price to pay for the ethical and political denunciation of biologism, racism and naturalism, etc'.[84] So there is never any question, in Derrida's work, of his adopting that facile post-structuralist line that preemptively celebrates the 'death of the author', the demise of the subject in whatever (Cartesian, Kantian or other) guise, and the necessity henceforth of managing without such delusive 'metaphysical' resources. What is thereby renounced is the very possibility of ethical thought, that is to say, of a thinking that would open questions beyond those allowed for by prevailing forms of consensus-based knowledge and belief.

Whether ethics might in some sense *precede* epistemology – thus reversing the order of priorities bequeathed to us by philosophy from Plato down – is the burden of Derrida's argument in his two sharply contrasted essays on Emmanuel Levinas, the one belonging to his earliest period, the other among his most recent productions.[85] There is, to be sure, a very marked shift of ground from the argument (in 'Violence and Metaphysics') that Levinas cannot ultimately make good his claims for an ethics of radical 'alterity', since it is only by analogy with our own experience that we can comprehend the experience of others, to the later essay where Derrida – whilst still critical of some aspects of Levinas's thought – none the less acknowledges that this relation to the other may precede and call into question all the resources of Western (epistemological or subject-centred) conceptuality.[86] This shift is bound up with other changes in the orientation of Derrida's thought which need not concern us here.[87] My point, more simply, is that his work represents a sustained engagement with questions – in particular this elusive but strictly *ineliminable* question of the subject – to which postmodernism and kindred variants of the 'linguistic turn' offer no more than a glibly dismissive response.

The same applies to those early writings – especially his books and essays on Husserl – where Derrida is concerned to adjudicate the issue between phenomenology and structuralism, since it is here (he argues) that the question is raised most acutely for philosophy, criticism and the present-day human sciences.[88] If 'a certain structuralism has always been philosophy's most spontaneous gesture', this is because the postulates of structuralist theory – its attachment to the ideals of system, method and conceptual rigour – are among the most deep-laid characteristics of Western (post-Platonic) epistemological thought. For Derrida, phenomenology constitutes a challenge to that tradition in so far as it seeks to offer an account of how meaning (or expression) can exceed the bounds of any finite, preexistent signifying structure, any theory of language or philosophy of mind that fails to allow for this moment of creative excess. Thus: '[i]t is always something like an *opening* which will frustrate the structuralist project ... What I can never understand, in a structure, is that by means of which it is not closed'.[89] And again, more eloquently:

The relief and design of structures appears more clearly when content, which is the living energy of meaning, is neutralized. Somewhat like the architecture of an uninhabited or deserted city, reduced to its skeleton by some catastrophe of nature or art. A city no longer inhabited, not simply left behind, but haunted by meaning and culture.[90]

Such passages are often passed over by commentators whose main interest is in Derrida's deconstructive reading of Husserl, his demonstration (seemingly to contrary effect) that Husserl is unable to articulate any theory of meaning and expression – any workable account of how *parole* may exceed the structural economy of *langue* – without falling back on a tacit appeal to precisely those constitutive structures.[91] What they thus fail to recognise is Derrida's insistence, here and elsewhere, that the Husserlian project of transcendental phenomenology is in no sense discredited (or rendered obsolete) by these problems that arise in the course of making good its own philosophical claims. Phenomenology and structuralism may indeed be opposed at the deepest level of governing presupposition, the level at which thinking encounters all manner of intractable antinomies or aporias. These include (by no means exhaustively) the conflicts of priority between *parole* and *langue*, expression and signification, genesis and structure, meaning and form, intuition and concept, history and event, language as that which enables the transcendence of pre-given meaning-horizons, and language as itself the ultimate horizon – the structural condition of (im)possibility – that calls such claims into question. But we should nevertheless be wrong, Derrida cautions, to think *either* that this is an endgame predicament in which phenomenology and structuralism have played each other off the field – arrived (so to speak) at a point of interlocked terminal aporia – *or* that we are left with the necessity of somehow choosing between these (strictly incompatible) projects of thought. For what each encounters at the limit is a moment of negative self-knowledge, a recognition that its own resources are inadequate, and hence that structuralism cannot help but draw upon phenomenological themes and motifs, while phenomenology – especially in its Husserlian transcendental mode – is likewise reliant on certain proto-structuralist concepts or terms of analysis. This is not to say that either project is invalid; rather, as Derrida contends, that they each represent one of the paths that thinking must pursue in response to the 'question of the subject' as posed by the conjunction of these two most rigorous forms of present-day philosophical critique.

Thus '[b]y virtue of its innermost intention, and like all questions about language, structuralism escapes the classical history of ideas which already supposes structuralism's possibility, for the latter naively belongs to the province of language and propounds itself within it'.[92] And again: what Husserl's investigations reveal – despite and against his express intent – is 'the principled, essential, and structural impossibility of closing a structural phenomenology'.[93] I should perhaps stress (for those unfamiliar with the essays in question) that these statements are the upshot of sustained close-reading and rigorous conceptual exegesis, and not – as with much that currently passes for 'deconstructive' criticism – the result of a foregone assumption that *all* truth-claims are ultimately 'undecidable', that *all* concepts (like the concept of structure) are sublimated metaphors, that subjectivity is *always and everywhere* an effect of language, etc. These slogans are of course common coin among the zealots of post-structuralist theory, where they substitute for anything that approaches the level of cogent philosophical argument. Thus Derrida's aim in the above-quoted passages is precisely to disarm such naive appropriations of his work by insisting on the need to respect those imperatives (of lucidity, rigour and critique) which he finds manifest in a thinker like Husserl. For the issue between phenomenology and structuralism is joined not only by those who would view themselves as belonging to one or the other camp, but also – as my quotations again make clear – *within the very texts* (including the texts of Husserl) which seem to espouse one side of that issue. It is precisely at such points of self-contestation – at the stage where thought comes up against the limits of its own project – that Derrida locates their exemplary value.

Thus if '[Husserl] had to navigate between the Scylla and Charybdis of logicizing structuralism and psychologistic geneticism', this is not to be seen as a disabling liability, a symptom of some deep-laid (though avoidable) confusion.[94] Nor can it be taken – as is often the case among Derrida's more enthusiastic, less circumspect commentators – for a sign that the discussion has now moved on, that Husserl's way of thinking is hopelessly *dépassé*, and that Derridean talk of 'différance' and 'supplementarity' is sufficient to dispel any lingering remnant of that old 'metaphysics of presence'. Such ideas have got around only on account of their not having read – or having largely forgotten – the specific contexts of argument and the passages of hard-pressed analytic commentary where Derrida establishes the pertinence of these otherwise meaningless neologisms. Thus *différance* is shown to function, in his reading of Husserl, as a name for that movement of differing-deferral whose trace may be discerned in the constant oscillation between structure and meaning, between 'indicative' and 'expressive' signs, or again – in Husserl's work on the modalities of time-consciousness – between the elusive (or illusory) moment of punctual, self-present consciousness and those moments of 'retention' and 'protention' (of past- and future-oriented awareness) in the absence of which thinking can achieve no concept of the 'living present'.[95] I apologize for this tortuous piece of summary exposition, but offer it as a sample of the difficulties – the often quite literally mind-wrenching problems of conceptual or logico-semantic grasp – encountered by any such attempt to recapitulate Derrida's arguments. Hence his resort to a term like *différance*, not (or not simply) as an adroit pun that combines the two senses 'difference' and 'deferral', but also as a compact reminder of those 'considerable labours of conceptual exegesis' – in Paul de Man's apposite phrase – which a deconstructive reading properly requires.

The same can be said of those other Derridean key-terms – *pharmakon* as it figures in his essay on Plato, 'supplementarity' (or the 'logic of the supplement') in his reading of Rousseau, *parergon* (the metaphor of framing or boundary-lines) in relation to issues of aesthetic autonomy in Kant's *Critique of Judgment* – all of which elude any form of summary explication.[96] However, this is *not* (and the point needs making very firmly) on account of their semantic 'richness', ambiguity, range of associative meanings, etc. Still less is it a matter of strategic imprecision, of Derrida's adopting a 'literary' approach to these texts which exploits a rhetoric of undecidability (or open-ended 'freeplay') in order to head off philosophical objections. In each case what is involved is the appeal to a wider context of argument where the terms acquire salience through a process of meticulously detailed analytic close-reading. It is only by pursuing their various chains of implication – their 'logical grammar', to adopt a more familiar (Wittgensteinian) idiom – that deconstruction can claim to locate those moments of aporia when a project like Husserl's comes up against its limits of conceptual grasp. This is why Derrida's work has been so ill-served by commentators (post-structuralists and literary theorists chiefly) who invoke *différance* as if its mere mention were enough to bring them out beyond 'logocentrism', the Western 'metaphysics of presence', and other such catch-phrase substitutes for a knowledge of the relevant texts from Plato to Husserl. It is also why his thought has little in common with the wider drift towards forms of all-purpose postmodern scepticism. If 'a certain structuralism' is indeed, as Derrida claims, 'philosophy's most spontaneous gesture', then this has to do with the absolute and principled necessity that thinking strive for the utmost degree of conceptual rigour. But it is equally the case – borne out by Husserl's analyses despite their aporetic character – that there will always be something that exceeds and frustrates the structuralist project of enquiry. And 'structuralism' in this context is not just the name for a contemporary (post-Saussurian) movement of thought which derives its main precepts from the field of semiology (or synchronic linguistics), and which can therefore be viewed by philosophers as largely irrelevant to their own concerns. Rather, it denominates one contemporary form of that 'logicizing' (rationalist) philosophy of mind, knowledge and language whose legacy is visible not only in Husserl but also – as I have argued – in the problematic aspects of a work like Chomsky's *Cartesian Linguistics*.

Of course this invites the straightforward rejoinder: that Chomsky from the outset defined his own project in explicit opposition to the structuralist paradigm and its various methodological shortcomings. But here, as with Husserl, on Derrida's account, there is a deeper level at which Chomsky can be seen to inherit all those vexing antinomies – determinism/freewill, structure/genesis, *langue/parole*, meaning/ system, etc – that assume their most salient present-day form in the issue between structuralism and phenomenology, but whose background encompasses the entire post-Cartesian history of epistemological debate. It has been my contention that such issues cannot be laid to rest by any version of the blandly accommodating line – or the 'linguistic turn' in its various forms – that would simply call an end to such debate. For as Derrida remarks, '[t]he passage beyond philosophy does not consist in turning the page of philosophy (which usually amounts to philosophizing badly), but in continuing to read philosophers *in a certain way*'.[97] This is partly for the reason – the negative reason, as it might appear – that any attempt to pass 'beyond' those inherited concepts and categories, to break with the resources or the logical grammar of (so-called) 'Western metaphysics', will always inescapably be couched in a language that takes its critical bearings from that same formative pre-history. Thus '[w]e can pronounce not a single destructive proposition which has not already had to slip into the form, the logic, and the implicit postulations of precisely what it seeks to contest'.[98] Each word in this lapidary sentence could be taken as a standing rebuke to those – post-structuralists and others – who deploy terms like *différance* as if they possessed some talismanic power to deconstruct the entire edifice of 'logocentric' reason quite aside from their operative force as manifest in the reading of particular texts. On the contrary, Derrida writes: '[t]he quality and fecundity of a discourse are measured by the critical rigour with which this relation to the history of metaphysics and to inherited concepts is thought'.[99]

Nowhere is this more apparent than in his work on philosophers like Kant and Husserl, those who maintain – like Derrida himself – a vigilant (but none the less enlightened) awareness of problems that arise to complicate the project of enlightenment critique. Such is the difference between a Kantian ethos of principled scepticism – an attitude that takes nothing on trust as regards the most important issues of knowledge and belief – and a postmodern outlook of wholesale sceptical disdain for the discourse of enlightened, truth-seeking thought. What deconstruction keeps open – as against all forms of dogmatic, unreflective or un-self-critical rationalism – is precisely this question of the subject as it figures in philosophers from Descartes and Kant to Husserl, Heidegger, and Levinas. I have perhaps said enough to indicate how Derrida sustains this 'essential and principled' dialogue, as for instance between epistemology and ethics (in the two essays on Levinas), between structure and genesis (Husserl), or again, between the different Kantian orders of cognitive understanding, practical reason, regulative ideas, determinate and reflective judgment, etc. For postmodernists like Lyotard these distinctions are so absolute – and the prospects of agreement in any given case so utterly remote – that the subject becomes just a nominal entity, or a floating ensemble of 'heterogeneous' language-games. For post-structuralists also it is the merest of illusions to revert to an obsolete (Kantian) standpoint as regards the 'transcendental unity of apperception', or the requirement that thinking involve something more than the flux of transient subject-positions as assigned by this or that constitutive 'discourse'. Quite simply, they would argue, we possess no critical grounds – no view from outside the current range of (albeit multiple and conflicting) positions – from which to adjudicate in matters of truth and falsehood or right and wrong. And the same goes for those in the Wittgensteinian, the neo-pragmatist and liberal-communitarian camps, arguing as they do – mostly by appeal to some version of the linguistic turn – that what counts as true or right for all practical purposes is always a product of existing (consensus-based) habits of belief. For in this case the subject is likewise deprived of any active (critical or questioning) role in the process by which such beliefs gain credence as a matter of *de facto* communal assent.

If there is one thing these thinkers won't entertain it is the idea – the Kantian regulative idea – that an appeal is always open to truth at the end of enquiry, or (in Habermas's terms) to an 'ideal speech-situation' where these issues might be raised in the context of a free and open democratic debate. In each case the upshot is a failure to conceive how the subject may exercise his or her powers of autonomous, principled and critical judgment with a view to promoting that *sensus communis* – or realm of enlightened participant exchange – which Kant offers as a measure of 'maturity' in questions of shared ethico-political concern. Hence Foucault's privatised version of autonomy, his 'strong-revisionist' reading of Kant – alongside Baudelaire – as the thinker who first pointed the way to a quest for 'authentic' ethical values conceived in purely individualist terms as a project of aesthetic self-fashioning.[100] Hence also those various latterday strains of counter-enlightenment thought whose rise has gone along with a demotion of the subject as source and guarantor of truth, and with the idea of language (or discourse) as the bottom-line of epistemological and ethical enquiry. These ideas have gained ground, on my submission, only as a result of that widespread anti-foundationalist orthodoxy that misconstrues Kant's thinking about the subject in Cartesian (essentialist) terms, and which thus makes of it a convenient target for all manner of routine debunking strategies. Then again there are those – Chomsky among them – who lay themselves open to just such criticism through their appeal to a narrowly rationalist (pre-Kantian) philosophy of mind and language, one that encounters all the deep-laid aporias which Kant addressed throughout the three *Critiques*. This is why the Chomsky-Foucault 'dialogue' – more precisely, their failure to engage in such dialogue – can be seen as symptomatic of a breakdown of communications in the wider (philosophical and ethico-political) sphere. For if Foucault can argue that Chomsky is still attached to a notion of the subject as pure, self-originating source of knowledge and truth, then he can also proceed – with at least some show of plausibility – to denounce what Chomsky regards as the vital role of critical intellectuals in exposing the lies and hypocrisies of government from a standpoint of reasoned and principled dissent. Nothing could more clearly illustrate the gulf of mutual incomprehension opened up by this entrenched conflict of viewpoints with regard to the legacy of enlightenment thought.

Of course I am not competent to assess Chomsky's work in the field of transformational-generative grammar, a field so specialized as to render such comment absurdly presumptuous. Nor would I in any way wish to detract from his inspiring example as one of the few – very few – public intellectuals who have consistently had the courage to stand up against the ideological self-images of the age. My point is that his arguments have had little impact on the currency of 'advanced' theoretical debate since they have been taken – if often on minimal acquaintance – as entailing an appeal to that 'naive' subject-centred epistemic paradigm which has yet to catch up with the linguistic turn in its various (e.g. Lacanian, Foucauldian, and postmodern-pragmatist) forms. What makes this situation yet more unfortunate is the fact that these latter modes of thought, despite their 'radical' claims, possess nothing like the force of impassioned moral and political conviction that motivates Chomsky's writings. Habermas presents a rather different case since his arguments *contra* post-structuralism and various affiliated movements of thought are developed in the context of a detailed questing-back into the philosophic discourse of modernity.[101] Together with Manfred Frank and other commentators of a broadly 'Frankfurt' persuasion he essays a critical genealogy of the new irrationalism, a reminder of the various paths not taken – and the episodes unwittingly repeated – by exponents of this counter-enlightenment trend.[102] Not that Habermas always lives up to his own best standards of interpretive conduct. In my judgment (and I have argued this case at greater length elsewhere) he offers little more than a travesty of Derrida's work, an account based largely on secondary sources and ignoring its close (if ambivalent) relation to the truth-claims and values of enlightenment critique.[103] But for the most part – especially when he writes about Foucault and his Nietzschean rhetoric of power/knowledge – Habermas provides a pinpoint diagnosis of the regressive tendencies manifest in this turn toward uncritical (pre-Enlightenment) forms of thought.

Habermas is also, like Chomsky, a 'public' intellectual who has consistently sought to relate these issues to the wider sphere of moral and political debate. If the relation is more convincingly argued in

Habermas's case it is because his philosophical sights are not fixed on that subject-centured (Cartesian) legacy of rationalist thought which has lately given rise to such a deal of confused and dead-end polemical strife. For it is with Kant, not Descartes, that Habermas starts out in his large-scale attempt to vindicate the claims of enlightenment critique as a *shared and collective* human enterprise, rather than a matter of the solitary thinker (the transcendental subject-presumed-to-know) arriving at truths through the individual exercise of unaided reason. From which it follows – postmodern scepticism notwithstanding – that such claims can survive both the anti-foundationalist onslaught and also (what often goes along with it) the 'linguistic turn' as a means of acknowledging their social, discursively-mediated character. For Habermas, as indeed for Kant, the point is not so much to reject any appeal to consensus values as to keep open the saving possibility of a genuine (enlightened) public sphere, a *sensus communis* redeemed from the various kinds of error, prejudice or distorting partiality that have so far prevented us from achieving such a goal. Of course this position is not without its problems when confronted with the typical postmodern-pragmatist (or liberal-communitarian) line of response. Thus it may well be argued, as by critics like Richard Rorty, that any talk of 'universal pragmatics' in the end comes down to just a minor variation on the standard pragmatist theme, i.e. a more 'principled' and high-sounding version of the appeal to what is (currently and contingently) 'good in the way of belief'.[104] In fact it seems to me that Habermas has lately yielded too much ground to the anti-foundationalist camp, as compared, for example, with an early book like *Knowledge and Human Interests* where his argument is both more Kantian in its philosophic orientation and more confidently premised on the values of enlightened (critical-emancipatory) thought. But this should not distract us from the main point at issue between Habermas and the apostles of postmodernity: namely, his commitment – early and late – to a Kantian conception of the intellectual's role in promoting the interests of reasoned debate on matters of moral and political conscience.

Hence – most recently – his interventions in the so-called *Historikerstreit*, the controversy occasioned by those right-wing revisionist historians who would deny the evidence (or minimise the extent) of Nazi wartime atrocities.[105] In denouncing these impostures Habermas is not – as Foucauldians might see it – assuming the role of an old-style 'universal intellectual', one who sets up as the conscience of his age merely on the strength of his own expertise in some specialised region of enquiry. On the contrary, what Habermas seeks to defend against its current (postmodernist and post-structuralist) detractors is precisely that Kantian regulative idea of the *sensus communis*, the public realm of informed participant debate wherein such truth-claims are offered and criticised according to the relevant criteria. As regards the 'revisionist' historians, this involves a range of normative standards – factual, evidential, methodological, ethical, socio-political etc – which between them constitute a means of assessing both the *truth* and the *truthfulness* (the good-faith condition) of any statement or version of events that claims historical warrant. Clearly these issues have a special urgency in the context of postwar German history. For Habermas they are crucially linked to continuing debates about the legacy of guilt and responsibility for Nazi war-crimes, and the role of memory – or historical awareness – as a guardian of collective conscience. They also raise complex ethical and political questions with regard to free speech and the limits of acceptable public discourse in a social-democratic order that is committed – so far as possible – to preserving such freedoms even for those who would exploit or abuse them to anti-democratic ends. Hence the importance (as Habermas argues) of maintaining a genuinely critical 'public sphere', a forum of exchange where these and other issues are openly raised through a process of active and informed participant debate. Only to the extent that such conditions exist can the state claim legitimate (democratically warranted) authority for placing some juridical constraint upon the public expression of extremist, racist, or – as in this case – mendacious and morally repugnant views.

Nor will these questions seem merely philosophical – or Habermas's stance just a species of arrogant intellectualism – if one considers (for instance) how Lyotard fares in the face of similar 'revisionist' claims advanced by the French historian Robert Faurisson.[106] On Faurisson's submission, we can have no knowledge, no *evidence* of what actually occurred in the gas-chambers at Auschwitz since there exist no survivors who can vouch for the facts as a matter of first-hand empirical witness. One might think this 'argument' so utterly absurd – such a squalid piece of sophistry in the service of current neo-fascist propaganda – as to place itself beyond the pale of civilised debate. On second thoughts one might begin, with heavy heart, to point out the irrelevance (and the patent bad faith) of Faurisson's alleged criteria; the massive accumulation of evidence from other (material, documentary, and testimonial) sources; the elementary blunder involved in adopting so crassly reductive or positivist a view of what counts as veridical warrant in such a case; and the wholesale dereliction of ethical values that results from a scepticism pushed to the point – as Orwell gloomily predicted – of annulling the difference between historical fact and ideological fiction. That such claims are advanced and widely (even seriously) discussed is no doubt a melancholy sign of the times, one indication among many of the depressed state of our present-day intellectual culture. But at least it may be said, of Habermas in particular, that this sceptical drift has not gone so far as to leave us without resources – philosophic and ethical resources – for exposing those claims to a vigorous rebuttal in the sphere of reasoned and principled debate.

For Lyotard, conversely, the last thing we should do when confronted with an argument like Faurisson's is to assess it according to our own presumptive standards of validity, justice, or truth. For we shall thereby fail to acknowledge the narrative 'differend' between his and our version of events, the need to suspend judgment – so Lyotard thinks – whenever two or more parties find themselves deeply at odds on some question of factual, ethical, or interpretative warrant. Moreover, there is a sense in which we wrong Faurisson by suppressing the discursive differential, the conflict of 'heterogeneous' language-games that afford no common adjudicative ground – no standpoint of impartial reason or truth – for sorting out the issue between them. Thus:

> one side's legitimacy does not imply the other's lack of legitimacy. However, applying a single rule of judgment to both in order to settle their differend ... would wrong (at least) one of them (and both if neither side admits this rule) ... A wrong results from the fact that the rules of the genre of discourse by which one judges are not those of the judged genre or genres of discourse.[107]

Quite simply, Faurisson is not interested in playing by the established (consensual) rules with regard to the protocols of scholarly enquiry, the respect for documentary sources, the critical sifting of evidence, and so forth. Nor does he offer his reading of the Holocaust as in any way subject to those normative 'phrase-regimes' that concern themselves on the one hand with *truth* as an object of disciplined historical research, and on the other with *justice* – justice to the victim – as arrived at through reflection on the facts of that history in the sphere of public (intersubjective) debate. Such appeals are quite without force in the case of an historian who flouts every ground-rule of the discipline (as well as every standard of humane or civilised moral judgment) in pursuit of his 'revisionist' line.

In short, we mistake what Faurisson is up to if we think to condemn him – to banish his work from the realm of 'competent', 'responsible' scholarship – by application of the usual criteria. Worse still: we run the risk that he will turn the argument around and accuse his accusers – those enlightened seekers-after-truth – of erecting their values into a universal law that unjustly ignores the differend, and which thus becomes repressive (or totalitarian) by its very nature. However, '[t]he historian need not strive to convince Faurisson if Faurisson is "playing" another genre of discourse, one in which conviction, or the obtainment of consensus over a defined reality, is not at stake ... Should the historian persist along this path, he will wind up in the position of victim'.[108] So the only response, as Lyotard sees it, is to operate always on the postmodern variant of Kant's categorical imperative, that is to say, the triple injunction: 'Let us wage war on totality', 'let us maximise the range of first-order pragmatic narratives', and 'let us save the honour of the name'.[109] And if this means granting an historian like Faurisson the benefit of the sceptical doubt – or treating even a name like 'Auschwitz' as possessed of no intrinsic historical, testamentary or moral significance – then we had best not flinch from such drastic conclusions. For '[w]hat you are calling bad will, etc, is the name you give to the fact that the opponent does not have a stake in establishing reality, that he does not accept the rules for forming and validating cognitives, that his goal is not to convince'.[110] In which case – again – one will play into Faurisson's hands by seeking either to refute his argument on factual-documentary grounds or to expose his 'bad will' by appealing to principles of justice, humanity, or shared moral outrage. For on Lyotard's account there is nothing that can justify those principles aside from their belonging to some particular (e.g. liberal-humanist) discourse, language-game, or cultural 'form of life'. And such a discourse will always give rise to injustice – to infractions of the narrative differend – if it presumes to extend its criteria of judgment over disputants (like Faurisson) who reject them *tout court*.

It is hard to know where to begin in disentangling this mess of philosophical confusions. Any adequate critique would have to go a long and (for present purposes) a needlessly distracting way around. It would take in – among other things – the familiar straw-man tactic whereby a narrowly positivist (or empiricist) conception of truth is set up as an easy target for the sceptic's routine dismissal; the Wittgensteinian appeal to language-games as a means of simply blocking any further argument on questions of truth, justice, or morality; the strain of ultra-nominalist thinking that treats *names* (as opposed to propositions, truth-claims, arguments, reasoned counter-arguments etc.) as the sole point of reference in any such dispute; the idea – debatably derived from Hume, shamelessly exploited by Faurisson, uncritically endorsed by Lyotard – that there exists an absolute, unbridgeable gulf between questions of fact and issues of ethical judgment; the current (postmodern/post-structuralist) doxa as regards the 'arbitrary' nature of the sign, the inscrutability of reference, the open-ended 'freeplay' of signification, and so forth; and – again most apparent in Lyotard's work – the perverse misreading of Kant that elevates the sublime as a figure of ultimate 'heterogeneity', a name for that which paradoxically 'presents the unpresentable', and hence for whatever exceeds or disconcerts the attempt to render justice in any given case. This last (and seemingly most specialized) issue is none the less crucial for any understanding of what is at stake in the current postmodernist drive to revoke the philosophic discourse of modernity. For, as Lyotard knows, the sublime is that point at which revisionist readings – whether of Kant or of post-Enlightenment historical events – can most readily take hold in the realm of intellectual debate. And they can then be harnessed to a generalized scepticism *vis-à-vis* the prospects for 'establishing reality', for 'attaining consensus over a defined area', or for dispelling those illusions – those forms of very active false consciousness – that presently constitute an obstacle to the emergence of any such enlightened public sphere.

Of course this is merely to flag some of the main points at issue. They all require a great deal more in the way of detailed analysis and critique, work that I have attempted elsewhere and that others – a significant number of philosophers and critical theorists – have likewise been drawn to undertake.[111] In this chapter my aim has been somewhat different: to examine the 'linguistic turn' as it figures across a range of present-day disciplines, and to suggest some alternative resources for critical theory. In its most extreme form – as with Lyotard – the result of such thinking is a *reductio ad absurdum* of the sceptical-relativist case, a dissolution of the Kantian public sphere into so many strictly incommensurable discourses, each disposing of its own *sui generis* criteria, and thus quite immune to criticism on factual, epistemic, or evaluative grounds. This position is arrived at by the grafting of late-Wittgensteinian themes ('language-games', 'forms of life', etc) onto a post-structuralist doctrine of the 'arbitrary' sign – a misconstrual of Saussure's working premise – and a Nietzsche-inspired attitude of radical mistrust with regard to all truth-claims or normative values. It goes along with that strain of theoretical anti-humanism (more exactly: that rejection of Cartesian rationalism in whatever residual guise) which has formed such a prominent feature of recent French thought. But the subject is no sooner demoted in this fashion – dismissed as just a figment of the liberal-humanist imaginary – than it returns (so to speak) with a vengeance, or under an aspect that bears all the hallmarks of serving as a regressive fantasy-substitute. Hence Foucault's protracted endeavour to articulate an ethics of autonomous self-creation, one that would break with notions of enlightened (intersubjective) reason and truth, and would discover its ideal in the ethos of *literary* modernism, or the project of strong-revisionist imagining exemplified by a poet like Baudelaire. I have argued that this project inherits all the problems and antinomies of Kantian critical philosophy, but that it offers nothing more than a dead-end response, a refusal to engage those problems constructively, and a retreat into various disabling postures of *au courant* postmodern scepticism.

Now at last there are signs – not least among its erstwhile exponents – that this whole anti-humanist line of talk has begun to show up as what in truth it always was, a massive and distorting simplification of the issues involved. The title of one recent volume of essays – *What Comes After the Subject?* – may serve, despite its coyly ambiguous phrasing, as a pointer to this welcome (if belated) recognition: that such talk is intellectually and morally bankrupt, since it sidesteps the three cardinal Kantian questions, 'What can I know?', 'What ought I to do?', and 'What may I reasonably hope for?'.[112] The linguistic turn has very often been a pretext for dismissing those questions out of hand, or – what amounts to much the same thing – for treating them (in Nietzschean-genealogical style) as so many obsolete topics thrown up by the delusive, quasi-transcendentalizing 'discourse' of Kantian-enlightenment thought. What remains deeply puzzling is the ease with which this orthodoxy captured the minds of so many otherwise intelligent philosophers and theorists.

NOTES

1. A.O. Lovejoy, 'On the Discrimination of Romanticisms', *Publications of the Modern Language Association of America*, Vol. XXXIX (1924), pp229-53; reprinted in Lovejoy, *Essays in the History of Ideas* (Baltimore: Johns Hopkins University Press, 1948).
2. Emile Benveniste, *Problems in General Linguistics* (Miami: Miami University Press, 1971). For an interesting, quirkish but broadly post-structuralist 'take' on Benveniste's ideas, see Roland Barthes, 'Why I love Benveniste', in *The Rustle of Language* (Oxford: Basic Blackwell, 1986); pp162-7.
3. J.L. Austin, *How To Do Things With Words* (London: Oxford University Press, 1962).
4. Shoshana Felman, *The Literary Speech Act: Don Juan with Austin, or seduction in two languages*, trans. Catherine Porter (Ithaca, N.Y.: Cornell University Press, 1983).
5. See especially Jacques Lacan, *Ecrits: a selection*, trans. A. Sheridan-Smith (London: Tavistock, 1977); also Lacan, *The Four Fundamental Concepts of Psychoanalysis*, trans. Sheridan-Smith (London: Hogarth Press, 1978). For an excellent brief introduction, see Malcolm Bowie, *Lacan* (London: Fontana, 1991).
6. These equations are developed most explicitly in Lacan, 'The Agency of the Letter in the Unconscious, or Reason since Freud', in *Ecrits* (op cit), pp146-78.
7. *Ibid*, p168.
8. For a shrewd account of Lacan's ambivalent (though mainly hostile) attitude to philosophy, see David Macey, *Lacan In Contexts* (London: Verso, 1988), especially pp75-120.
9. Jürgen Habermas, *Knowledge and Human Interests*, trans. Jeremy J. Shapiro (London: Heinemann, 1972).
10. Lacan, 'Seminar on "The Purloined Letter" ', trans. Jeffrey Mehlman, *Yale French Studies*, No. 48 (1973), pp39-72.
11. Habermas, *The Philosophical Discourse of Modernity: twelve lectures*, trans. Frederick W. Lawrence (Cambridge: Polity Press, 1987).
12. See for instance Rainer Nägele, 'Freud, Habermas and the Dialectic of Enlightenment: on real and ideal discourses', *New German Critique*, Vol. XXII (1981), pp41-62.
13. See especially Habermas, *Theory of Communicative Action*, Vols. 1 & 2. trans. Thomas McCarthy (Boston: Beacon Press, 1984 and 1989).
14. See for instance Richard Rorty, *Consequences of Pragmatism* (Minneapolis: University of Minnesota Press, 1982) and *Contingency, Irony, and Solidarity* (Cambridge: Cambridge University Press, 1989); also Stanley Fish, *Doing What Comes Naturally: change, rhetoric, and the practice of theory in literary and legal studies* (Oxford: Clarendon Press, 1989).
15. For a recent example see Francis Fukuyama, *The End of History and the Last Man* (London: Heinemann, 1992).
16. I develop these arguments at greater length in Norris, *Uncritical Theory: postmodernism, intellectuals and the Gulf War* (London: Lawrence &

Wishart and Amherst, Mass.: University of Massachusetts Press, 1992).
17. Michel Foucault, *The Order of Things: an archaeology of the human sciences* (London: Tavistock, 1970). See also Foucault, *The Archaeology of Knowledge*, trans. A. Sheridan-Smith (London: Tavistock, 1972).
18. Foucault, *The Order of Things* (*op cit*), p387.
19. See especially Foucault, *Language, Counter-Memory, Practice: selected essays and interviews*, Donald F. Bouchard and Sherry Simon (eds) (Ithaca, N.Y.: Cornell University Press, 1977) and *Power/Knowledge: selected interviews and other writings* (Brighton: Harvester Press, 1980).
20. Roland Barthes, *S/Z*, trans. Richard Miller (London: Jonathan Cape, 1975).
21. These essays are collected in Barthes, *Image, Music, Text*, trans. Stephen Heath (London: Fontana, 1977).
22. See Foucault, *Madness and Civilization: a history of insanity in the age of reason*, trans. Richard Howard (New York: Mentor Books, 1971); *The Birth of the Clinic: an archaeology of medical perception*, trans. A. Sheridan-Smith (New York: Vintage Books, 1973); *Discipline and Punish: the birth of the prison*, trans. A. Sheridan-Smith (New York: Pantheon, 1977); *The History of Sexuality*, Vol. 1 (*An Introduction*), trans. Robert Hurley (New York: Pantheon, 1978).
23. See the late essays and interviews collected in *The Foucault Reader*, Paul Rabinow (ed) (Harmondsworth: Penguin, 1984); also *The Final Foucault*, James Bernauer and David Rasmussen (eds) (Cambridge, Mass.: M.I.T. Press, 1988).
24. Foucault, 'What Is Enlightenment?', in Rabinow (ed), *The Foucault Reader* (*op cit*), pp32-50.
25. Rorty, 'Moral Identity and Private Autonomy: the case of Foucault', in *Essays on Heidegger and Others* (Cambridge: Cambridge University Press, 1992), pp193-8.
26. *Ibid*, p198.
27. Foucault, 'On the Genealogy of Ethics: an overview of work in progress' (interview with Paul Rabinow and Hubert Dreyfus), in Rabinow (ed), *The Foucault Reader* (*op cit*), pp340-72; p350.
28. Foucault, 'What Is Enlightenment?' (*op cit*), p46.
29. *Ibid*, p50.
30. Foucault, 'Polemics, Politics and Problematizations' (interview with Paul Rabinow), in *The Foucault Reader* (*op cit*), pp381-90; p390.
31. *Ibid*, p388.
32. Foucault, 'What Is Enlightenment?' (*op cit*), p43.
33. Foucault, 'On the Genealogy of Ethics' (*op cit*), p352.
34. Foucault, 'What Is Enlightenment?' (*op cit*), p42.
35. *Ibid*, p45.
36. Claude Lévi-Strauss, 'History and Dialectic', in *The Savage Mind* (London: Weidenfeld & Nicolson, 1972), pp245-69.
37. See M.A.K. Halliday, *Explorations in the Functions of Language* (London: Edward Arnold, 1973); *System and Function in Language: selected papers*, G.R. Kress (ed) (London: Oxford University Press, 1976); *Language as Social Semiotic* (London: Edward Arnold, 1978).

38. See Umberto Eco, *A Theory of Semiotics* (Bloomington, Ind.: Indiana University Press, 1971) and *Semiotics and the Philosophy of Language* (London: Macmillan, 1984).
39. Hubert L. Dreyfus, *What Computers Can't Do: the limits of artificial intelligence*, rev. ed. (New York: Harper & Row, 1979).
40. See for instance Noam Chomsky, *Rules and Representations* (New York: Columbia University Press, 1980); Daniel C. Dennett, *The Intentional Stance* (Cambridge, Mass.: MIT. Press, 1987) and *Consciousness Explained* (London: Allen Lane, 1991); Jerry A. Fodor, *Psychosemantics: the problem of meaning in the philosophy of mind* (MIT Press, 1987) and *Representations: philosophical essays in the foundations of cognitive science* (Brighton: Harvester Press, 1981); John R. Searle, *Intentionality: an essay in the philosophy of mind* (Cambridge: Cambridge University Press, 1983) and *Minds, Brains and Science* (London: BBC Publications, 1984).
41. See Noam Chomsky, *Syntactic Structures* (The Hague: Mouton, 1957); *Current Issues in Linguistic Theory* (Mouton, 1964); *Aspects of the Theory of Syntax* (Cambridge, Mass.: MIT Press, 1965); *Topics in the Theory of Generative Grammar* (Mouton, 1966); *Studies on Semantics in Generative Grammar* (Mouton, 1972).
42. Chomsky, *Language and Responsibility* (based on conversations with Mitsou Ronat), (New York: Pantheon, 1979); also *Problems of Knowledge and Freedom* (New York: Pantheon, 1971); *Knowledge of Language: its nature, origin and use* (New York: Praeger, 1986); and *Language and Problems of Knowledge* (Cambridge, Mass.: MIT Press, 1988).
43. See for instance Chomsky, *American Power and the New Mandarins* (Harmondsworth: Penguin, 1969); *For Reasons of State* (New York: Pantheon Books, 1973); *The Fateful Triangle: the United States, Israel and the Palestinians* (Boston, Mass.: South End Press, 1983); *On Power and Ideology*, (South End Press, 1987); *Language and Politics* (Montreal: Black Rose Books, 1988); *Necessary Illusions: thought control in democratic societies* (London: Pluto Press, 1989).
44. Chomsky, *Cartesian Linguistics: a chapter in the history of rationalist thought* (New York: Harper & Row, 1966).
45. Chomsky, 'Review of B.F. Skinner's *Verbal Behavior*', *Language*, Vol. XXXV, No. 1 (1959).
46. See Pierre Bourdieu, *Homo Academicus* (Cambridge: Polity Press, 1988) and *Language and Symbolic Power*, trans. Gino Raymond and John B. Thompson (Polity Press, Cambridge 1991).
47. Michael Oakeshott, *Rationalism in Politics, and other essays* (London: Methuen, 1962).
48. See for instance Roger Scruton, *The Meaning of Conservatism* (Harmondsworth: Penguin, 1980).
49. Immanuel Kant, *Critique of Pure Reason*, trans. N. Kemp Smith (London: Macmillan, 1933).
50. Kant, *Critique of Practical Reason*, trans. L.W. Beck (Indianapolis: Bobbs-Merrill, 1975).
51. Onora O'Neill, *Construction of Reason: explorations of Kant's practical philosophy* (Cambridge: Cambridge University Press, 1989).

52. *Ibid*, p29.
53. See for instance Michael J. Sandel, *Liberalism and the Limits of Justice* (Cambridge: Cambridge University Press, 1982); also Sandel, *Liberalism and its Critics* (Oxford: Basil Blackwell, 1984).
54. G.W.F. Hegel, *Philosophy of Right*, trans. T.M. Knox (London: Oxford University Press, 1952).
55. Bernard Williams, *Ethics and the Limits of Philosophy* (London: Fontana, 1985); Michael Walzer, *Spheres of Justice* (Oxford; Basil Blackwell, 1983).
56. See Rorty, *Contingency, Irony, and Solidarity* (*op cit*) and Fish, *Doing What Comes Naturally* (*op cit*).
57. Fukuyama, *The End of History and the Last Man* (*op. cit.*).
58. Peter Winch, *Ethics and Action* (London: Routledge & Kegan Paul, 1972), p55.
59. O'Neill, *Construction of Reason* (*op cit*), p175.
60. *Ibid*, p25.
61. Some of these texts are collected in Hans Reiss (ed), *Kant's Political Writings* (Cambridge: Cambridge University Press, 1970) and L.W. Beck, R.E. Anchor and E.L. Fackenham (eds), *Kant: on history* (Indianapolis: Bobbs-Merril, 1973).
62. O'Neill, *Constructions of Reason* (*op cit*), p16.
63. Jean-François Lyotard, *The Differend: phrases in dispute*, trans. Georges Van Den Abeele (Manchester: Manchester University Press, 1988).
64. Christina Howells, 'Conclusion: Sartre and the deconstruction of the subject', in Howells (ed), *The Cambridge Companion to Sartre* (Cambridge: Cambridge University Press, 1992), pp318-52; p322.
65. Cited by Howells (*ibid*), p323.
66. See for instance the essays collected in Eduardo Cadava, Peter Connor and Jean-Luc Nancy (eds), *Who Comes After the Subject?* (London: Routledge, 1991).
67. See Lyotard, *The Differend* (*op cit*); also 'Complexity and the Sublime', in Lisa Appignanesi (ed), *Postmodernism* (London: ICA Documents/Free Association Books, 1989), pp19-26 and *The Inhuman: reflections on time*, trans. Geoff Bennington and Rachel Bowlby (Cambridge: Polity Press, 1991).
68. See for instance Dick Hebdige, *Hiding in the Light: on images and things* (London: Routledge, 1988); Hugh Silverman (ed), *The Textual Sublime* (Albany, N.Y.: State University of New York Press, 1990); and Slavoj Zizek, *The Sublime Object of Ideology* (London: Verso, 1990).
69. Jean-François Lyotard and Jean-Loup Thébaud, *Just Gaming*, trans. Wlad Godzich (Manchester: Manchester University Press, 1986).
70. O'Neill, *Constructions of Reason* (*op cit*), p85.
71. *Ibid*, p85.
72. *Ibid*, p85.
73. *Ibid*, p19.
74. Joseph Graham, *Onomatopoetics: theory of language and literature* (Cambridge: Cambridge University Press, 1992). See also note 76, below.
75. Thomas A. Pavel, *The Feud of Language: a history of structuralist thought* (Oxford: Basil Blackwell, 1990).

76. In his *Onomatopoetics* (*op cit*) Joseph Graham argues that literary theory has run into all kinds of confusion through its over-reliance on an inadequate (Saussurean) paradigm of linguistic structure, and its failure to take account of more recent developments in cognitive psychology, artificial intelligence, grammatico-semantic theory, etc. Hence – according to Graham – its eager embrace of such modish doctrines as the 'arbitrary' sign, the radical indeterminacy of meaning, the open-ended 'freeplay' of interpretation, and rhetoric (quite apart from logic or grammar) as the sole horizon of linguistic intelligibility. Much better had these theorists acquired some knowledge of, for instance, Jerry Fodor's work on the structures of cognitive-semantic representation, work that might have saved them a deal of misplaced pseudo-philosophical endeavour. (See references to Fodor, n. 40 above.) For what then becomes clear is the need to distinguish between issues of interpretation at the depth-grammatical level (where understanding is constrained by determinate structures of cognitive and logico-semantic grasp), and those other – more subjective or culture-specific – forms of interpretive activity which are not thus constrained and which therefore involve at least some measure of hermeneutic licence. Where post-structuralism errs is in taking these latter as the paradigm case for *all* interpretation, and hence (Graham argues) reducing language to an endless game of rhetorical substitutions, deconstructive aporias, proliferating signifiers, 'unlimited semiosis', and so forth.

His case seems to me both well-argued and a needful corrective to many of those confusions that have bedevilled recent literary theory. At the same time it raises a new set of problems by adopting what I have here described as a latterday version of the Cartesian-rationalist standpoint. That is, it invokes the kind of 'black-box', compartmentalised philosophy of mind and language that construes these issues in artificial isolation from the wider (social and ethical) context of communicative utterance. And in so doing – I would also contend – Graham ignores the very real differences of theory and principle between, on the one hand, post-structuralism, postmodernism, neo-pragmatism and suchlike varieties of wholesale sceptical creed, and on the other deconstruction with its far more articulate philosophical grasp of the questions thus raised. Nevertheless his book is a welcome contribution and one that leaves post-structuralists with less excuse for proffering Saussure – or their own highly selective reading of Saussure – as the last word in linguistic wisdom.

77. Roland Barthes, 'The Death of the Author', in *The Rustle of Language*, trans. Richard Howard (Oxford: Basil Blackwell, 1986), pp49-55; Michel Foucault, 'What is an Author?', trans. Josué V. Harari, in Harari (ed), *Textual Strategies: perspectives in post-structuralist criticism* (Ithaca, N.Y.: Cornell University Press, 1979), pp141-60; also Foucault, 'Afterword: the Subject in Power', in Hubert L. Dreyfus and Paul Rabinow, *Michel Foucault: beyond structuralism and hermeneutics* (Brighton: Harvester Press, 1982), pp208-26. For an informative and vigorously-argued treatment of this topic, see Sean Burke, *The Death and Return of the Author* (Edinburgh: Edinburgh University Press, 1992).

78. See especially – from a range of philosophical perspectives – Andrew Bowie, *Aesthetics and Subjectivity from Kant to Nietzsche* (Manchester: Manchester University Press, 1990); Anthony J. Cascardi, *The Subject of Modernity* (Cambridge: Cambridge University Press, 1992); Stanley Corngold, *The Fate of the Self: German writers and French theory* (New York: Columbia University Press, 1986); Peter Dews, *Logics of Disintegration: post-structuralist thought and the claims of theory* (London: Verso, 1987); Manfred Frank, *What Is Neostructuralism?*, trans. Sabine Wilke and Richard Gray (Minneapolis: University of Minnesota Press, 1989); Jürgen Habermas, *The Philosophical Discourse of Modernity* (*op cit*); Gillian Rose, *Dialectic of Nihilism: post-structuralism and law* (Oxford: Basil Blackwell, 1984).

79. 'Noam Chomsky and Michel Foucault: human nature, justice *versus* power', in Fons Elders (ed), *Reflexive Water: the basic concerns of mankind* (London: Souvenir Press, 1974), pp133-97.

80. See Habermas, *Theory of Communicative Action* (*op cit*).

81. See especially Jacques Derrida, 'Parergon', in *The Truth in Painting*, trans. Geoff Bennington and Ian McLeod (Chicago: University of Chicago Press, 1987); 'Economimesis', trans. Richard Klein, *Diacritics*, Vol. XI, No. 2 (Summer 1981), pp3-25.

82. On this aspect of Derrida's work, see Rodolphe Gasché, *The Tain of the Mirror: Derrida and the philosophy of reflection* (Cambridge, Mass.: Harvard University Press, 1986); also Irene Harvey, *Derrida and the Economy of Differance* (Bloomington, Ind.: Indiana University Press, 1986).

83. Derrida, 'The Ends of Man', in *Margins of Philosophy*, trans. Alan Bass (Chicago: University of Chicago Press, 1982).

84. Derrida, *De l'esprit: Heidegger et la question* (Paris: Editions Galilée, 1987), p20. Cited in Howells, *op cit*, p70.

85. Derrida, 'Violence and Metaphysics', in *Writings and Difference*, trans. Alan Bass (London: Routledge & Kegan Paul, 1978), pp79-153; 'En ce moment même dans cet ouvrage me voici', in *Psyché: inventions de l'autre* (Paris: Editions Galilée, 1987).

86. See Emmanuel Levinas, *Totality and Infinity*, trans. A. Lingis (Pittsburgh, Pa.: Duquesne University Press, 1969); *Otherwise than Being, or beyond essence*, trans. A. Lingis (The Hague: Martinus Nijhoff, 1981).

87. Some of the best commentary on this 'turn' in Derrida's thought – albeit from a standpoint at variance with my own – may be found in Simon Critchley, *The Ethics of Deconstruction* (Oxford: Basil Blackwell, 1991).

88. See especially Derrida, *'Speech and Phenomena' and Other Essays on Husserl's Theory of Signs*, trans. David B. Allison (Evanston, Ill.: Northwestern University Press, 1973); also 'Force and Signification' and 'Structure and Genesis', in *Writing and Difference* (*op cit*), pp3-30 & 154-68.

89. Derrida, 'Genesis and Structure', p160.

90. Derrida, 'Force and Signification', p5.

91. See Derrida, *Speech and Phenomena* (*op cit*).

92. Derrida, 'Force and Signification' (*op cit*), p4.

93. Derrida, 'Genesis and Structure' (op cit), p162.
94. Ibid, p158.
95. See Derrida, 'Différance', in Speech and Phenomena (op cit); also Edmund Husserl, The Phenomenology of Internal Time-Consciousness, trans. James S. Churchill (Bloomington, Ind.: Indiana University Press, 1964).
96. Derrida, 'Plato's Pharmacy', in Dissemination, trans. Barbara Johnson (London: Athlone Press, 1981, pp61-171; (on Rousseau) Of Grammatology, trans. Gayatri C. Spivak (Baltimore: Johns Hopkins University Press, 1976); 'Parergon', in The Truth in Painting (op cit).
97. Derrida, 'Structure, Sign and Play in the Discourse of the Human Sciences', in Writing and Difference (op cit), pp278-93, p288.
98. Ibid, pp280-1.
99. Ibid, pp282.
100. Foucault, 'What is Enlightenment?' (op cit).
101. Habermas, The Philosophical Discourse of Modernity (op cit).
102. Manfred Frank, What Is Neostructuralism? (op cit).
103. Christopher Norris, 'Deconstruction, Postmodernism and Philosophy: Habermas on Derrida', in Norris, What's Wrong with Postmodernism: critical theory and the ends of philosophy (Hemel Hempstead: Harvester-Wheatsheaf and Baltimore: Johns Hopkins University Press, 1991), pp49-76.
104. See Rorty, 'Habermas and Lyotard on Postmodernity', in Essays on Heidegger and Others (Cambridge: Cambridge University Press, 1991), pp164-76.
105. Jürgen Habermas, The New Conservatism: cultural criticism and the historians' debate, ed. and trans. Shierry Weber (Cambridge: Polity Press, 1989).
106. Lyotard, The Differend (op cit).
107. Ibid, p13.
108. Ibid, p19.
109. See Lyotard, The Postmodern Condition: a report on knowledge, trans. Geoff Bennington and Brian Massumi (Manchester: Manchester University Press, 1984).
110. Lyotard, The Differend (op cit), pp18-9.
111. See Christopher Norris, The Truth About Postmodernism (Oxford: Basil Blackwell, 1993); also Norris, What's Wrong with Postmodernism (op cit) and Uncritical Theory (op cit).
112. Cadava, Connor and Nancy (eds), Who Comes After the Subject? (op cit).

2

RAISING THE TONE: DERRIDA, KIERKEGAARD AND THE RHETORIC OF TRANSCENDENCE

I MUST WE MEAN WHAT WE SAY? DECONSTRUCTION AND THE 'APOCALYPTIC TONE'

'Apocalypse': etymologically a shedding of veils, a revelation of truths hitherto concealed, a coming-to-light of some sacred or secret wisdom vouchsafed only to the elect few. This is the realm of hermeneutics, rather than philosophy, to the extent that philosophy has mostly been thought of – at least since Socrates – as a process of reasoned and disciplined enquiry aimed toward establishing valid propositions in the sphere of enlightened understanding. And indeed the philosophers have not taken kindly to the 'apocalyptic tone', regarding it as a renegade or upstart discourse, a mode of address that ignores all the protocols, all the criteria and validity-conditions that properly determine what shall count as a competent (good-faith) contribution to debate. These characters offend against reason and justice alike by claiming a privileged access to truth that renders them exempt from any such requirements. Moreover, their language is so cryptic and obscure – so akin to the rapturous afflatus of the poets, prophets and other enthusiasts – that it brooks no correction from the critical tribunal of plain-prose reason. They can wax eloquent on any topic you care to name without the least show of supporting argument or proof that they know what they are talking about. Worse than that, they affect an arrogant belief that they, and they alone, have attained true wisdom through this power of mystical-intuitive insight that rejects any challenge on grounds of mere logic, consistency, or evidential warrant.[1]

In short, the 'apocalyptic tone' is nothing more than a species of rhetorical imposture, a strategy for evading peer-group review among those – the genuine philosophers – who submit their judgment to the *sensus communis* of informed participant exchange. So little do its zealots care for such debate that they positively glory in the gulf of mutual incomprehension – the lack of any shared grounds for discussion – between their own rhapsodic-inspirational style and the kinds of philosophising mostly carried on in the academies, the journals, or other such reputable quarters. Quite simply, they think themselves above such commonplace or workaday standards of assessment, presuming as they do – on no better authority than sheer intuitive self-evidence – that what is true or right is what is revealed to them through possession of the requisite hermeneutic skills.[2] Hence the long series of philosophical put-downs, from Plato's dialogues – where Socrates is shown running expert dialectical rings around the poets, rhetoricians, sophists and other such false claimants to truth – to the latest bout of hostilities between thinkers in the Anglo-American 'analytic' camp and those, like Derrida, who are taken to exemplify the worst excesses of that whole misbegotten 'continental' tradition of thought. The idioms may have changed, and the lines of demarcation been drawn rather differently from time to time. Nevertheless the charge-sheet remains much the same if one compares (say) Plato's case against the poets – and more crucially, those who mix the genres of poetry and philosophy – with the typical response of analytic philosophers when invited to air their views on the topic. Here again it is primarily a question of style, of the choice – as these latter see it – between, on the one hand, a language that respects the philosophical requirements of clarity, precision, and the good-faith will to communicate, and on the other a language (Derrida's) that exploits the maximum possible degree of obscurity, bafflement, and high-toned 'literary' pretension. By the same token such pseudo-philosophy is held to constitute a standing affront to all those regulative notions (of truth, method, conceptual adequacy, argumentative rigour, etc) which define the very nature of the philosophic enterprise, and in the absence of which – so it is urged – any jumped-up charlatan can always lay claim to the truth as revealed to his or her powers of unaided intuitive vision.

Hence the frequent tonings of moral outrage – the talk of corrupting influence, of 'nihilism', irrationalism, decadence and so forth – which reached a climax in the recent campaign to prevent Derrida from receiving an honorary doctorate at Cambridge.[3] One may suspect that such opinions very often went along with a determined refusal to read Derrida's work, since to do so would clearly place these parties at risk of succumbing to that virulent contagion. But despite its more absurd aspects this episode provides a useful index of the defences that philosophy still seeks to muster against any intrusion of the 'apocalyptic tone' as perceived – with whatever degree of distorting prejudice – by those within the current professional fold. What makes the case still more interesting is the fact that Derrida has always maintained a highly complex, ambivalent yet critical relation to that 'tone' in its various modalities, sometimes through a kind of multi-layered intertextual dialogism such that those opponents might almost be forgiven for lumping him together with the latterday zealots and mystagogues.[4] But those opponents are demonstrably wide of the mark when they fail to observe how Derrida is *citing* certain instances of apocalyptic discourse, and how they thus come to figure, in the analytic idiom, as 'mentions' rather than 'uses' of the tone or style in question. That is to say, we shall get Derrida wrong if we think to read his arguments straight off from the page without first asking such elementary questions – 'elementary' at least for literary critics – as: what is the function of this utterance in context? what determines where the relevant context(s) begin or end? who is speaking here and to what (overt or implied) purpose? how are we to take the various signs of non-coincidence between manifest meaning and meaning as construed with ironic reference to those same texts that Derrida is citing or mentioning? For we shall otherwise end up in the unfortunate position of those novel-readers who naively assume that any statement not attributed to some (named or identified) fictive character must therefore reflect the author's own views on this or that topic of thematic concern.

Of course this may be taken as yet further evidence – if any were needed – that Derrida's work scarcely merits serious (philosophical) attention. For it can always be assigned to that hybrid genre of so-called 'literary theory' which treats philosophy, in Richard Rorty's phrase, as just another optional 'kind of writing' on a level with poetry, fiction, *Kulturgeschichte* or what have you, and which is therefore best left to those tender-minded (or muddle-headed) types who nowadays congregate in departments of Comparative Literature.[5] But whatever its justice as applied to some of Derrida's less philosophically informed disciples, this view is quite inadequate in his own case. For nobody has gone further towards thinking through the relationship that exists between philosophy, literature, and the 'apocalyptic tone'. And he has done so *not* – as neopragmatists like Rorty would approvingly claim, along with detractors like Jürgen Habermas – in a spirit of post-philosophical scepticism that sets out simply to demolish or collapse such generic boundary-markers.[6] On the contrary: the questions that Derrida raises with regard to the 'apocalyptic tone' are questions that have haunted the discourse of philosophy from Plato to Kant, Husserl, J.L. Austin, and even (or especially) those who would nowadays exclude it *de jure* from the forum of 'serious' intellectual debate. What is distinctive about Derrida's work – and what has often provoked such fierce antagonism – is the way that he both enacts (or mimics) that tone through all manner of 'literary' allusions, citations, parodic references, etc, and at the same time subjects it to a deconstructive reading of the utmost philosophical acuity. In Austin's terms his writing is both *performative* and *constative*: a putting-into-play of various speech-act modalities (among them the discourse of revealed or apocalyptic truth) while maintaining a certain critical reserve, a capacity to stand back and remark their more wayward, extravagant or questionable forms.

It is this calculated mixing of genres – this extreme virtuosity of style allied to a constant reflexive critique of its own performative implications – which Derrida's opponents have mostly written off as so much 'literary' verbiage. Small wonder that his texts have caused great offence to exponents of a would-be systematic speech-act theory – notably John Searle – who unlike Derrida (and indeed unlike Austin) wish to draw a firm disciplinary line between performatives and constatives, standard and non-standard ('deviant') cases, 'felicitous' and 'infelicitous' modes of utterance, 'ordinary language' as properly deployed in the conduct of our everyday lives and those other speech-act genres – literature among them but also, more vexingly, the discourse of 'ordinary language' philosophy – that cite such examples in a different (artificial or deviant) context of usage, and which thus tend always to suspend or problematise the usual speech-act conventions.[7] For it was Austin – not Derrida – who first remarked on this tendency of performatives to 'play Old Harry' with received philosophical ideas, among them (to begin with) the truth/falsehood distinction and then, as he followed out the logic of his own argument, the very possibility of assigning any firm categorical status to constative and performative modes. This is why the best, most intelligent and responsive readings of Austin are those that decline to take refuge in the comforts of system and theory, and which follow his example by remaining alert to the various anomalies, deviant cases, communicative 'misfires', etc, that can always arise to complicate the project of speech-act philosophy. For as Derrida insists – again *contra* Searle – it is only by taking account of such 'marginal' instances that theory is able to define the requirements of normal (felicitous or good-faith) performative utterance. Which is also to say that one will never come up with an exhaustive set of criteria – of necessary and sufficient conditions – whereby to establish what should rightfully count as a genuine, authentic example of the kind.

Hence the oscillation, in Austin's text, between sincerity-conditions based on the idea that speakers should genuinely *mean what they say*, and contextual criteria which make it a matter of uttering the appropriate form of words in the right situation, with adequate authority, institutional warrant or whatever. In each case there will always be instances that give room for doubt, that are simply undecidable by any such appeal to intentions or validating context. And this applies above all to that most problematical genre of discourse which Derrida – taking his cue, as it happens, from a little-known polemic by Kant – refers to as the 'apocalyptic tone'.[8] For it is here that philosophy (and speech-act theory in particular) comes up against the greatest imaginable challenge to its powers of conceptual grasp. After all, what use is the appeal to sincerity-conditions – to good-faith utterance or speaker's intent – in the case of a discourse that acknowledges no such criteria, whose truth is a matter of inward revelation (whether vouchsafed directly through divine grace or through the inspired reading of scripture), and which therefore renders such questions wholly redundant? What room is there for talk of utterer's meaning, speech-act implicature, commitment to honour one's word, etc, if the apocalyptic tone is *by very definition* such as to suspend all notions of assignable origin, all attempts to construe it in subjective, intentionalist, or humanly accountable terms? And again: what is to count as a relevant context where the speech-act in question (or the genre of discourse) is one that would claim to transcend all the limiting conditions of historical place and time?

Not that Derrida wishes us to take such claims on faith, or to be understood himself as practising a form of divinatory textual hermeneutics. Nor should he be taken as suggesting – with regard to

Austin – that issues of context or speaker's intent are utterly beside the point, since language is always and everywhere subject to this kind of radical undecidability. On the contrary: he knows that in most situations, and for most practical purposes, we do get along quite reliably on the basis of imputing good-faith intentions (or reckoning with their possible absence), and also by taking due stock of the relevant contextual factors. For otherwise we could never make a start in understanding even the simplest of verbal communications, let alone those immensely complex forms of utterance that constitute the domain of philosophical argument. So his opponents are wrong – Searle and Habermas among them – when they think to catch Derrida out by invoking the standard *tu quoque* argument deployed against sceptics down through the ages, that is to say, by pointing out that he requires his own work to be read with a decent regard for context, generic constraints, authorial intentions etc, while (supposedly) allowing himself all manner of hermeneutic licence with the works of others. What they ignore is Derrida's reiterated point: that the claim to respect those imperative values can become a pretext for simply reproducing the established interpretive tradition, and thus remaining blind to any discrepant or anomalous details in the text that would threaten to disrupt that prevailing consensus view. For it is precisely in the 'margins of philosophy' – in those aspects which are deemed marginal on the standard (doxastic) account – that an alert reading may hope to gain access to philosophy's 'unthought axiomatics', its hitherto occulted systems of value and priority.[9] Such is at any rate Derrida's contention, a case borne out (as I have argued at length elsewhere) by readings that exhibit the highest qualities of philosophical rigour, acuity, and insight.[10]

It is important to be clear about this since the critics have gained some polemical mileage from the idea of deconstruction as a variety of all-out (and hence self-refuting) scepticism. One could assemble quite a dossier of statements – beginning with some well-known passages from *Of Grammatology* – where Derrida very firmly rejects any idea that deconstruction can somehow dispense with the standards of interpretive validity, of right reading, of consistency, logic, or truth.[11] Nor can these be written off as mere pious declarations patently at odds with Derrida's actual practice. For what typifies his writing at best – as in the books and essays on Plato, Rousseau, Kant, Husserl, Austin and others – is a scrupulous attentiveness to the letter of the text, combined with a keenness of analytic insight that is seldom matched in the commentary of mainstream exegetes.[12] That his arguments so often run counter to the received wisdom – raising questions that understandably provoke strong resistance among those wedded to the orthodox view – is scarcely good reason for rejecting them out of hand. And this applies even (or especially) to those instances where the question has to do with such deep-grained philosophical assumptions as the priority of literal over metaphoric meaning, the principle of sufficient reason, the existence of determinate felicity-conditions for the various classes of speech-act, or again – subsuming all of these – the privilege traditionally accorded to logic and grammar (as opposed to 'mere' rhetoric) in the analysis of language under its truth-functional aspect. In each case Derrida arrives at his heterodox (and often counter-intuitive) conclusions through a process of meticulous textual close-reading allied to a detailed working-through of the rhetorical *and* the logico-grammatical complexities involved. Such is his procedure – to cite just a few examples – when analysing the relation between concept and metaphor in his essay 'White Mythology', when examining Husserl's phenomenological distinction between 'expressive' and 'indicative' signs, or when expounding the strange (but none the less rigorously demonstrable) 'logic of supplementarity' that inhabits Rousseau's various writings on language, culture, civil institutions, and the genealogy of morals.[13] Commentators may well baulk at Derrida's findings, especially when these are taken out of context or cited – as too often happens – in reductively encapsulated statements of the kind 'there is nothing outside the text', 'all concepts are metaphors', 'all interpretation is misinterpretation', etc. But such readings find no warrant in Derrida's work, least of all in those texts (like the essay on Austin or his second-round response to John Searle) where the argument turns explicitly on questions of context and authorial intent. For it is here, more than anywhere, that Derrida is at pains to dissociate deconstruction from any version of the free-for-all hermeneutic creed – promoted by some of his literary-critical admirers – which would cheerfully bid farewell to such irksome constraints upon the infinitised 'freeplay' of textual meaning.

II PLATO, DERRIDA, HABERMAS

So much by way of cautionary preamble, lest it be thought that Derrida exploits the 'apocalyptic tone' as yet another ruse (along with *différance*, 'dissemination', intertextuality and the like) for deflecting attention from his own failure to offer cogent or adequate philosophical arguments. What it does serve to emphasise – perhaps more pointedly than any of those other terms – is the problem that philosophy has always encountered with speech-acts, discursive genres or modes of utterance that cannot be assigned with confidence to any one (e.g. constative or performative) category. Hence Plato's chief objection to the poets, sophists and other purveyors of a false (unphilosophical) wisdom. All very well had these characters preserved a due modesty with regard to their own inferior role, their task of providing occasional solace or instruction in the arts of public speaking. But this was not at all the limit of their ambition. Rather, they imposed upon ignorant or credulous minds by mixing up various sorts of true-seeming statement – moral *sententiae* and so forth – with a hopeless farrago of myth, metaphor, personification and suchlike deceptive tropes. So the wise (philosophically instructed) lawmaker had no choice but to counsel their speedy banishment from the well-ordered republic, albeit with token expressions of regret. And he was also obliged – as part of this same exercise in intellectual hygiene – to set about purging philosophy of those residual poetic elements that compromised its own dedication to the interests of virtue, justice, and truth. Of course the issue was by no means closed, as witness the long succession of brooding commentaries – most recently by Iris Murdoch – that have sought to re-adjudicate this 'ancient quarrel' between poetry and philosophy.[14]

Among them must be counted Derrida's remarkable essay 'Plato's Pharmacy', his deconstructive reading of the *Phaedrus* as a dialogue which implicitly pursues that quarrel through all manner of oblique, allegorical, and self-reflexive strategy.[15] For the essay is concerned not only with speech *versus* writing as a problematic topos in the legacy of Platonist thought. It also has to do with that whole complex of associated themes – origins, presence, truth, *mimesis*, the paternal *logos* of authorized knowledge as against its upstart progeny, rhetoric and metaphor – which together provide an interpretive matrix for what has seemed to many commentators a somewhat unconvincing or loosely-constructed piece of argument. In particular, it casts fresh light on that troublesome episode in the *Phaedrus* where Plato resorts to an Egyptian myth about the origins of writing, despite his own strictures on mythic explanation as a pre-philosophical (and hence highly suspect) form of pseudo-knowledge. What Derrida is thus able to show is firstly the structural complicity that exists between these

various opposed pairs of terms (speech/writing, *logos/doxa*, concept/
metaphor, reason/rhetoric, philosophy/myth, etc), and secondly the
way that those same oppositions are destabilised – rendered strictly
'undecidable' – by Plato's recruitment of myth, metaphor and other
such 'literary' devices as a necessary adjunct to his own philosophical
argument. The ambivalence of the key-term *pharmakon* (writing as
both 'poison' and 'cure') is just one among the numerous textual signs
that Plato is here drawn into issues of language, knowledge and
representation that in some way exceed his conceptual resources for
determining the philosophic outcome in advance. Which is also to say –
as many readers have felt – that the stylistic qualities of Plato's writing
(his images, metaphors, flights of allegorical invention) are such as to
qualify his overt allegiance to Socrates' teaching, and to place him in the
poets' party despite his doctrinal unwillingness to acknowledge the fact.

I would not of course claim that this summary does justice – or anything like it – to the extraordinary subtlety, the intricate detail and the
sheer analytical intelligence brought to bear in Derrida's reading of
Plato. But there are several points that may usefully be stressed by way of
leading us back to the 'apocalyptic tone' and its significance for Derrida's
work. One is its kinship with those 'literary' elements – myth, rhetoric,
metaphor, etc – which likewise involve an appeal beyond the Socratic
tribunal of reason and truth as established through a process of disciplined dialectical thought. Another is the way that this 'ancient quarrel'
has been played out repeatedly down through the history of Western
philosophical debate, from Kant's polemic against the mystagogues, the
hierophants and adepts of revealed religious truth, to those current
denunciations of Derrida's work – by Habermas, Searle and Iris Murdoch among others – which take him to task for adopting an irrationalist
stance (a contemporary update of the 'apocalyptic tone') quite beyond
the pale of reputable, truth-seeking discourse.[16] And lastly, there is the
notion of his having 'deconstructed' the distinction between philosophy
and literature, thus exposing philosophy (as Plato feared) to all the alien
intrusions of a mystical afflatus – an 'inner voice' of revealed, self-
authenticating truth – that would block any appeal to the *sensus communis* of enlightened inter-subjective debate. On this account the tonings of
apocalypse that occasionally surface in Derrida's work – no matter how
ironically qualified or hedged about with intertextual allusions – must be
seen as gestures intended to promote a species of hermeneutic mystery-
mongering or a wholesale irrationalist creed.

Hence Habermas's oft-repeated charge against Derrida: that his 'philosophy' regresses to a phase in the pre-Kantian history of thought when religion, so far from being properly confined within the 'limits of reason alone', was permitted to encroach upon domains of thought where it had no right to obtrude. 'If this suspicion is not utterly false', Habermas writes, 'Derrida returns to the historical locale where mysticism once turned into enlightenment.'[17] And he does so in order to revoke the philosophical discourse of modernity, to undermine the truth-claims of enlightenment critique, and to level those various genre-distinctions – as between epistemology, ethics, and aesthetics, or thought in its problem-solving, moral-evaluative, and poetic or 'world-disclosive' aspects – which have served at least since Kant as a regulative framework for the conduct of genuine (responsible) enquiry. What this charge amounts to is the grave accusation: that Derrida has promoted just *one* of those aspects – the 'world-disclosive' – to a point where it effectively dissolves all the others into so many forms of metaphoric or poetico-rhetorical discourse, devoid of any normative or critical force. Thus:

> [t]he rhetorical element occurs *in its pure form* only in the self-referentiality of the poetic expression, that is, in the language of fiction specialized for world-disclosure. Even the normal language of everyday life is ineradicably rhetorical; but within the matrix of different linguistic functions, the rhetorical elements recede here ... The same holds true of the specialized languages of science and technology, law and morality, economics, political science, etc. They, too, live off the illuminating power of metaphorical tropes, but the rhetorical elements, which are by no means expunged, are tamed, as it were, and enlisted for special purposes of problem-solving.[18]

What Derrida simply ignores, on Habermas's account, is this process of increasing specialization within and between discourses, this attainment of a differential 'public sphere' wherein the various languages can expect to be assessed each according to its own evaluative criteria, its appropriate validity-conditions, or distinctive orders of truth-claim. So far from respecting such differences, Derrida 'holistically levels these complicated relationships in order to equate philosophy with literature and criticism'.[19] From which it follows, yet more damagingly, that '[h]e fails to recognize the special status that both philosophy and literary criticism, each in its own way, assume as mediators between expert cultures and the everyday world'.

In Habermas's view it is here – through their various 'mediating' roles – that such (relatively) specialized discourses can feed back into the currency of ordinary language with the effect of enhancing its capacity for informed, responsible, or discriminating judgment. But in so doing they must also retain some degree of autonomy, some critical distance that sets them apart from both 'expert cultures' (science, law, political theory etc) and the language of the 'everyday world'. And this is where Derrida goes so disastrously wrong, according to Habermas.

> Because [he] over-generalizes this one linguistic function – namely, the poetic – he can no longer see the complex relationship of the ordinary practice of normal speech to the two extraordinary spheres, differentiated, as it were, in opposite directions. The polar tension between world-disclosure and problem-solving is held together within the functional matrix of ordinary language; but art and literature on the one side, and science, morality, and law on the other, are specialized for experiences and modes of knowledge that can be shaped and worked out within the compass of *one* linguistic function and *one* dimension of validity at a time.[20]

I have perhaps said enough already to indicate why this is a false (or at any rate very partial and misleading) account of Derrida's work. It ignores – among other things – his continued engagement with the legacy of Kantian-enlightenment thought; his insistence (*contra* postmodern 'textualists' like Rorty) that deconstruction can never justifiably dispense with the values of truth, right reading, and interpretive responsibility; and above all the precise analytical grasp that Derrida brings to his writings on metaphor, on the rhetorical (performative) aspects of philosophic discourse, and on the 'ancient quarrel' – resumed with such partisan vigour by Habermas – between philosophy and literature. In short, there is good reason for Derrida's sharp-toned rejoinder to Habermas, Searle and others who would accuse him of muddying philosophical distinctions, or of failing to respect those elementary protocols which they (his opponents) are curiously apt to abandon when confronted with Derrida's texts.[21]

But my concern here is not so much to vindicate Derrida's case as to ask just what it is about his writing that has engendered this latest resurgence of polemics around deconstruction and its perceived threat to the conduct of serious, civilized philosophical debate. The most obvious starting-point for any such enquiry is Derrida's essay 'Of an

Apocalyptic Tone Recently Adopted in Philosophy', a text that not only rehearses the issue as raised by philosophers from Plato to Kant, but which also includes some sidelong reflections on this age-old 'contest of the faculties' in its present-day guise. However, that essay is such a gift for my purpose that I shall defer the pleasure of expounding it for just a while longer, and preface my discussion with some further remarks about the 'literary' reading of philosophic works. For it is this question that most exercises critics like Habermas and Searle, committed as they are to a definite view of the proper relationship between 'ordinary' (or 'everyday') language on the one hand, and on the other those relatively 'specialized' languages – philosophy among them, but also (more problematically) poetry and fiction – whose benefits are available only on condition that they observe the requisite division of discursive domains. With Searle, this requirement takes the form of a speech-act philosophy that aims to define the criteria for felicitous (good-faith) performative utterance, together with a theory of fictive (literary) discourse which specifies the ways in which such language departs from those same real-world standards of veridical utterance.[22] For Habermas – who always has Heidegger in view as the chief modern enemy of enlightenment – it is more a matter of preventing the metaphorical (or 'world-disclosive') aspect of poetic language from overreaching its competence to the point of annulling all distinctions between those realms.

Thus in Derrida's work, as Habermas construes it,

> Linguistically mediated processes within the world are embedded in a *world-constituting* context that prejudices everything; they are fatalistically delivered up to the unmanageable happening of text-production, overwhelmed by the poetic-creative transformation of a background designated by archi-writing, and condemned to be provincial.[23]

What provokes this charge – as so often in philosophy's troubled dealings with poetry and metaphor – is the idea of a language wholly given over to the 'apocalyptic tone' of some inner revelation, some voice of inspired (self-authenticating) utterance that defies all the standards of rational accountability. And it also has to do with those issues that Derrida raises with regard to Austinian speech-act theory. For in the case of such apocalyptic language one can never know for sure *who is speaking*, in the name of what authority, with what precise intent (or institutional warrant), in fulfilment of what obscure prophecies, or with cryptic allusion to how many source-texts, arcane prefigurings, typological correspondences, and so forth. It is as if – to take up Habermas's argument – philosophy were in danger of being thrown back to a stage of unthinking pre-enlightenment faith when intuition (not reason) was the oracle of truth, and when the mere appeal to scripture (Derrida's *archi-écriture*) sufficed to silence any criticism. Or again, it would risk endorsing that strain of post- or counter-enlightenment thought which abandoned the imperatives of critical reflection and embraced various forms of quasi-transcendental monism, whether grounded (like Fichte's idealist variant) in the all-positing world-creating subject or else (like Schelling's) in the idea of nature – the 'objective' pole of this pseudo-dialectic – as the ultimate horizon of being and truth. 'Unabashedly', Habermas writes,

> and in the style of *Ursprungsphilosophie*, Derrida falls back on this *Urschrift* which leaves its traces anonymously, without any subject ... As Schelling once did in speculating about the timeless temporalizing inter-nesting of the past, present and future ages of the world, so Derrida clings to the dizzying thought of a past that has never been present ... He too [like Heidegger] degrades politics and contemporary history to the status of the ontic and the foreground, so as to romp all the more freely ... in the sphere of the ontological and of archi-writing.[24]

Such might indeed be the consequence if Derrida were arguing – as he doesn't – that concepts or truth-claims are *nothing but* sublimated metaphors; that philosophy is *purely and simply* a 'kind of writing'; and that there is no appeal beyond the rhetorical (or 'literary') aspect of philosophic discourse. One could cite any number of passages from his work – especially from 'White Mythology' – that go clean against this vulgar-deconstructionist line. It is, to say the least, ironic that Habermas takes no account of them while he criticises Derrida for supposedly infringing all the maxims and ground-rules of communicative reason or good-faith dialogical exchange.

III KIERKEGAARD *EN ABIME*

Still one has to ask: can there be any reason in principle – as distinct from reasons of professional self-esteem – for supposing that philosophy need have no truck with such 'literary' notions as narrative voice, the unreliable narrator, or the implied author and his/her counterpart, the implied reader? The example of Kierkegaard is perhaps most telling in this respect since he adopts a whole range of oblique narrative strategies – multiple viewpoint, repetition, incongruous perspectives, unstable irony, pseudonymous authorship, etc – in order to confound any straightforward reading that would pass directly from the 'words on the page' to ascriptions of authorial intent. Of course this is not the whole story, since Kierkegaard (according to his own retrospective account in *The Point of view for My Work as an Author*) was from the outset fully in control of his literary production, deploying such strategies always in the service of a higher self-justifying cause, that of revealed religious truth.[25] Thus his ultimate design was to point a way *through and beyond* these stages of aesthetic indecision – of artfully suspended judgment – to a moment when at last all pretences would be set aside, when Kierkegaard would speak *in propria persona* (as in the 'edifying' or 'upbuilding' discourses), and when the reader would confront a necessary choice between 'authentic' or 'inauthentic' modes of existence.

Such is at any rate Kierkegaard's claim, his challenge to the unregenerate *hypocrite lecteur* who might well be tempted to value the 'aesthetic' productions (especially Volume One of *Either/Or*) above anything belonging to the ethical stage – like Judge William's virtuous reflections in Volume Two – or even (worse yet) above the works of redemption authored by Kierkegaard *ipse*.[26] At this point art must indeed conceal art, or literature disown – by all the means at its disposal – whatever might still be construed as in need of 'literary' (narrative or rhetorical) decoding. For eternal salvation, no less, depends upon the reader's capacity to perceive this qualitative difference of realms, this need to pass over – by an existential 'leap of faith' – from the aesthetic domain of ambiguity, irony, unreliable narration and so forth, to a hermeneutic quest for truth as revealed to those with the requisite powers of inward or spiritual understanding. Failing that, his authorship will stand condemned in every aspect of its intricate development. It will be shown up as a vain and delusive enterprise, not only at the ultimate (all-justifying) stage of religious conversion, but also as providing – in the aesthetic or pseudonymous works – such a range of pretexts for sceptical readers who can then claim Kierkegaard as one of their own, an ironist and aesthete *malgré lui* whose powers of literary invention got the better of his merely didactic ('edifying') purpose. And nothing could be worse, from

Kierkegaard's viewpoint, than for his authorship to suffer this perverse misconstrual in matters that bear upon the reader's prospects of attaining salvation through faith.

This is why he goes to such lengths, in *The Point of View*, to explain what prompted his various modes of oblique or pseudonymous narration, to justify those writings with reference to a higher (providential) sense of governing intent, and to caution any reader drawn to the idea that maybe the *entirety* of Kierkegaard's authorship can be read as a species of aesthetic (or 'literary') production. In his own day this was the approach of those romantic ironists, Friedrich Schlegel among them, who saw no end – and no ethical objection – to the enticing prospect of an infinitised irony that would undermine every last standard of interpretive validity or truth.[27] And the same would apply, give or take a few shifts of rhetorical idiom, to the present-day exponents of deconstruction in its literary or ultra-textualist guise. Such readings are the Devil's work, Kierkegaard implies, since they acknowledge no difference – no absolute requirement to choose – between the aesthetic way of life conjured up so brilliantly in the 'Seducer's Diary' of *Either/Or*, Volume One, and the religious vocation that involves a total break with such frivolous 'life-styles' or cultivated forms of self-deception. For the stakes in this matter are pitched uncommonly high. On Kierkegaard's account the issue of right reading – or true divination of authorial intent – becomes nothing less than a touchstone of spiritual grace, a means of separating the sheep from the goats among his various (more or less receptive or educable) readers. As with Milton, his writings are intended for that elect group of individuals, fit though few, who will not be seduced by aesthetic blandishments or mere story-telling interest. To put it bluntly, this author will see you damned if you persist in mistaking his purpose, as for instance by reading a work like *Fear and Trembling* – Kierkegaard's sombre meditation on the parable of Abraham and Isaac – as if it were just another piece of fictive experiment, handy material for literary talk about the 'implied author', levels of irony or textual *mise-en-abîme*, frame-narratives, the 'rhetoric of dubious authority', or suchlike tools of the trade.[28] For to do so is to side with the romantic ironists of his time – and the canny deconstructors of our own – in treating the most serious choices of existence as if they were fictive episodes contrived to the end of mere aesthetic delectation.

And yet, as Kierkegaard ruefully acknowledges, there is a sense in which his writings are sure to be misread on account of those same duplicitous strategies (or techniques of literary indirection) which should properly lose their seductive appeal once the reader has been brought to this stage of true religious inwardness. Thus: 'I held out *Either/Or* to the world in my left hand, and in my right the *Two Edifying Discourses*; but all, or as good as all, grasped with their right hand what I held in my left'.[29] In other words, what can prevent the 'sophisticated' reader from ignoring Kierkegaard's overt professions of intent, rejecting the idea of a providential 'governance' at work throughout the authorship, and choosing to treat the *entirety* of that authorship – first-person 'edifying' works included – as so many literary texts that call for expert hermeneutical treatment? This problem has three main aspects, all of them tending to compound the difficulty of taking Kierkegaard at his word, or following him through the 'stages of existence' set down for the benefit of his good-faith reader in *The Point of View*. To begin with there is the awkward fact – noted by Adorno, among others – that the first-person discourses are often plain boring, delivered in a heavily didactic, repetitive and moralizing style which apparently goes out of its way to repel those readers who have already been seduced by the artfulness of Kierkegaard's pseudonymous (literary) writings.[30] Second, there is the problem that attends all uses of irony as a propaedeutic technique: namely, that of knowing for sure when the irony is supposed to have an end and give way to the voice of authentic, self-authorised, first-person truth. Of course Kierkegaard was acutely aware of this problem, having devoted much of his life's work to a sustained engagement with the various practitioners of irony, from Socrates to Friedrich Schlegel.[31] But this is not to say – as *The Point of View* would so strenuously seek to convince us – that on an adequate reading (i.e. one attuned to its deepest governing intent) the authorship provides indubitable warrant for distinguishing these two modes of utterance. Nor does one have to be a romantic ironist like Schlegel (or a thoroughgoing sceptical debunker like Stanley Fish) in order to perceive this difficulty with Kierkegaard's position.[32] For it is here that the third major problem arises: in the fact that Kierkegaard has himself offered a whole range of highly effective strategies – ironic, rhetorical, 'literary', aesthetic, proto-deconstructive and so forth – by which to subvert (or to render 'undecidable') any such clear-cut distinction. And these are likely to exert all the more appeal when contrasted with what Adorno describes, not unfairly, as the 'loquacious boredom', the 'tiresome and unpleasant reading', and the 'verbosity of an interminable monologue' that often overtake the *Edifying Discourses*.[33] In which case Kierkegaard would indeed be at risk not only of failing to separate the sheep from the goats among his target readership, but also – much worse – of excluding from the fold a sizable number of likely or potential converts.

The 'apocalyptic tone' is never far away when Kierkegaard's critics (and Kierkegaard himself) seek to clarify this issue of authorial intent in relation to his literary strategies on the one hand, and his claims of divine or providential 'governance' on the other. After all, what authority can they (or he) possess to pronounce on the authentic meaning of his work unless guided by some ultimate voice of truth beyond all the obstacles and mazy detours which that work places in their way? Only at this moment of revealed truth will the literary production cease – along with the pseudonyms, aesthetic devices, narrative alibis, ironic disclaimers, etc – and the authorship assume its true vocation as a work of first-hand spiritual witness. For otherwise there is simply no end to what 'literature' can get away with; no end, that is, to the strategies of self-evasion that readers may practise by taking with their left hands what Kierkegaard offers with his right. But the question remains: can even the good-faith reader who seeks to comprehend Kierkegaard's edifying purpose be certain of not falling prey to the snares of aesthetic illusion or literary semblance? What makes this question so urgent for Kierkegaard is the necessity, as he sees it, that *all* communication must nowadays adopt such an oblique approach to matters of serious concern, since the 'present age' is so far given over to irony, fictive role-playing, and other forms of inauthentic existence. 'If the apostle's personal character is one of noble and pure simplicity (which is the condition for being the instrument of the Holy Spirit), that of the reviser is his ambiguous knowledge.'[34] And again: '[i]f the apostle is in a unique and good sense entirely in the power of providence, the reviser is in the same power in an ambiguous sense.'[35] But the time is not propitious for 'apostles', at least, not for those who refuse all commerce with the secular spirit of the age. For only the 'reviser' – the adroit exponent of ambiguity, irony and aesthetic indirection – can hope to communicate effectively with readers who share his or her unfortunate plight, that of living in an epoch whose chief characteristic is the excess of self-conscious reflection over authentic commitment.

Hence another crucial tenet of Kierkegaard's thought, most conveniently summarised in a passage from *The Point of View*:

> Teleological suspension in relation to the communication of truth (i.e.,
> to suppress something for the time being that the truth may become
> truer) is a plain duty to the truth and is comprised in the responsibility a
> man has before God for the reflection bestowed upon him.[36]

This 'suspension' has been in effect – or so we are now given to
understand – at every point in the pseudonymous authorship. Its
purpose (and sole justification) was Kierkegaard's avowed intent of
coaxing the reader onward and up through the various stages of
aesthetic, ironic, reflective, and ethical awareness, to that moment of
ultimate choice between 'religiousness A' and 'religiousness B', or the
dictates of conventional Christian observance as against the starkly
uncompromising faith enjoined by a work like *Fear and Trembling*.
For there would then be no need of further prevarication, the reader
having at last won through to a state of authentic inwardness and grace
whereby to comprehend the edifying works at their true (albeit
aesthetically unappealing) worth.

Fear and Trembling is the crucial test-case here, since it deploys
every means to interpellate that reader – to set him or her up, so to
speak – in a position that allows of no possible escape-route from the
choice between those two kinds of religiousness. Thus Kierkegaard
subjects the parable of Abraham and Isaac to a series of speculative or
experimental readings, all but one of them tending to soften or
humanise its ethico-religious implications. Of the various sermons that
might be preached on this theme, most would take the decently
accommodating line of assuming that God or Abraham (or both) were
from the outset looking for some way to save Isaac, some happy issue
out of Abraham's hideous predicament. Their aim, in other words, is
to commensurate the orders of divine providence and human
understanding, or to offer a more 'civilized' account of the parable that
seeks to bridge the otherwise appalling gulf between God's command
to Abraham (that he should sacrifice Isaac) and Abraham's agony of
conscience as viewed from the natural standpoint of fatherly love, of
familial and ethico-social responsibility, or even of 'religiousness A' as
a perspective that takes due account of those secular interests. But
having entertained a number of such conjectural readings, Kierkegaard
– or rather his pseudonym, 'Johannes de Silentio' – rejects them as
simply not measuring up to the demands of the biblical narrative. What
we should see in them, rather, is a series of instances designed to
illustrate (and implicitly discredit) that easygoing form of religious

belief that the Sunday-best preachers and their right-thinking audience would substitute for the rigours of authentic Christian faith. It is at this point that 'religiousness A' (with its residues of Hegelian *Sittlichkeit* or civic-institutional morality) passes over into the bleak and comfortless terrain of Kierkegaard's 'religiousness B'.

Thus the only adequate reading of the parable is one that discounts its saving *dénouement*, that rejects any form of sentimentalizing pathos or 'human' appeal, and which moreover insists on Abraham's absolute willingness to carry out the sacrifice, along with God's inscrutable purpose in willing that this should be the case. Nor should the reader be tempted to suppose that God, in his divine prescience, must surely have known all along that an alternative object of sacrifice would present itself, and therefore that the test of Abraham's faith would not involve the actual killing of his son. For this is just another strategy of evasion, an interpretive ruse designed to get God off the hook, as it were, from the viewpoint of secular ethics or 'religiousness A'. There is simply no room, as Kierkegaard reads it, for applying any principle of charity or best-case scenario that would reconcile this parable to our everyday notions of virtue, decency, or civilized conduct. Any reader who seeks to do so – with whatever good motive, humanly considered – is thereby signalling his or her failure to comprehend both the parable itself and Kierkegaard's own strenuous exercise in the hermeneutics of faith.

And yet, as I have remarked, this text cannot be counted among the 'edifying' works, at least according to the standard distinction (as laid down in *The Point of View*) between pseudonymous and first-person modes of discourse. Johannes de Silentio is the 'knight of faith', a would-be convert at the highest preparatory stage, but one whose approach is philosophical and reflective, rather than grounded in the absolute certitude of revealed religious truth. In the words of one commentator, *Fear and Trembling*

> is written in the form of an indirect religious communication from the poetic perspective ... [Thus] Johannes confesses from the outset that he cannot understand the faith of Abraham. Compared to the Hegelians who want to go beyond Christian faith, Johannes could only imagine faith ... The 'knight of faith' is only a hero of imagination unable to empower the leap of faith or to sustain a poised faith that does not vaccilate continually between leap and fall. Kierkegaard wants the reader with a religious disposition – one who already knows Bible

stories and who worships regularly – to acknowledge that it is one thing to know stories of faith heroes, but it is quite another to experience genuine faith. Faith is the highest passion, but how is such faith attained? For the receptive reader the book might initiate a quest with a seriousness of intent transcending the trivialising effect of those who would 'go beyond faith'.[37]

This is of course a fideistic commentary that takes Kierkegaard very much at his word concerning the various choices of existence. Thus it proceeds in accordance with his own directives as to how his texts should be read, what purposes governed his project from the outset, and where exactly the dividing-line falls between indirect ('aesthetic' or 'reflective') productions and works of achieved religious inwardness or faith. By the same token – and likewise at Kierkegaard's behest – it implicitly reproves those non-compliant readers (Hegelians, aesthetes, romantic ironists, speculative thinkers of various persuasion) who reject his advice and treat the entire authorship as fit material for subtilised techniques of interpretive self-evasion. What they ignore is the absolute requirement that one accept his strong providentialist account as offered in *The Point of View*, and that one not take refuge – like present-day sophisticates – in such notions as the 'implied author' or 'implied reader'. For these again provide any number of convenient bolt-holes for the secular exegete keen to avoid facing up to that moment of choice between the aesthetic, the ethical and the religious realms of existence.

And yet, as Kierkegaard is uncomfortably aware, his readers might be thought to have every excuse for missing the point, since the authorship provides so many opportunities for communicative breakdown or cross-purpose understanding. Like some of Jesus's more cryptic parables, it seems almost wilfully designed to place obstacles in the way of those interpreters – the great majority – who lack the prerequisite spiritual grace to divine its authentic meaning.[38] 'To them that have, shall more be given; but from those that have not, shall that little they have be taken away.' For it is a feature of apocalyptic writings in whatever (religious or quasi-secularised) mode that their truth is meant only for those few elect readers who are somehow already in possession of that truth as a matter of divinatory skill or hermeneutic foreknowledge. And in Kierkegaard's case this exclusion zone is drawn with uncommon severity and rigour. It does not apply only to the unregenerate hedonists who preferred Volume

One of *Either/Or*, and whose interests were no doubt reflected in the much higher sales of that volume when printed separately, as well as in the fact that one particular section – the 'Diary of a Seducer' – has on occasion been published as a separate text. From Kierkegaard's viewpoint there is not much to choose between these seekers after mere erotic titillation and those other, albeit more sophisticated types who perversely insist on applying the wrong (i.e. aesthetic or literary) criteria when they interpret his ethico-religious writings. They are all of them displaying that same disastrous failure to remark the qualitative shift that occurs – at least on the fideist account – as Kierkegaard abandons his various techniques of ironic, indirect or pseudonymous communication and engages his reader at the level of authentic first-person address. Whatever their motive such readers place themselves utterly beyond reach of Kierkegaard's redemptive ministry. And they do so, he speculates, more often through excess of hermeneutic or interpretive subtlety than through sheer obtuseness or failure to grasp the plain sense of what he is saying.

But there is a further problem here if the reader then asks what *authority* Kierkegaard can offer for his claim that these texts give access to a truth, an order of spiritual wisdom beyond any pleasures or stimulus to be had by reading them as if they belonged to the aesthetic production. For that reader could adduce several arguments in support of his or her revisionist stance. First (and most familiar): Kierkegaard's declared intentions are not the last word on this matter, since the authorship might always turn out to have meanings more oblique, ambiguous or rewardingly complex than anything that Kierkegaard overtly or willingly acknowledged. This standpoint is commonplace among literary critics though not so much among philosophers. Second: the very character of Kierkegaard's writings – their degree of rhetorical and narrative complexity – is such as to preclude any confident appeal to his governing purpose as supposedly manifest in this or that passage of express authorial comment. From which it follows (third) that an ethics of reading gets no direct purchase on Kierkegaard's work, since we may in fact do him an injustice – interpret that work at less than its full creative or indeed philosophical stretch – if we privilege those passages of first-person statement that would narrow the range of possibilities elsewhere.

Of course Kierkegaard *ipse* does everything in his power to represent this as a bad-faith response, a retreat to aesthetic or literary grounds of judgment which thereby disqualifies the reader from attaining a genuine understanding of his work. But one could just as well argue that the principle of charity extends to moral issues also, since Kierkegaard's writings and his troubled life-history (in particular the break with his fiancée, Regina Olsen) scarcely make an edifying spectacle if one takes him at his word in *The Point of View*. For on this account Kierkegaard, like Eliot's Tiresias, knew and foresuffered all that would be subsequently enacted in the course of his dealings with Regina. It requires us to believe that the whole sad affair – the courtship, the engagement, the self-lacerating break – was embarked upon from the outset (like Kierkegaard's erotic, pseudonymous, or literary productions) as a kind of controlled experiment with the various possibilities of indirect discourse, an episode whose charms were coterminous with the 'aesthetic' stage, and whose upshot marked his point of transition to authentic inwardness and faith. Thus Regina is to be sacrificed, like the Isaac of *Fear and Trembling*, in order that Kierkegaard/Abraham can thereby vindicate his own elect calling and his readiness to endure the utmost degree of moral and social disgrace in pursuit of that high vocation. All in all – and despite his fervent protestations to the contrary – one might feel justified on ethical as well as on aesthetic grounds in rejecting Kierkegaard's version of events and treating *The Point of View* as an ingenious piece of narrative fiction or (what amounts to much the same thing) as an *ex post facto* self-justifying account contrived to place a providentialist gloss on his own past actions.

This reading would of course go flat against Kierkegaard's claim to have been guided always – in every last detail of his life and authorship – by that supreme 'governance' whose instrument and mouthpiece he aspired to become. But at least it would present him in a morally and humanly preferable light, that is to say, as having suffered these prophetic delusions only after the event, and not as having planned the whole episode with Regina as part of some monstrously elaborate ruse under the pretext of divine guidance. Moreover, it would answer more fully to our sense that Kierkegaard is often saved from his own worst devices – from arrogance and self-righteous zeal – by precisely those 'literary' doubts and scruples that charcterise the pseudonymous texts. This applies above all to *Fear and Trembling*, where Johannes de Silentio plays the role of doubting intermediary, and where the sheer inhuman harshness of Kierkegaard's teaching (his interpretation of the Abraham and Isaac narrative) is at least somewhat offset by the presence of one who confesses himself unable to fathom this mystery.

With *The Point of View* likewise there is reason to maintain (on what I have called this ethico-interpretive 'principle of charity') that the work is better read with a measure of scepticism – of ironic reserve – as regards its more self-assured intentionalist claims. Only thus can one avoid attributing to Kierkegaard a degree of premeditated cruelty in his relations with Regina which finds a parallel in his willingness to seduce the reader through forms of cunningly contrived aesthetic beguilement which leave him or her perpetually at risk of nothing less than eternal damnation. Much better – one might think – to discount his protestations of divinely authorised purpose, and to regard *all* his works – the 'edifying' discourses included – as subject to a high degree of motivational ambivalence.[39]

At least this approach will have much to recommend it for secular readers who remain unconvinced by his claim to speak as God's proxy, or as the voice of a 'governance' whose purpose is at first revealed obscurely, through various devices of aesthetic indirection, and then – at the last – in the authentic accents of divine inspiration or a certain 'apocalyptic tone'. For it is only by invoking this God-given surety as the last refuge behind aesthetic appearances – as an ultimate source of meaning and truth beyond all the fallible devices of human understanding – that Kierkegaard can justify his having adopted such a range of seductive 'literary' stratagems. Once remove that presumptive ground of appeal and the authorship will then be open to assessment in literary-aesthetic and secular-ethical terms. That is to say, we shall value it either for its brilliance of rhetorical and narrative execution, or – on the principle of charity – for the extent to which (borrowing a phrase from William Empson on Milton) Kierkegaard's intensely ambivalent moral feelings can be seen as 'crying out' against the demands of his 'appalling theology'.[40] In fact these approaches – the aesthetic and the ethical – are by no means incompatible, despite his great effort (from the God's-eye perspective of achieved religious inwardness) to hold them apart as qualitatively distinct existential stages on life's way. For a secular criticism is perfectly entitled to reverse Kierkegaard's express order of priorities, to esteem the complications of his pseudonymous authorship, and to count it a *positive virtue* in narrators like Johannes de Silentio that they maintain such a doubting or ambiguous attitude in the face of those inhuman sacrificial demands that God places upon Abraham and Kierkegaard (not to mention Isaac and Regina). The 'apocalyptic tone' would then figure as an instance of destructive messianic delusion, albeit to some extent redeemed – in Kierkegaard's case – by the countervailing presence of an 'implied author' whose feelings (and whose complex narrative strategies) are engaged to quite contrary effect. What is thereby lost to Kierkegaard in terms of his self-avowed governing purpose is more than made up for – so these critics might claim – by respecting not only the 'literary' aspect of his work but also its range of ethical defences against that illusory voice of conscience.

IV BETWEEN PHENOMENOLOGY AND STRUCTURALISM

No doubt such a reading can easily lean over into the kind of all-forgiving yet ultimately cynical wisdom summed up in the tag *tout comprendre, c'est tout pardonner*. It can also give rise to that deconstructive variant which Paul de Man exploits to ingenious (if ethically dubious) effect in his rhetorical dismantling of the truth-claims advanced in a text like Rousseau's *Confessions*.[41] For according to de Man it is always the case that such discourse has a 'literary' component, a tendency to generate narrative pretexts for the author to mount a self-admiring display of his or her exemplary readiness to confess. It is thus forever 'undecidably' suspended between the factual and the fictive, the referential and the rhetorical, or the constative and performative modes of utterance. 'There is never enough guilt around for the textual machine to excuse', no end of this desire – on the author's part – to recall (or invent) ever more shameful episodes whereby to exhibit his truth-telling credentials. But as the scandalous revelations pile up so the suspicion inevitably grows – 'inevitably' at least on de Man's ultra-sceptical view – that what is offered is not so much a piece of honest self-reckoning as a roundabout means of excusing the utterer through the sheer weight of self-reproach. 'The more there is to be exposed, the more there is to be ashamed of; the more resistance to exposure, the more satisfying the scene, and, especially, the more satisfying and eloquent the belated revelation, in the later narrative, of the inability to reveal.'[42] For one can never be sure of the speech-act genre to which such utterances belong; whether they are an instance of good-faith confession (owning up to some veritable fact of past experience), or whether – as de Man would more often have us believe – they are a fictive contrivance adopted for the sake of absolving the confessor from his present feelings of obscure and unfocused guilt. Thus it is possible 'to face up to any experience (to excuse any guilt) because the experience always exists simultaneously as fictional discourse and as empirical event'.[43] Moreover, when we read such narratives, 'it is never possible to decide which possibility is the right one'. In which case there is always the risk that such discourse 'will indeed exculpate the confessor, thus making the confession (and the confessional text) redundant as it originates'.[44]

In de Man's late (and so far unpublished) essay 'The Concept of Irony' there is a curious – not to say outrageous – remark to the effect that the entire modern discipline of *Germanistik* grew out of a refusal to read Friedrich Schlegel's novel *Lucinde*.[45] What de Man has in mind, more generally, is the failure to engage with that vertiginous mixture of eroticism and romantic irony which Schlegel's interpreters had managed to contain by resorting to reductive (i.e. 'thematic') modes of analysis, readings which ignored the spiralling complexity – the moments of rhetorical *mise-en-abîme* – engendered by the novel's endlessly shifting and elusive ironic stance. His point was aimed partly against proponents of 'stable' irony like Wayne Booth, those who thought to offer a worked-out method, a set of interpretative techniques for reliably detecting the presence of ironic intent and thus convincing readers (themselves included) that they wouldn't be cast in the embarrassing role of victim, fall-guy, or dupe.[46] Such attempts would always fail, so de Man argued, when confronted with the kind of radically *un*stable irony exemplified not only in Schlegel's fiction but wherever language in its figural ('tropological') aspect threatened to exceed the interpreter's powers of self-assured hermeneutic grasp. But his hyperbolic claim about the avoidance of Schlegel among professional *Germanisten* would apply more justly to the way that Kierkegaard has been conspicuous by his absence in most quarters of present-day philosophico-literary debate. And the reasons, I think, have to do quite as much with the 'apocalyptic tone' as with Kierkegaard's own propaedeutic uses of irony – of that same seductive and dangerously potent resource – by way of countering enthusiasts like Friedrich Schlegel.

This is not just an issue of two opposed styles (the ironic and apocalyptic) whose antagonism results from the former's appeal to an ethos of secularised sceptical doubt and the latter's to an order of religious or intuitive truth beyond the furthest reach of unaided human intellect. For one thing, the relationship between them is much more complex, making it often very difficult if not impossible to tell (as with

Kierkegaard) whether a statement is intended ironically or whether it issues – as we are meant to believe – from some transcendent source of self-authorised meaning and truth. For another, there is a sense in which *all* understanding of language, philosophical and literary alike, is caught up in this tension between what Derrida calls 'hyperbole and finite structure'.[47] Booth's idea of 'stable irony' – and the problems he encounters in making it stick – can then be understood as a hard-pressed attempt to contain such exorbitant linguistic perspectives (ironic and apocalyptic alike) within a reassuring framework that allows the interpreter to ignore their more wayward or unsettling implications. It is in this sense that, in Derrida's words, 'a certain structuralism has always been philosophy's most spontaneous gesture'.[48] But at the same time philosophers – like literary theorists – have often been aware of that within language that cannot be brought under adequate concepts or reduced to the order of some abstract explanatory paradigm. This issue has been joined by just about every party to the long-running debate between philosophy and literature down through the history of Western thought. Such was Plato's quarrel with the poets, his reproach that they substituted mere inspiration (along with delinquent figures like metaphor and allegory) for the serious business of philosophic argument and truth-seeking enquiry. That Plato himself made liberal use of those figures – not to mention other such 'literary' devices as dialogue, mimesis, myth, imagery, personification, etc – is of course one of the puzzles that has exercised his commentators from Philip Sidney to Iris Murdoch and Derrida. The 'ancient quarrel' was resumed by Aristotle, who found more reason to respect poetry for its different kind of truth-telling virtue, but who did so strictly on the terms laid down by his commitment to a methodological ideal of high formalist rigour. Thereafter it was mainly theorists of the sublime – from Longinus to Shelley and their latest postmodern progeny – who contested that approach in a language much given to apocalyptic tonings and gestures.[49]

But the issue, as I say, is one that recurs in a range of philosophical contexts beyond this debate between classicism and romanticism as rival interpretive paradigms. It is often within reach of the larger question: how far is it possible to theorise (or conceptualise) the conditions of possibility for language, given the excess – the creative surplus – of *parole* over *langue*, or of utterer's meaning over that which (in some sense) precedes and enables every act of utterance? Nowadays this question is posed most acutely in the wake of Saussure's influential re-statement of linguistic aims and priorities. But it remains problematic for those (like Chomsky) who reject a good deal of Saussure's theoretical programme, and who would shift the emphasis from *langue* to *parole*, or from language considered in its abstract generality to language as a matter of speakerly 'competence', of the way that speakers can generate a huge (potentially infinite) range of well-formed grammatical utterances from a finite stock of 'deep' syntactic structures.[50] For this still gives rise to a version of the old freewill/determinism issue, a problem – to put it very crudely – in reconciling Chomsky's account of these ultimately rule-governed (recursive) structures with our intuitive sense of what it actually feels like to talk straight ahead and sort out the grammar as we go along.[51] As with Saussure – who is quite explicit on this point – the antinomies are not so much resolved or transcended as conveniently shelved for the purpose of attaining a clearer, more adequate explanatory grasp. But they are always liable to resurface and generate perplexity at the level of reflective philosophical thought. Under various descriptions – *langue* and *parole*, structure and genesis, system and meaning, 'indicative' and 'expressive' signs – they constitute the range of binary terms that figure so often as problematic *topoi* in Derrida's early books and essays.[52] Thus the 'apocalyptic tone' is just one example – albeit an extreme case – of the tension that exists between 'hyperbole and finite structure', or the individual speech-act (idiomatically construed) and those constitutive structures – whether of Saussure's *la langue* or Chomsky's 'competence' – that presumably subtend every such utterance.

Of course it is not a question, for philosophy at least, of simply choosing one or the other perspective. Like Kant's antinomies (or their Derridean equivalent, the aporias discovered in a deconstructive reading) they each follow by the strictest necessity from certain likewise ineliminable presuppositions about the topic in hand. All the same it is difficult not to pose the issue in terms of an either/or choice between alternate possibilities, in consequence of which there have emerged entire schools of philosophico-linguistic thought. That is to say, language can either be conceived (on the structuralist-systemic model) as a closed repertoire of signifying elements, a purely differential economy of sound and sense, or again (following the expressivist or phenomenological path) as a field of open-ended creative possibility where every new utterance somehow transcends those structures of preconstituted meaning. On the first view it is assumed that any adequate linguistic theory will have to go by way of a structuralist *ascesis* which, faithful to Saussure, treats language as an object of scientific study and which thus – for this purpose – brackets all questions of speaker's intent, context of utterance, idiomatic variations, linguistic creativity, etc. On the second (adopted sometimes by Husserl but also, more consistently, by Merleau-Ponty) it is only by taking account of those moments of expressive transcendence – the way that meaning surpasses or exceeds all the limits of established sense – that philosophy can do justice to language and other forms of human creative potential.[53] 'The relief and design of structures', Derrida writes,

> appears more clearly when content, which is the living energy of meaning, is neutralised. Somewhat like the architecture of an uninhabited or deserted city, reduced to its skeleton by some catastrophe of nature or art. A city no longer inhabited, not simply left behind, but haunted by meaning and culture.[54]

But we should be wrong, he cautions, to set this up as a straightforward conflict of interpretations between structuralism (or the tyranny of concepts) on the one hand and phenomenology (or the claims of creative transcendence) on the other. For what emerges from Derrida's reading of Saussure and Husserl – taking these as the most 'advanced' and 'rigorous' proponents of each tradition – is the fact that their projects exist in a relationship of close and reciprocal dependence, each of them deconstructing the other's preconceptions through a process of mutual interrogative exchange.

Thus '[b]y virtue of its innermost intention, and like all questions about language, structuralism escapes the classical history of ideas which already presupposes structuralism's possibility, for the latter naively belongs to the province of language and propounds itself within it'.[55] And again: '[i]t is always something like an *opening* which will frustrate the structuralist project ... What I can never understand, in a structure, is that by means of which it is not closed'.[56] This impossibility of closure has to do with the expressive surplus in language – the movement beyond all pre-given codes and structures of signification – which involves an appeal to intention or utterer's meaning, and which therefore cannot be interpreted (much less conceptualised) according to the *a priori* dictates of structuralist method. All of which will appear, on a cursory reading, to place Derrida very firmly in the phenomenological camp. But it is also the case – as argued in his various writings on Husserl – that the project of transcendental phenomenology must itself have recourse to certain structuralist (or proto-structuralist) concepts if it is to offer any workable account of how language articulates those meanings in the public sphere of communicative utterance. Husserl may have wished – and explicitly required – that 'expressive' signs should take priority over mere 'indicative' uses of language, since the former are genuinely meaningful (imbued, so to speak, with the animating spirit of utterer's intent), while the latter belong to a lifeless realm of conventionalised routine signification.[57] However, this distinction proves impossible to maintain, since it is precisely by virtue of its 'indicative' aspect – its partaking of a generalised 'iterability' or capacity to communicate meaning quite aside from any present intention in the utterer's mind – that language exists as a medium of public (intersubjective) exchange. If expression *always and everywhere* exceeds the limits of structural analysis – and this by an intrinsic necessity of language – still there is no escaping the obverse conclusion: that expressive signs can only acquire meaning as elements in a pre-given structural economy of differential terms and relationships.

In short, Husserl 'had to navigate between the Scylla and Charybdis of logicising structuralism and psychologistic geneticism'. His project required that he open up 'a new direction of philosophical attention', one that might permit 'the discovery of a concrete, but nonempirical, intentionality, a "transcendental experience" which would be "constitutive", that is, like all intentionality, simultaneously productive and revelatory, active and passive'.[58] Which brings us back to the apocalyptic tone and its role as a standing provocation to philosophy. A 'provocation', that is, in the twofold sense that it calls forth enquiry into issues of language, meaning, utterer's intention, 'expressive' *vis-à-vis* 'indicative' signs, etc, and also that it conjures up deep-laid anxieties concerning philosophy's competence to resolve or adequately address those issues. For the antinomies that characterise language as conceived by Husserl – 'simultaneously productive and revelatory, active and passive' – are those that emerge to more disquieting effect when language takes the apocalyptic turn towards a mode of utterance that seemingly defies all the normative constraints upon good-faith rational discourse. Hence (as I have argued) the 'ancient quarrel' between philosophy and poetry, one that rumbles on in our current faculty wars and whose echoes are clearly audible when a thinker like Habermas reproaches Derrida for wilfully blurring that genre distinction, or for allowing language in its poetic ('world-disclosive') aspect to override the interests of conceptual clarity and reasoned philosophical debate. What Habermas chiefly objects to – like Plato before him – is the idea of a language 'simultaneously productive and revelatory, active and passive', or laying claim to an order of imaginative truth beyond any appeal to utterer's intent or suchlike regulative notions. It is one thing for poets to enjoy a certain privilege in this matter of not knowing precisely what they mean, or not always meaning precisely what they say. But it is quite another – so Habermas maintains – for philosophers (or those who abuse that title) to comport themselves stylistically in a way that insinuates doubts as to just who is speaking and with what argumentative warrant.

This is Derrida's theme in the essay that I mentioned earlier, 'Of an Apocalyptic Tone Recently Adopted in Philosophy' (hereafter *AT*). The title is taken over in modified form from a little-known pamphlet by Kant, 'Von einem neuerdings erhobenen vornehmen Ton in der Philosophie'.[59] The word 'apocalyptic' might seem a loose – not to say a downright tendentious – rendering of what appears in the latest English translation as a 'newly raised superior' tone. But this is one of Derrida's points in the essay: that when Kant attacks the purveyors of apocalypse, the fake illuminati, the mystagogues, adepts and apostles of the inner light, he is also attacking their lordly pretensions and their refusal to abide by the civilised rules of open democratic debate.[60] Thus 'they scoff at work, the concept, schooling; to what is given they believe they have access effortlessly, gracefully, intuitively or through genius, outside of school' (*AT*, p34). It is on these grounds that Habermas criticises Derrida: for breaking faith with the entire post-Kantian tradition of enlightenment thought – the 'philosophical discourse of modernity' – and thereby reverting to what he (Habermas) regards as a kind of irrationalist mystery-mongering.[61] It takes no very subtle or sagacious reading to perceive this as the polemical subtext of Derrida's essay, a strategy that would substitute Habermas for Kant, or – not to personalise the issue quite so crudely – which would play off the present-day upholders of enlightenment against the 'apocalyptic tone' in its latest modality. Thus everything that Kant has to say about Jacobi and other such perverters of reason and truth is reproduced point for point in the charge-sheet that Habermas draws up by way of countering deconstruction and its supposedly malign influence.[62] That he gets Derrida wrong on just about every issue – relying for the most part on secondary sources or a cursory reading of the texts in question – is a case that I have argued at length elsewhere and which Derrida presents most forcefully in his 'Afterword: toward an ethic of discussion'.[63] At the moment my concern is not so much with the philosophic rights and wrongs of this quarrel as with Derrida's oblique re-staging of it through the return to Kant and his *Auseinandersetzung* with an earlier phase of counter-enlightenment thought. For in all the vast corpus of Derrida's writings to date there is no other text that engages so revealingly with the 'apocalyptic tone' and its unsettling effect on the discourse of self-assured reason and truth.

This is *not* to say – as a simplified reading might have it – that Derrida sides with Jacobi as against Kant, or with those who would appeal to the privilege of genius (of intuitive or revelatory access to truth) as against the merely prosaic virtues of conceptual exegesis and critique. After all, in Derrida's words, paraphrasing Kant:

> [t]he hierarchized opposition of work to gift, of intuition to concept, of genius's mode to scholar's mode ... is homologous to the opposition between aristocracy and democracy, eventually between demagogic oligarchy and authentic rational democracy. Masters and slaves: the overlord reaches with a leap and through feeling what is immediately given him; the people work, elaborate, conceive (*AT* p34).

Of course it will be pointed out (with some justice) that this passage – like so much else in the essay – exploits a kind of ventriloquist effect, an instance of *oratio obliqua* (or 'free indirect style') that cannot reliably be taken as expressing Derrida's thoughts on the matter, any more than is the case with Kierkegaard's pseudonymous writings. Which is also to say, in Habermasian terms, that this discourse mixes up the genres of philosophy and literature, that it exploits the so-called 'apocalyptic tone' as a pretext for not responsibly meaning what it says or saying what it means. Here again Kant's polemic prefigures the issue between Habermas and Derrida. What he finds so irksome in the mystagogues is their habit of constantly 'raising the tone' to a pitch of quasi-sublime inspirational address where it becomes impossible to determine who is speaking, or how far the utterance takes rise from a realm of cryptic intertextual citations. For nothing is more elusive – and more resistant to philosophical treatment – than this question of the tonal nuances and differences that inhabit every discourse beyond a certain point of rhetorical complexity.

On the standard view such problems can safely be assigned to the margins of philosophy, or to those (maybe in departments of rhetoric, comparative literature, or the history of ideas) who are simply not up to the serious business of first-order philosophic argument. This was clearly Kant's attitude and it is one that lives on among a good few subscribers to the current analytic line. 'Through what is called neutrality of tone, philosophical discourse must also guarantee the neutrality or at least the imperturbable serenity that should accompany the relation to the true and the universal' (*AT*, p29). Which means that philosophy should have no truck with those tonal perturbations – those voices of unassignable origin – that might otherwise call its authority into doubt. For one would then have to raise quite a number of difficult questions concerning (for instance) the operative difference between citation, paraphrase and satire in Derrida's treatment of Kant, or the problem of ascertaining where Kant himself passes over from a rehearsal of the 'apocalyptic tone' to a satire on its lordly pretensions. What if Kant were less in control of this parodic performance – along with all its tonal ambiguities – than he and the mainstream exegetes would have us believe? What if it should turn out that those 'partisans of intellectual intuition', before and after Kant, were not so much lacking or ignoring the lesson of his critical philosophy as perceiving an unresolved issue at its very heart, the issue that Kant himself attempted to cordon off in his treatment of the aesthetic sublime as a modality of somehow (paradoxically) 'judging without concepts?'. And again: what if the 'apocalyptic tone' were just an extreme (hyperbolic) instance of the problem that philosophy has always confronted in accounting for its own authoritative voice, its privileged relation to truth?

From Plato to Habermas, these questions have been posed most often in relation to a certain idea of literature (or poetry) as that which speaks in an alien voice, which threatens to disrupt the composure of philosophical discource, and must therefore be kept off bounds for the purposes of genuine truth-seeking thought. But their insistence on the point – like Kant's anxiety to discredit the apocalyptic tone – is evidence enough that this insecurity is not so easily laid to rest. Will it always be possible, Derrida asks, 'to listen to or detect the tone of a philosopher, or rather (this precision is important) the so-called or would-be philosopher?' (*AT* p29). The usual response – spelled out most explicitly in John Searle's rejoinder to Derrida – is to assert 'yes indeed', and back up the claim by invoking criteria of good-faith utterance, serious intent, speech-act felicity, philosophic competence, etc.[64] These criteria are then taken as adequate grounds for excluding certain parties (e.g. Derrida) from the forum of qualified professional debate. And they are also tacitly invoked when it comes to deciding – in the case of (say) Wittgenstein or Austin – which passages should be read as 'seriously' meant, as expressing the author's considered or principled views, and which as examples of language 'going on holiday' (in Wittgenstein's phrase), or of its tendency in Austin to generate puzzles which speech-act theory should supposedly resolve.

This is not the place for a detailed exposition of Derrida's exchange with Searle. Sufficient to say that it creates real problems – and problems that Austin was himself quick to recognise – with any direct appeal to context, utterer's meaning or authorial intent as criteria for settling such issues.[65] Other commentators (Shoshana Felman on Austin and Henry Staten on Wittgenstein) have shown to what extent the texts of so-called 'ordinary language' philosophy are capable of a reading markedly at odds with the mainstream interpretive view.[66] Nor are such readings – as Searle would have it – mere instances of the bad habit, among literary theorists, of ignoring the plain sense of things and cultivating puzzles and perplexities just for the hell of it. On the contrary: they play the orthodox interpreters clean off the field not only by virtue of their greater attentiveness to 'literary' nuances of style, metaphor, irony, oblique narrative voice, intertextual allusion and so forth, but also on account of their raising questions – eminently philosophical questions – with regard to the conditions of possibility for a worked-out theory of speech-act implicature. And among those questions perhaps the most crucial is that of Austin's (or Wittgenstein's) tonal range, their adoption of numerous – so to speak – ventriloquist devices by way of conducting an unmarked dialogue between the various viewpoints on offer.

Of course there is no genuine problem here for those who assuredly know in advance what Austin has to say about the criteria for good-faith performative utterance, or what Wittgenstein thought on the topic of private languages. But in each case there is enough disagreement – both among the commentators and between discrepant passages of the original text – to suggest that this assurance is somewhat misplaced. Moreover, it is precisely in the matter of tone (or of knowing what should count as 'serious', good-faith utterance) that their writings solicit such diverse interpretations. For, as Derrida remarks, 'a tone can be mimicked, feigned, faked ... I shall go as far as to say *synthesised*'. And again:

> a tone can be taken, and taken from the other. To change voice or mimic the intonation of the other, one must be able to confuse or induce a confusion between two voices, two voices of the other and, necessarily, of the other within oneself (*AT* p34).

Such was Plato's charge against the poets: that they feigned all manner of authoritative utterance (knowledge by acquaintance, by reason, or sheer unaided intuition) while offering not the least show of proof that they actually knew what they were talking about. And for Kant likewise the 'apocalyptic tone' was just the kind of shifty rhetorical ruse – along with metaphor and other such figural diversions – that permitted philosophers (or pseudo-philosophers) to evade the requirements of good-faith rational debate. These charlatans 'play the overlord' and 'give themselves airs' by thus setting up, in oracular style, to pronounce upon matters that exceed the capacity of even the best, most competent philosophical minds. For according to Kant in his essay *The Conflict of the Faculties*, philosophy has its place in the parliament of reason as belonging to the 'lower' faculty, the tribunal concerned strictly with issues of theoretical truth and falsehood.[67] It is thereby distinguished from those other disciplines (theology preeminent among them, but also medicine and law) which occupy the 'higher' faculty, and whose role it is to adjudicate on questions 'most serious for existence'.

Of course it may be argued that Kant is just pretending here; that he means us to read between the lines (as it were) and make allowance for the forms of renewed political and religious censorship that were coming into force at the time when he wrote this essay. Indeed, it is almost impossible to read such utterances straight if one considers how far Kant's critical philosophy extends beyond the limits of 'theoretical' enquiry in this restrictive sense of the term. In which case the text should perhaps be read as a satire on those in authority (the politicians, theologians, and censors) who might be so simple-minded as to take its pronouncements at face value. But then there is the problem – familiar from Austin – of maintaining any firm or principled distinction between constative and performative modes of discourse. For on Kant's submission it is the privilege of those in the 'higher' faculty to 'represent the power whose official instrument they are', and thus to promulgate edicts or laws in the name of that authorising power. That is to say, they possess the performative warrant to enforce or legitimise such sovereign commands. Philosophy, on the other hand, 'has the right to inspect everything touching on the truth of theoretical (constative) propositions but no power to give orders' (*AT* p35). In the parliament of reason it 'occupies the bench on the left', by which Kant means – in a usage dating from the French revolutionary epoch and still current today – the role of those who criticise government in a freely dissenting but non-executive capacity. Where the mystagogues give most offence is therefore by 'hoist[ing] themselves above their colleagues or comrades', and 'wrong[ing] them in their inalienable right to freedom and equality regarding everything touching on reason alone' (p35). For such presumption not only deprives philosophy of its proper (critical or dissident) voice *vis-à-vis* the dictates of established authority and power. It also runs the risk that philosophy will be subject to further – more repressive or arbitrary – forms of censorship on account of its straying across this line between the constative and performative domains.

As I say, there is good reason to suppose that Kant is not entirely in earnest when he counsels philosophers to accept this rather shuffling and evasive *modus vivendi*. All the same it is an attitude not without parallel in the present-day context of government concern to dissuade intellectuals from confusing their proper vocation (their scholarly, academic or specialised business) with matters of a wider socio-political import. Hence – among other things – the revived fashion for those 'end-of-ideology' arguments which first broke surface in the late-50s climate of intensified Cold War propaganda, and which have lately been deployed to much the same effect by ideologues of a 'New World Order' premised on the global triumph of capitalist liberal democracy.[68] Such writings display what can only be described as an inverse relation between the pressures of ideological recruitment that bring them into being and the overt protestations of neutrality, disinterest, scholarly objectivity, etc, that make up their rhetorical stock-in-trade. In other words they exemplify – in almost pathological form – that confusion between the constative and performative modes that Kant thinks so harmful to philosophy. And yet there is a sense in which Kant's own writings prefigure this current sleight of hand by advising (with whatever ironic or duplicitous intent) that philosophers stick to their appointed sphere and not allow their thinking to be compromised by linkage with any such extraneous interests. For those interests can all the more easily be smuggled in under cover of a rhetoric that professes the virtues of critical detachment or a strictly non-partisan devotion to reason and truth. Which is also to say that the exercise of power in its linguistic (performative) aspect is never more subtly efficacious than when joined to a philosophy – or an ideology – that admits of no dealing with such practical affairs.

V KANT, DERRIDA, LYOTARD

Derrida has made this point in a number of essays examining the kinship between Kant's doctrine of the faculties – especially his idea of aesthetic disinterest as a touchstone of reason in its 'pure' or politically disengaged form – and the way that this doctrine persists in the modern division of intellectual labour (university departments or research-programmes) into so-called 'pure' and 'applied' disciplines.[69] For it is always the case that this distinction can be seen to break down when set against the sheer multiplicity of interests – government funding, research grants, peer-group review, incentives or disincentives of various kinds – which motivate scholars even in the humanities (and even, as Derrida remarks at one point, in fields like linguistics, semiotics, or literary theory). To put it simply: why would – for instance – the US Navy invest in such a range of unlikely research projects if not with a view to certain 'deferred profits' or the possibility (however remote) of long-term practical yield? In short, there is a good deal of mystification about Kant's doctrine of the faculties, whether construed in terms of his critical philosophy as a teaching with regard to the well-regulated uses of reason, or again – with reference to his other, more exoteric works – as addressing philosophy's public role and its relation to the modern (faculty-based) system of school or university education. Derrida's essays are very much concerned with these wider pedagogical issues, especially in the context of French government moves to reduce the amount of philosophy teaching at *lycée* or secondary-school level. For this question of the 'right to philosophy' – who is qualified to teach it, to study it (and from what 'proper' age), or to pronounce with authority in its name – is always within reach of the Kantian claim for philosophy's imperative (but duly circumscribed) entitlement to speak on matters of public concern.

   It is also bound up with the 'apocalyptic tone' and Kant's abhorrence of that tone when it intrudes upon the discourse of philosophical reason. What provokes his indignation – as we have seen – is the fact that these charlatans bring philosophy into disrepute by thus laying claim to powers and prerogatives that don't rightfully belong to them. Moreover, they invite an ever-ready suspicion among those in power (a suspicion voiced preemptively by Plato, Kant and Habermas) that such arrogant liberties of tone or style go along with a will to subvert all forms of orderly civic existence. 'This leap toward the imminence of a vision without concept, this impatience turned toward the most crypted secret sets free a poetico-metaphorical overabundance.' And again:

> Not only do they [the exponents of this tone] confuse the voice of the oracle with that of reason. They do not distinguish either between pure speculative reason and pure practical reason; they believe they *know* what is solely *thinkable* and reach through feeling alone the universal laws of practical reason (*AT*, p37).

Here we are very close to Habermas's insistence on the bad consequences – philosophical, ethical and socio-political – that must flow from any attempt (like Derrida's, as Habermas construes it) to dissolve the generic boundary-distinction between philosophy and literature. Nor are such anxieties altogether unfounded, as Derrida would himself be quick to concede. For we should be wrong to think that this issue of the apocalyptic tone is one that philosophers have blown up out of all proportion, or that it is only of pressing concern to those – like Kant and Habermas – who take a highly compartmentalised view of philosophy's proper scope and remit. On the contrary: what sets Derrida apart from Jean-François Lyotard and other celebrants of the postmodern sublime is his refusal to issue apocalyptic statements about the 'end of modernity', the demise of enlightenment reason, or other such modish *idées recues*.

This refusal was already quite explicit in his essay 'The Ends of Man' (1968), where Derrida took issue with the then emergent strain of anti-humanist or counter-enlightenment rhetoric.[70] But it should be evident to any careful reader of his work that he insists always on *thinking through* the antinomies of philosophic discourse, and not – like the current postmodernists – treating them as so many welcome pretexts for dancing on modernity's grave. Nor is this position abandoned when Derrida takes stock of the 'apocalyptic tone', its various performative or speech-act modalities, and its challenge to the more questionable certitudes of Kantian thought. Thus: '[w]e cannot and we must not – this is a law and a destiny – forego the *Aufklärung*, in other words, what imposes itself as the enigmatic desire for vigilance, for the lucid vigil, for elucidation, for critique, and truth' (*AT, p51*). And this principle holds even if such truth can be shown, as the sentence continues, to 'keep within itself some apocalyptic desire, this time as desire for clarity and revelation'. On the one hand there is no conceived of enlightenment – of the access to truth through reason or critique – without at the same time conceiving that truth as somehow revealed to the knower's mind in a state of receptive grace, or through some form of intellectual intuition. But it is equally the case – as Kant argues – that such appeals must always be suspect, issuing as they do from a source of self-authorised inward conviction which respects none of the established procedures for assessing their validity-claims.

Hence the well-known problems with Plato's epistemology, his idea of knowledge as arrived at both through *anamnesis* (the 'unforgetting' of truths once known to the soul before its fall into mortal ignorance) and also as determined through a process of reasoned dialectical exchange. These are not the kinds of problem that can be made to disappear by any sorting-out of logical grammar or Wittgensteinian recourse to 'ordinary language' as a happy deliverance from all our self-induced puzzles and perplexities. They are installed at the heart of philosophical enquiry despite all the various attempts to resolve them from one or another perspective. What Derrida brings out is the impossibility of maintaining a firm, categorical distinction between these orders of discourse, as Kant wished to do and as other philosophers – from Plato to Habermas – have likewise strenuously argued. Their metaphorical kinship is enough to suggest that terms like 'enlightenment' and 'revelation' (or 'clarity' and 'vision') cannot be rigorously held apart through any such act of *a priori* stipulative judgment. And this applies just as much to the present-day issue between those (like Habermas) who would seek to defend the 'philosophic discourse of modernity' and those whom they regard – wrongly in Derrida's case – as betrayers of that same tradition. Thus, in Derrida's words,

> Kant speaks of modernity, and of the mystagogues of his time, but ... it could be demonstrated that today every slightly organized discourse is found or claims to be found on both sides, alternately or simultaneously ... Each of us is the mystagogue and the *Aufklärer* of another (*AT*, p45).

And he further suggests that his audience will surely perceive, 'without [my] having to designate explicitly, name, or draw out all the threads, how many transpositions we could indulge in on the side of *our* so-called modernity' (p45). His aim here is not (or not only) to turn the tables on those – like Habermas – who would play the *Aufklärer* to his (Derrida's) typecast role as heir to the 'mystagogues' or perverters of reason. Rather, it is to show how every such appeal to enlightenment as a source of countervailing truth- and validity-claims will always at some point have recourse to a language that (metaphorically or implicitly) invokes the 'apocalyptic tone'.

No doubt it is naive to suppose – as some have understood Derrida to argue – that *just because* many philosophical concepts can be shown to derive from forgotten or sublimated metaphors (including the very terms 'concept' and 'metaphor'), *therefore* philosophy is metaphorical through and through, or just a 'kind of writing' that chooses to forget its own mythologico-poetic origins. For these figures of thought can always be taken up into other, more specialised (philosophical or scientific) registers where they perhaps retain something of their original sense but acquire along with it a genuine cognitive, conceptual or explanatory force. Besides, as Derrida points out, any discussion of metaphor – including such claims for its omnipresence within philosophy – will necessarily draw upon *concepts* of metaphor that have been elaborated by philosophers from Aristotle down, or else by rhetoricians and literary theorists whose thinking is still a part of that same tradition.[71] So we get Derrida wrong if we take him to be arguing *simply* that 'all concepts are metaphors', all philosophy a species of literature, all truth-claims merely a form of rhetorical or fictive contrivance, etc. And the same applies to those kindred pairs of quasi-antithetical terms – enlightenment/revelation, constative/ performative, reason/intuition and their various cognates – whose structural genealogy Derrida traces in Kant's riposte to the mystagogues. For here also it is not so much a question of collapsing the difference between them as of perceiving the *internal* fault-lines that exist on both sides of this dispute. Hence what he calls the 'old solidarity of these antagonists or protagonists', the way that each draws upon the other's metaphorical and conceptual resources while continuing to denounce its imperious truth-claims.

We have seen this already in Derrida's reading of Husserl, more specifically in his demonstration of the problems that arise when Husserl strives to justify his *de jure* distinction between 'expressive' and 'indicative' signs.[72] What prevents him from so doing – on the *de facto* evidence supplied by certain crucial passages in his own text – is the impossibility of drawing that distinction with the degree of conceptual or philosophic rigour that Husserl himself explicitly requires. The point will perhaps bear repeating here since it clarifies much of what Derrida has to say about the 'apocalyptic tone' and its relation to the discourse of Kantian enlightened critique. If the expressive dimension of language must in some sense be thought of as surpassing the indicative (structural) aspect, and thus as exceeding all the bounds of conceptual accountability, then it is also the case – conversely – that this indicative dimension is the *condition of possibility* for language in general, expressive signs included. But one cannot make sense of this latter requirement without once again encountering the limits of any such structuralist project, the moment when critical reflection discovers the 'absolute, principled and rigorous impossibility of closing a structural phenomenology'. For it is only in so far as utterer's meaning transcends those pre-given structures of sense that language can communicate anything beyond the banalities of routine (indicative) exchange.

In which case, Derrida asks, 'wouldn't the apocalyptic be a transcendental condition of all discourse, of all experience even, of every mark or every trace? And the genre of writings called "apocalyptic" in the strict sense, then, would be only an example, an exemplary revelation of this transcendental structure' (*AT*, p 57). For what the discourse of apocalypse gives us to think is the way that *all* language – every instance of expressive utterance – means something more than could ever be grasped through a structural or a rigorously theorised phenomenological account of its signifying forms and modalities. Moreover, this follows necessarily from the kind of transcendental deduction that Kant (and Husserl after him) regarded as a precondition for establishing the validity of any such enterprise. That it turns out to generate certain unresolvable aporias in the project of phenomenological enquiry is not to say that this project is misguided, or that they might be laid to rest by some further effort of conceptual clarification. Rather, these problems will always reemerge when philosophy reflects on the strictly aporetic relation between language conceived as a realm of open-ended expressive possibility and language as a domain of pre-constituted signifying structures. The apocalyptic *genre*, as Derrida describes it, is therefore a striking (if exorbitant) case of this 'exemplary revelation' which disconcerts the more self-assured projects of structural linguistics, speech-act theory, or transcendental phenomenology.

One likely objection at this point is that Derrida is playing fast and loose with the term 'transcendental'. Thus he seems to be using it both in the technical, Kantian sense ('predicable of all categories', or 'presupposed by any act of judgment') and also in the sense more familiar to mystics and claimants of a spiritual wisdom 'transcending' the powers of plain-prose reason. So it is – the objector might claim – that Derrida can pass off his otherwise patently absurd line of argument concerning the affinity (or deep-laid collusion) between the 'lucid vigil' of enlightenment thought and the visionary transports of apocalypse. It would amount to nothing more than a variety of metaphorical free association, or a deconstructive variant of the age-old fallacy (the so-called 'proof by etymology') that thinks to uncover deep philosophical truths by delving back into the remote pre-history of this or that privileged lexical item. To accuse Derrida of promoting this mystified jargon of authenticity is to ignore – among other things – his express reservations with regard to such thinking in the essay 'White Mythology', and his various criticisms of Heidegger on precisely that account.[73] What he does seek to show is the way that certain (seemingly antithetical) topoi – like the two meanings of 'transcendental' or the 'end of philosophy' as it figures in the discourse of apocalypse, but also, just as insistently, in Kantian thought – are more closely related than appears on the standard (doxographic) account. Thus:

> [i]f Kant denounces those who proclaim that philosophy has been at an end for two thousand years, he has himself, in marking a limit, indeed the end of a certain type of metaphysics, freed another wave of eschatological discourses in philosophy. His progressivism, his belief in the future of a certain philosophy, indeed of another metaphysics, is not contradictory to this proclamation of ends and of the end (*AT*, p 48).

For it is possible to demonstrate, on Derrida's submission, that for every prominent item in the discourse of Kantian enlightenment critique there is not only an analogous metaphor but a corresponding strategy of argument deployed by those who lay claim to a knowledge that transcends all the limits of reason. And this applies no less to the 'transcendental' turn which stands as one of Kant's most distinctive contributions to philosophic thought. Here also, what is revealed – in

Kant as in Husserl – is the strict *impossibility* that reason alone should provide the ultimate self-justifying ground for its own legislative truth-claims.[74]

Of course it is the case – as Derrida would not deny – that Kant's entire project in the three *Critiques* (and also in polemical writings like his essay 'Of an Apocalyptic Tone') was aimed toward establishing lines of demarcation between the faculties of pure reason, theoretical understanding, practical reason, and aesthetic judgment, each assigned to its own legitimate domain. And this in turn means the end of a certain mode of philosophising: namely, that of speculative metaphysics in its pre-critical or conceptually overweening form.[75] Thus there is – one might think – all the difference in the world between talk of closure that promises a new (more constructive) beginning and that which proclaims an end to every notion of enlightened, truth-seeking thought. Again, Derrida acknowledges the point and doesn't for one moment ask us to view them as minor variations on the same underlying theme. Enlightenment is not an option in the sense that one could choose – reasonably or responsibly choose – to reject all its critical imperatives and bid farewell to the philosophic discourse of modernity. 'No doubt', Derrida writes, 'one can think – I do – that this demystification must be led as far as possible, and the task is not modest.' Indeed, 'it is interminable, because no one can exhaust the overdeterminations and the indeterminations of the apocalyptic stratagems' (*AT*, p 59). Critique is always necessary since without it – if thinking is persuaded to suspend its 'lucid vigil' – then the claimants to revealed truth can impose all manner of dogmatic falsehood (or morally repugnant doctrine) in the name of some god-given superior wisdom. But it will underestimate the adversary discourse (and also risk falling into its own kind of dogmatism) if it fails to acknowledge these 'stratagems' and 'overdeterminations' that complicate the issue between them.

Such, as I have argued, is the case with Kierkegaard's *Fear and Trembling*, a text whose humanly appalling implications are to some extent questioned – if not countermanded – by the presence of a doubting or reflective narrator. But the problem is more acute with those varieties of postmodern thought which raise the quasi-Kantian sublime into a principle of absolute heterogeneity between various language-games, speech-act genres, ethical codes, etc.[76] For the upshot of this ultra-relativist stance is to leave moral judgment suspended over the void of an ultimate undecidability, a situation where nothing could possibly count as a valid reason for or against any given ethical commitment. Lyotard provides a set-piece example when questioned by his interlocutor (Jean-Loup Thébaud) as to whether he condoned the action of the Baader-Meinhof group in murdering a West German industrialist on account of his complicity (as they saw it) with the military-industrial complex and the agencies of state-sponsored violence.[77] Or again: did he think it wrong that the resources of a German computer network should be placed at the disposal of US surveillance and intelligence-gathering operations? 'Yes, absolutely', Lyotard responds, 'I can say that this is my opinion. I feel committed in this respect.'[78] But when Thébaud (very reasonably) presses the issue a bit further – requesting that Lyotard support his 'opinion' with at least some show of reasoned or principled justification – then the dialogue runs up against a sheer brick wall. 'If you ask me why I am on that side, I think that I would answer that I do not have an answer to the question "why" and that this is of the order of ... transcendence.'[79] Not of course in any religious or quasi-mystical sense of the word, he hastens to assure us, but in the sense that – with a glance toward the Kantian sublime – '[w]hen I say "transcendence", it means: I do not know who is sending me the prescription in question'.[80] True to his own postmodernist lights Lyotard insists on the absolute incommensurability of 'language-games' and the mistake – indeed, the manifest injustice – of supposing that any one such game (e.g. the cognitivist discourse of factual warrant or liberal-enlightenment talk of 'reasons' or 'principles') could rightly set up as judge of any other. For in so doing we suppress the 'differend' or the point at issue between them, and thus inflict a wrong upon one or other (or indeed upon both) parties.

Hence Lyotard's triple nominalist-pragmatic-postmodern injunction: first, that we should 'save the honour of the name' (refuse to abstract from the particulars of localised context-specific utterance); second, that we should seek to multiply the range of 'first-order natural pragmatic narratives'; and third, that we should 'wage war on totality' in the form of those prescriptive ('meta-narrative') schemas that claim access to some ultimate truth at the end of enquiry.[81] Clearly the issues are presented in such a way as to close all exits for the well-intentioned reader save that marked 'postmodernism'. As so often in these debates it is a straw-man position that Lyotard is attacking, a compound made up in roughly equal parts of Hegelian historicism, enlightenment doctrine in its most uncritical (pre-Kantian) guise, and a crypto-theological notion of truth as arrived at through intuitive access or inward revelation. All the more ironic – though entirely predictable, for reasons I have touched on above – is the way that Lyotard himself has recourse to a rhetoric of 'transcendence' (a language with markedly Kierkegaardian overtones) in order to contest what he wrongly perceives as the 'totalising' truth-claims of enlightenment critique. For there is, quite simply, no other way that his argument can go once it has thrown out the idea that ethical judgments might be capable of reasoned and principled discussion on the basis of informed factual understanding. Such is the position that Lyotard arrives at by grafting a 'radical' (post-structuralist) variant of Wittgenstein's language-games doctrine on to an inflationary reading of the Kantian sublime as that which creates an insuperable gulf between cognitive and evaluative orders of discourse. Up to a point this idea might be thought to find warrant in Kant's writings. No doubt the sublime in its aesthetic modality serves as a useful *analogical* means whereby to suggest the crucial distinction between determinate (cognitive or phenomenal) judgments and those of a non-determinate (ethical, reflective or speculative) character. But to treat it as a touchstone of absolute 'heterogeneity' – a standing rebuke to any talk of ethical reasons, principles, or justifications – is the kind of (surely wilful) misconstrual that provokes real doubt as to Lyotard's competence as a reader of Kant. For as I have argued elsewhere – in company with other commentators – nothing could be more alien to Kant's thinking than this sort of irrationalist dogma raised into a pretext for totally divorcing ethics from the realm of shared (intersubjectively validated) arguments and truth-claims.[82]

On the face of it Derrida is driving toward conclusions very similar to those of Lyotard. Thus he remarks that Kant has difficulty in distinguishing between the 'voice' of practical reason – of the moral law within us – and those other kinds of voice that the mystagogues hear in their self-induced states of delusive visionary trance. 'What condition does Kant lay down for those who, like himself, declare their concern to speak the truth, to *reveal* without emasculating the *logos*?' (*AT*, p46). Most importantly, they must follow Kant's strict precept in refusing that voice any form of sensuous or quasi-phenomenal embodiment, any recourse to images – idolatrous representations – that would compromise its absolute purity. The *Aufklärer* then has this much in common with the mystagogue: that both have to strive against a constant tendency to devalue moral law by lessening its remoteness from the realm of mere desire or physical inclination. So it is that 'Kant first asks them to get rid of the veiled goddess before which they both tend to kneel' (p46). If there is room for some kind of negotiated 'truce' – as Derrida puts it, again paraphrasing Kant – then its terms will have to do with this shared liability and the need on both sides to resist its more seductive blandishments. Thus, Kant very reasonably asks them

> no longer to personify the moral law or the voice that incarnates it. No longer, he says, should we personify the law that speaks in us, above all, not in the 'aesthetic', sensible, and beautiful form of this veiled Isis. Such will be the condition for understanding/hearing the moral law itself, the unconditioned ... In other words, and this is a trenchant motif for thought of the law or of the ethical today, Kant calls for placing the law above and beyond, not the person, but personification and the body, above and beyond, as it were, the sensible voice that speaks in us, the singular voice that speaks to us in private, the voice that could be said in his language to be 'pathological' as opposed to the voice of reason (*AT*, p46).

This passage would bear a good deal of explication, not least – as the metaphors clearly imply – in terms of its bearing on recent debate about the Kantian ('formalist') tradition of ethical thought and the way that it privileges 'masculine' ideals of pure, disembodied rationality over 'feminine' qualities of nurturing, empathy, intuitive insight and the like.[83] What is thus excluded or driven out of mind in Kant's uneasy truce with the mystagogues is 'precisely the body of a veiled Isis, the universal principle of femininity, murderess of Osiris all of whose pieces she later recovers except for the phallus' (p46). Of course such a reading will carry little weight with those who maintain a contemporary ('analytic') version of Kant's strict refusal to allow mere metaphors – or sensuous analogues of whatever kind – to play any role in the conduct of genuine philosophical argument. All the same, Derrida asks, 'grant me at least this: that the truce proposed between the two declared defenders of a non-emasculated *logos* supposes some exclusion. It supposes some *inadmissible*. There is an excluded middle and that will be enough for me' (p46).

One possible reading of Derrida's essay would construe this passage – along with many others – as rhetorically asserting the claims of that 'excluded middle' against all the strictures of Kantian philosophy and its various lineal descendants. The point would then be to subvert all the truth-claims vested in a discourse of logocentric (or 'phallogocentric') reason, whose effect is to silence any voice from outside its privileged domain. And should the question be raised as to whence this voice might issue – with what authority, reasonable warrant, ethical justification, etc – then his response might appear to place Derrida in the company of those, like Lyotard, who reject such demands and treat ethics as belonging to 'the order of transcendence'. Then his essay would align itself on one side only (the distaff side, so to speak) of the axis that runs between all those binary distinctions: constative/ performative, reason/rhetoric, concept/metaphor, logic/intuition, masculine/feminine, etc. On this account Derrida rejects the terms of any 'truce' or provisional concordat that might claim to reconcile the parties by discovering a measure of common ground in their agreement to maintain the law of excluded middle. It casts him, in effect, as protagonist of an ethics that would raise the 'apocalyptic tone' – or language in its performative/revelatory aspect – to a point of radical incommensurability with every last ground-rule, every precept or criterion for the conduct of 'serious' philosophical debate. And one could then go on to claim (as some feminists have) that deconstruction thus conceived is a needful corrective to that whole male-dominated discourse of reason and truth which has sought to monopolise the conversation from Socrates to Kant and beyond.

But this is to ignore the countervailing argument that runs through Derrida's essay, an argument none the less compelling for the fact that it is here rehearsed or played off against the apocalyptic tone. For there is, *contra* Lyotard, no question of simply turning the page on enlightenment or abandoning those critical resources – those interests of reason or reflective judgment – that characterise the philosophic discourse of modernity. 'Several times', Derrida writes,

> I have been asked why (with a view to what, to what ends, and so on) I had *taken on* an apocalyptic tone and put forward apocalyptic themes. That is how they have often been qualified, sometimes with suspicion, and above all, I have noticed, in the United States where people are always more sensitive to phenomena of prophetism, messianism, eschatology, and apocalypse-here-now. That I have multiplied the distinctions between closure and end, that I was aware of speaking of discourse *on* the end rather than announcing the end, that I intended to analyze a genre rather than practise it, and even when I would practise it,

to do so with that ironic genre clause I tried to show never belonged to the genre itself; nevertheless, for the reason I gave a few minutes ago, all language on apocalypse is also apocalyptic and cannot be excluded from its object (*AT*, pp60-1).

At this point one can well imagine an exasperated reader – Habermas perhaps – who simply loses patience with Derrida's ventriloquist strategy and asks 'Well, which is it to be?'. For he does rather appear to be having it both ways, running with the hare and the hounds, or maintaining the need for analysis, critique and the 'lucid vigil' of enlightenment thought while denying that these values can ever be detached from the residual presence of a certain 'apocalyptic tone'. Thus on the one hand – in company not only with the mystagogues but also with postmodernists like Lyotard – he rejects the idea that any discourse 'on' or 'of' apocalypse could attain the level of meta-linguistic grasp required to analyse such phenomena without having resort to their own language of revelation, unconcealment, 'transcendence', and the like. On the other he requires us not to be such simple-minded readers – or so much in thrall to the myth of authorial presence – as to take his rehearsals of the apocalyptic tone (that is to say, his citations, performative enactments, parodies, intertextual allusions, etc) for evidence that Derrida is 'practising' that genre, rather than seeking to analyse its effects. 'No doubt one can think – I do – that this demystification must be led as far as possible, and the task is not modest.' Indeed, it is a strictly interminable task, and this because – as we have already noted – 'no one can exhaust the overdeterminations and the indeterminations of the apocalyptic stratagems (*AT*, p59).

All the same we should be wrong to count this just a piece of ingenious 'textualist' chicanery, a pretence of even-handedness adopted in order to head off his earnest-minded philosophical detractors while continuing to practise those same stratagems. For it is – or it should be – quite clear to the attentive reader of Derrida's text that there is more going on at the level of analysis and critique than could possibly be accounted for on these terms. To read him as endorsing (or uncritically practising) the genre of 'apocalypse-here-now' is equivalent to the claim that his essay is *performative* through and through, that its rhetoric – in Rorty's terms – goes 'all the way down', and therefore that we miss the whole point if we assess it according to standards which Derrida is manifestly out to subvert.

What this amounts to is a failure to remark the difference between deconstruction and postmodernism, at least when the latter is construed – on Lyotard's submission – as a discourse that renounces all ideas of reason, truth or critique, and which takes as its governing maxim the strictly nonsensical notion of judging somehow 'without criteria'. For the upshot, as we have seen, is Lyotard's quasi-Kierkegaardian leap of faith, his refusal to offer any justification of ethical or political commitments save by remarking that they 'belong to the order of transcendence', and are therefore beyond all reach of reasoned or principled debate. Whatever its appeal for the latterday mystagogues – postmodernists and enthusiasts of the pseudo-Kantian sublime – this notion is quite without warrant either in Kant or in Derrida's reading of Kant. No doubt there is a genuine puzzle – familiar at least since Hume – as to how we pass from an 'is' to an 'ought', or – in Kantian terms – how principles translate into lower-level maxims of practical reason, and then again, how these latter apply to the exercise of judgment in particular instances where circumstantial knowledge (along with the appeal to precedent) plays a necessary role. Still it is the case, as neither would deny, that we can and do negotiate this two-way passage whenever moral judgment is brought to bear upon some issue of real-world responsibility or choice. Any theory – like Lyotard's – which erects Hume's puzzle into a sheer rule that we cannot or should not is thereby committed to an ethics of 'transcendence' with very marked apocalyptic overtones.

So it is important that we not misinterpret Derrida when he asks (rhetorically, no doubt): 'wouldn't the apocalyptic be a transcendental condition of all discourse, of all experience even ... 'so that 'the genre of writings called "apocalyptic" in the strict sense would then be only an example, an *exemplary* revelation of this transcendental structure'? (*AT*, p60). Such a passage might well be taken as further confirmation that critics like Habermas are right when they charge Derrida with simply collapsing the 'genre-distinction' between philosophy and literature, or – what amounts to much the same thing – with promoting a rhetoric (an 'apocalyptic tone') that summarily revokes the philosophic discourse of modernity. It would then be a matter of patiently remarking his various (more or less wilful) confusions: of showing, for instance, how the term 'transcendental' has a quite different sense when Kant deploys it in the context of an argument directed *against* against the fake illumati and their overweening claim to have privileged access to a knowledge 'transcending' the limits of critical reason. Or again, it might entail taking issue with his notion that merely to demonstrate the presence of metaphorical (or rhetorical) elements in a philosophic text is somehow to subvert that text's generic identity and prove that philosophy is just a 'kind of writing' or a sub-set of the genre 'literature'. However these are readings so utterly at odds with the range, depth and philosophical acuity of Derrida's work that they need not detain us here. More relevant to ask what exactly is at issue when he speaks of 'another limit of demystification', a limit 'perhaps more essential', and one that would 'distinguish a deconstruction from a simple progressive demystification in the style of the Enlightenment' (p60).

For it is here that Derrida most explicitly measures his distance from that potent strain of irrationalist thought – apocalyptic, revelatory, performative, rhetorical, postmodernist, etc – which adopts, as with Kierkegaard or Lyotard, a stance of *absolute and principled indifference* to the claims of mere reason or humane ethical judgment. And yet, as he remarks, there is a sense in which 'each of us is the mystagogue and the *Aufklärer* of another', so that Kant – even Kant – is driven to evoke the 'moral law' in a language heavy with apocalyptic images and motifs. Thus:

> The veiled goddess for whom we of both parties bend our knees is the moral law within us, in its inviolable majesty. We do indeed perceive her voice and understand very well her commands. But when we are listening we are in doubt whether it comes from man, from the perfected power of his own reason, or whether it comes from another, whose nature is unknown to us and speaks to man through this, his own reason (cited in *AT* p47).

For some – Lyotard among them – this uncertainty can only be resolved in favour of an ethics that would have us judge always 'without criteria', that is to say, by harkening to the dictates of an inner voice whose 'inviolable majesty' Kant contravened when he held it subject to the precepts and maxims of practical reason. Hence his (Lyotard's) constant invocation of the Kantian sublime as that which somehow 'presents the unpresentable', and which thus lies beyond the furthest limits of judgment in its determinate (epistemic) or reflective (ethical and political) modes. At this point the mystagogue has clearly won out over the *Aufklärer*, or the adept of 'apocalypse-here-now' over anyone who would still deludedly cling to the notion of an ethics whose claims might yet be redeemed in the Kantian 'parliament' of intersubjective reason, dialogue, and critique. For Derrida, conversely, there is no question of endorsing this Kierkegaardian leap to a standpoint of unconditional faith – or quasi-sublime revelation – which counts such ideas a world well lost in its rush to abandon the exposed high ground of enlightenment thought. Nor can his reflections be taken lightly at a time when oracular truth-claims of various sorts (including a rhetoric of national destiny with marked religious and apocalyptic overtones) are once again playing a prominent role in the discourse of ethics and politics.

NOTES

1. For an informative survey, see Frederick C. Beiser, *The Fate of Reason: German philosophy from Kant to Fichte* (Cambridge, Mass.: Harvard University Press, 1987).
2. See for instance Immanuel Kant, 'On a Newly Raised Superior Tone in Philosophy', trans. Peter Fenves, in Fenves (ed) *On the Rise of Tone in Philosophy: Kant and Derrida* (Baltimore: Johns Hopkins University Press, 1992).
3. For a representative sampling, see 'Reflections on the Derrida Affair', *The Cambridge Review*, Vol. 113, October 1992.
4. See especially Jacques Derrida, 'Of an Apocalyptic Tone Recently Adopted in Philosophy', trans. John P. Leavey, in Harold Coward and Toby Foshay (eds), *Derrida and Negative Theology* (Albany, NY: State University of New York Press, 1992), pp. 25-71.
5. Richard Rorty, 'Philosophy as a Kind of Writing', in *Consequences of Pragmatism* (Minneapolis: University of Minnesota Press, 1982), pp89-109.
6. Jürgen Habermas, *The Philosophical Discourse of Modernity: twelve lectures*, trans. Frederick Lawrence (Cambridge: Polity Press, 1987).
7. See J.L. Austin, *How to Do Things with Words* (London: Oxford University Press, 1963); Jacques Derrida, 'Signature Event Context', *Glyph*, Vol. I (Baltimore: Johns Hopkins University Press, 1977), pp172-97; John R. Searle, 'Reiterating the Differences', *Glyph*, Vol. I, pp198-208; Derrida, 'Limited Inc abc', *Glyph*, Vol. II (1977), pp162-254.
8. Kant, 'On a Newly Raised Superior Tone' (*op cit*).
9. See especially Derrida, *Margins of Philosophy*, trans. Alan Bass (Chicago, Ill.: University of Chicago Press, 1982).
10. See for instance Christopher Norris, *Derrida* (London: Fontana, 1987) and 'Limited Think: how not to read Derrida', in *What's Wrong With Postmodernism* (Hemel Hempstead: Harvester-Wheatsheaf, 1990), pp134-63.
11. Derrida, *Of Grammatology*, trans. Gayatri C. Spivak (Baltimore: Johns Hopkins University Press, 1977), p158.

12. In addition to the above-cited works of Derrida see particularly *'Speech and Phenomena' and Other Essays on Husserl's Theory of Signs*, trans. Richard P. Leavey (Evanston, Ill.: Northwestern University Press, 1972); *Writing and Difference*, trans. Alan Bass (London: Routledge & Kegan Paul, 1978); 'Plato's Pharmacy', in *Dissemination*, trans. Barbara Johnson (Chicago, Ill.: University of Chicago Press, 1981), pp61-171; and on Kant, 'Parergon', in *The Truth in Painting*, trans. Geoff Bennington and Ian McLeod (Chicago, Ill.: University of Chicago Press, 1987), pp15-147.

13. See Derrida, 'White Mythology: metaphor in the text of philosophy' in *Margins of Philosophy* (*op cit*), pp207-71; also *Speech and Phenomena* (*op cit*) and *Of Grammatology* (*op cit*).

14. Iris Murdoch, *The Fire and the Sun: why Plato banished the poets* (London: Oxford University Press, 1977).

15. Derrida, 'Plato's Pharmacy' (*op cit*).

16. See Habermas, *The Philosophical Discourse of Modernity* (*op cit*) and Searle, 'Reiterating the Differences'; also Iris Murdoch, *Metaphysics as a Guide to Morals* (London: Chatto & Windus, 1992).

17. Habermas (*op cit*) p184.

18. *Ibid*, p209.

19. *Ibid*, p207.

20. *Ibid*, p207.

21. See especially Derrida, 'Afterword: toward an ethics of conversation', in *Limited Inc*, 2nd edn. (Evanston, Ill.: Northwestern University Press, 1989), pp111-54.

22. See John R. Searle, *Speech Acts: an essay in the philosophy of language* (Cambridge: Cambridge University Press, 1969) and *Expression and Meaning: studies in the theory of speech acts* (Cambridge University Press, 1979).

23. Habermas (*op cit*) p204.

24. *Ibid*, pp179-81.

25. Søren Kierkegaard, *The Point of View for My Work as an Author*, trans. Walter Lowrie (London: Oxford University Press, 1939).

26. Kierkegaard, *Either/Or*, Vols. I & 2, trans. David F. Swenson and Lillian M. Swenson (New Jersey: Princeton University Press, 1971).

27. See Friedrich Schlegel, *'Lucinde' and the fragments*, trans. Peter Firchow (Minneapolis: University of Minnesota Press, 1971) and *Dialogue on Poetry and Literary Aphorisms*, trans. Ernst Behler and Roman Struc (University Park & London: University of Pennsylvania Press, 1968). See also Kierkegaard, *The Concept of Irony*, trans. Lee M. Capel (Bloomington, Ind.: Indiana University Press, 1968).

28. Kierkegaard, *Fear and Trembling*, trans. Walter Lowrie (New York: Anchor books, 1954).

29. Kierkegaard, *The Point of View* (*op cit*), p20.

30. T.W. Adorno, 'On Kierkegaard's Doctrine of Love', in Paula Kepos (ed), *Nineteenth-Century Literature Criticism* (Detroit: Gale Research Inc., 1992), pp192-9.

31. Kierkegaard, *The Concept of Irony* (*op cit*).

32. See especially Stanley Fish, 'Short People Got No Reason to Live: reading

irony', in *Doing What Comes Naturally: change, rhetoric, and the practice of theory in literary and legal studies* (Oxford: Clarendon Press, 1989), pp180-96.

33. Adorno, 'On Kierkegaard's Doctrine of Love' (*op cit*), p193.
34. Kierkegaard, *The Last Years: Journals, 1853-5*, ed. and trans. Ronald Gregor Smith (London: Fontana, 1958), p200.
35. *Ibid*, p201.
36. Kierkegaard, *The Point of View* (*op cit*), p18.
37. Janet Forsythe Fishburn, 'Soren Kierkegaard, Exegete', in Paula Kepos (ed), *Nineteenth-Century Literature Criticism* (*op cit*), pp259-66; p264.
38. On this aspect of the Gospels, see Frank Kermode, *The Genesis of Secrecy* (Cambridge, Mass.: Harvard University Press, 1979).
39. I explore these possible alternative readings in Norris, 'Fictions of Authority: narrative and viewpoint in Kierkegaard's writing', *The Deconstructive Turn: essays in the rhetoric of philosophy* (London: Methuen, 1983), pp85-106.
40. William Empson, *Milton's God* (London: Chatto & Windus, 1961).
41. Paul de Man, 'Excuses (*Confessions*)', in *Allegories of Reading: figural language in Rousseau, Nietzsche, Rilke, and Proust* (New Haven: Yale University Press, 1979), pp278-301.
42. *Ibid*, p285.
43. *Ibid*, p293.
44. *Ibid*, p295.
45. For further discussion, see Norris, 'De Man Unfair to Kierkegaard? an allegory of (non)-reading', in *Deconstruction and the Interests of Theory* (London: Pinter Publishers and Norman, Okl.: Oklahoma University Press, 1988), pp156-86.
46. See Wayne Booth, *A Rhetoric of Irony* (Chicago: University of Chicago Press, 1974).
47. Derrida, 'Cogito and the History of Madness', in *Writing and Difference* (*op cit*), pp31-63; p60.
48. Derrida, ' "Genesis and Structure" and Phenomenology', in *Writing and Difference* (*op cit*), pp154-68; p159.
49. See for instance Peter de Bolla, *The Discourse of the Sublime: readings in history, aesthetics and the subject* (Oxford: Basil Blackwell, 1989); Jean-François Lyotard, *The Differend: phrases in dispute*, trans. Georges van den Abbeele (Minneapolis: University of Minnesota Press, 1987); Slavoj Zizek, *The Sublime Object of Ideology* (London: Verso, 1989).
50. See Noam Chomsky, *Cartesian Linguistics* (New York: Harper & Row, 1966); *Language and Mind* (New York: Harcourt, 1972); *Language and Problems of Knowledge* (Cambridge, Mass.: M.I.T. Press, 1988).
51. See for instance Chomsky, *Problems of Knowledge and Freedom* (New York: Pantheon, 1971); *Reflections on Language* (New York: Pantheon, 1975); *Language and Responsibility* (New York: Pantheon, 1979).
52. See especially 'Force and Signification' and 'Genesis and Structure', in *Writing and Difference* (*op cit*),pp3-30 and 154-68.
53. See for instance the essays collected in Maurice Merleau-Ponty, *Sense and Non-Sense*, trans. H.L. and P.A. Dreyfus (Evanston: Northwestern

University Press, 1964); *Signs*, trans. R.C. McCleary (Northwestern U.P., 1964); *Themes from the Lectures at the Collège de France*, trans. J. O'Neill (Northwestern U.P., 1970).

54. Derrida, 'Force and Signification' (*op cit*), p5.
55. *Ibid*, p4.
56. Derrida, 'Genesis and Structure' (*op cit*), p160.
57. See Derrida, *Speech and Phenomena* (*op cit*).
58. Derrida, 'Genesis and Structure' (*op cit*), p158.
59. Immanuel Kant, 'Von einem neuerdings erhobenen vornehmen Ton in der Philosophie', in Kant, *Gesammelte Schriften*, ed. Royal Prussian Academy of Sciences (Berlin: Gruyter, 1923), Vol. VIII, p387-406. For details of English translation see Note 2, above.
60. Derrida, 'Of an Apocalyptic Tone Recently Adopted in Philosophy' (details in Note 4, above). All further references given by *AT* and page-number in the text.
61. Habermas, *The Philosophical Discourse of Modernity* (*op cit*).
62. See Beiser, *The Fate of Reason* (*op cit*) for a detailed account of these chapters in the history of enlightenment (and counter-enlightenment) thought.
63. See Derrida, 'Afterword: towards an ethic of conversation', in *Limited Inc* (*op cit*); also Norris, 'Deconstruction, Postmodernism and Philosophy: Habermas on Derrida', in *What's Wrong with Postmodernism* (*op cit*), pp49-76.
64. Searle, 'Reiterating the Differences' (*op cit*).
65. Derrida, 'Signature Event Context' (*op cit*) and *Limited Inc* (*op cit*).
66. Henry Staten, *Wittgenstein and Derrida* (Lincoln, Nebr. & London: University of Nebraska Press, 1984); Shoshana Felman, *The Literary Speech-Act: Don Juan with Austin, or seduction in two languages*, trans. Catherine Porter (Ithaca, NY: Cornell University Press, 1983).
67. Kant, *The Conflict of the Faculties*, trans. Mary J. Gregor (New York: Abaris, 1979).
68. See for instance Daniel Bell, *The End of Ideology* (Glencoe, Ill.: University of Illinois Press, 1960) and – for a postmodern update on the same theme – Francis Fukuyama, *The End of History and the Last Man* (London: Secker & Warburg, 1992).
69. See especially Derrida, 'The Principle of Reason: the university in the eyes of its pupils', *Diacritics*, Vol. XIII, No. 3 (Fall 1983), pp3-20; 'Mochlos, ou le conflit des facultés', *Philosophie*, No. 2 (April 1984), pp21-53; 'No Apocalypse, Not Now (full speed ahead, seven missives, seven missiles)', *Diacritics*, Vol. XIV, No. 2 (Summer 1984), pp20-31; 'The Age of Hegel', trans. Susan Winnett, *Glyph Textual Studies*, New Series, Vol. I (Minneapolis: University of Minnesota Press, 1986), pp3-35. Some of these are collected – along with other texts – in Derrida, *Du Droit à la philosophie* (Paris: Minuit, 1990).
70. Derrida, 'The Ends of Man', in *Margins of Philosophy* (*op cit*), pp109-36.
71. See Derrida, 'White Mythology: metaphor in the text of philosophy' (*op cit*).
72. Derrida, *Speech and Phenomena* (*op cit*).

73. Derrida's many statements of indebtedness to Heidegger have led some commentators to deny or play down the extent of these differences between deconstruction and the project of 'fundamental ontology'. See for instance Derrida, 'The Ends of Man' (*op cit*); *Spurs: Nietzsche's styles*, trans. Barbara Harlow (Chicago, Ill.: University of Chicago Press, 1979); *Of Spirit: Heidegger and the question*, trans. Geoff Bennington and Rachel Bowlby (University of Chicago Press, 1989); also – from a different but related standpoint – '*Geschlecht*: sexual difference, ontological difference', trans. Ruben Berezdivin, *Research in Phenomenology*, Vol. VIII (1983), pp65-83.

74. See also Derrida, 'The Principle of Reason' (*op cit*).

75. Immanuel Kant, *Critique of Pure Reason*, trans. N. Kemp Smith (London: Macmillan, 1933).

76. See especially Jean-François Lyotard, *The Differend* (*op cit*).

77. Jean-François Lyotard and Jean-Loup Thébaud, *Just Gaming*, trans. Wlad Godzich (Minneapolis: University of Minnesota Press, 1986).

78. *Ibid*, p69.

79. *Ibid*, p69.

80. *Ibid*, p69.

81. See Lyotard, *The Postmodern Collection: a report on knowledge*, trans. Geoff Bennington and Brian Massumi (Minneapolis: University of Minnesota Press, 1984).

82. See my chapter 'Kant Disfigured' in Christopher Norris, *The Truth About Postmodernism* (Oxford: Basil Blackwell, 1993).

83. See for instance Andrea Nye, *Feminist Theory and the Philosophies of Man* (London: Routledge, 1989); Luce Irigaray, *Speculum of the Other Woman*, trans. Gillian C. Gill (Ithaca, NY: Cornell University Press, 1985); Genevieve Lloyd, *The Man of Reason: 'male' and 'female' in Western philosophy* (Minneapolis: University of Minnesota Press, 1984); Michèle Le Doeuff, *The Philosophical Imaginary*, trans. Hugh Tomlinson (London: Athlone Press, 1991).

3

SPINOZA, MARX, ALTHUSSER: 'STRUCTURAL MARXISM' TWENTY YEARS ON

I ALTHUSSER AGAINST POST-STRUCTURALISM

The essays by Althusser collected in *Philosophy and the Spontaneous Philosophy of the Scientists** were written during the period 1965 to 1978, a period that witnessed what is nowadays thought of, not without a certain wry nostalgia, as the rise and fall of 'structural Marxism'.[1] Indeed they span very nearly the entirety of Althusser's once highly visible career as a leading left intellectual and spokesman for various more or less dissident positions within the French Communist Party. Despite the waning of his intellectual star since the early 1980s, Althusser remains one of the handful of Marxist theoreticians who have set the agenda for current debate even – or especially – among those most zealous in rejecting his ideas. Gregory Elliott's informative introduction to the collection and his skilful choice of texts compose something like a running commentary on Althusser's complex theoretical visions and revisions. This is particularly useful at a time when 'left' intellectuals are queuing up – alongside the usual assortment of right-wing pundits – to declare that events in Eastern Europe spell the end of Marxism as a coherent political philosophy. Small wonder that the current purveyors of high post-modernist fashion tend to evoke Althusser's name in a tone of mock-rueful disdain. For it was he, more than anyone over the past three decades, who sought both to vindicate the truth-claims of

* This essay is a review article prompted by the publication of Louis Althusser, *Philosophy and the Spontaneous Philosophy of the Scientists, and other essays*, Gregory Elliott (ed), Verso 1990.

Marxist theory through a labour of rigorous conceptual critique, and to understand the various massive deformations that had overtaken that theory when translated into party-line precept and practice. It is good to have these essays as a standing reminder of Althusser's extreme philosophical acuity, his impressive range of socio-historical reference, and – not least – the sheer remoteness of his thinking from the fads and buzzwords of current 'radical' debate.

Above all, they should serve to dispel the myth that Althusser's project was so closely tied to the fortunes of French structuralism that the demise of that movement (or its oft-chronicled mutation into various 'post-structuralist' derivatives) inexorably swept his ideas along with it. In fact there is not a single reference here to Saussure, Barthes, Greimas, Lacan, Derrida, Foucault or any of the thinkers who standardly figure in the intellectual background to stocktaking accounts of Althusserian Marxism. Only Lévi-Strauss gets a passing mention, and that by way of endorsing Paul Ricoeur's polemical point that when structuralists start to philosophise, then their thinking amounts to nothing more (or nothing less) than 'Kantianism minus the transcendental subject'. Of course there were significant points of contact, among them the emphasis (derived from Saussurean linguistics) on immanent or 'synchronic' modes of analysis, and also the affinity that Althusser noted between his own account of ideological recruitment – that is to say, the process by which subjects are 'interpellated' into the roles pre-assigned to them by this or that social mechanism of identification – and Lacan's reworking of Freudian psychoanalysis in terms of the Imaginary and Symbolic orders.[2] Moreover, Althusser clearly played a leading part in the rejection of humanist (or subject-centred) epistemologies which ensued upon the structuralist 'linguistic turn' and the markedly anti-Hegelian bias that went along with this movement of thought. So there is some basis for the widespread idea – widespread at least among lapsed converts, post-mortem analysts, *Screen* devotees and other such partial witnesses – that 'structural Marxism' was just the most extreme variant of that promised revolution in the human sciences whose failure led on to the current revolt against theory in whatever shape or form. On this account Althusser figures in retrospect as a deluded (albeit resourceful) spokesman for that dead-end 'enlightenment' or rationalist tradition of which structuralism – in its classic or 'scientistic' mode – was a final and inevitably short-term phase.

As I say, these essays should do much to discredit the received (i.e.

postmodernist or post-structuralist) idea of what Althusserian Marxism was all about. For if there is one thing that comes across consistently here it is Althusser's striking lack of concern with such localised topics of debate, and his engagement with issues that reach far back into the history – indeed, the pre-history – of Marxist philosophical thought. Anyone who scans the index with an eye for 'Saussure', 'Lacan' and the rest will most likely be surprised to find 'Spinoza' (not to mention Epicurus, Aristotle, Descartes, Hume, Berkeley, Kant, Hegel, Husserl, etc) among the most frequently cited entries. Thus one cannot begin to grasp what Althusser means when he talks about 'ideology' or the 'spontaneous ideology of the scientists' unless one understands the Spinozist distinction between *knowledge of imagination* and the knowledge that derives from adequate (theoretically elaborated) concepts or ideas.[3] Indeed he made a point of acknowledging this debt in numerous passages of *For Marx* and *Reading Capital*,[4] passages that must have been wholly opaque to those whose philosophical reading was confined to the currency of structuralist source-texts and primers. It is explained most fully in the course of his essay 'A Marxist in Philosophy', based on Althusser's spoken defence of his submission for the degree of *doctorat d'Etat* at the University of Picardy, and published in this volume for the first time in English translation. Thus:

> I would say that Marx – not only the Marx of the 1857 *Introduction*, which in fact opposes Hegel through Spinoza, but the Marx of *Capital*, together with Lenin – is in fact on close terms with Spinoza ... I obviously also had in mind an echo of Spinozist 'production', and I drew on the double sense of a word which beckoned both to labour, practice, and to the display of truth ... [Thus] I concluded that perceptions and images were treated by Marx as abstractions, and I attributed to this abstraction the status of the concrete or of experience as you find it in Spinoza's first level of knowledge – that is, in my language, the status of the ideological ... But there did remain this borderline case of a purely ideological raw material, a hypothesis which allowed me to introduce the science/ideology distinction, and the epistemological break, which Spinoza, long before Bachelard, inserted between his first and second levels of knowledge ... This distinction is indubitably present in Marx's text, as is the reference to the work of elaboration and the diversity of its moments, and the distinction between the thought-concrete and the real object, of which it gives us knowledge (224-5).

I have quoted this passage at length not only because it brings out the Spinozist connection with particular clarity and force, but also to convey the sheer distance that separated Althusser's thinking from 'structuralism' in its wider, trans-disciplinary and linguistically oriented mode. For these essays make it clear that what Althusser describes at one point as his brief 'flirtation' with structuralist theory was indeed nothing more than that, the result of his drawing for tactical purposes on a body of ideas that otherwise exerted little influence on his thought. And this makes it all the more ironic that commentators should now link the fate of 'structural Marxism' to an episode in the history of intellectual fashion which Althusser was among the first to criticise on jointly philosophical and political grounds.

Where the structuralists erred was precisely in the grounding proposal of their enterprise, that is to say, the idea that truth and reality were constructed entirely in and through language, or by way of those signifying codes and conventions that language imposed upon the raw data of experience. Hence Althusser's agreement with Ricoeur that structuralism can indeed be fairly described as 'Kantianism minus the transcendental subject', or idealist philosophy re-cast to take account of the linguistic turn ushered in by thinkers like Saussure, Hjelmslev and Jakobson. For their own part, these thinkers adopted certain basic principles (like Saussure's doctrine of the 'arbitrary' sign, his indifference to language in its referential aspect, or the structural priority attached to *langue* over *parole*, the 'synchronic' over the 'diachronic', etc), but did so strictly as a matter of intra-disciplinary method, and without any thought of erecting such precepts into a full-blown philosophy of mind, knowledge or the human sciences at large. But their ideas were taken up by theorists in other fields – notably literary criticism – who ignored these specific conditions of pertinence and based all manner of far-reaching claims on a few, suitably striking pronouncements taken out of context. Thus Saussurean linguistics found itself weirdly transmogrified into a 'radical' theory of writing and reading – most brilliantly expounded in Barthes's *S/Z* – which managed to equate the 'arbitrary' nature of the sign with the notion of an open-ended textual freeplay (or unlimited semiosis) blissfully released from all the cramping bourgeois conventions of the 'classic realist text'.[5] So it was that the structuralist dream of method gave way to a heady post-structuralist ethos in which systematic 'theory' rapidly lost its erstwhile appeal. And from this point it was no great distance to the current crop of postmodernist gurus like Baudrillard who would consign critical theory, along with all its dubious intellectual antecedents – Marxism, modernism, philosophy, enlightenment thinking in general – to the scrapheap of dead or moribund ideas.[6]

In a sense this was nothing more than the working-out of inherent liabilities and defects that had always characterised the structuralist project, and which came of its resort to an all-purpose model of linguistic description devised for quite other (discipline-specific) ends. In particular, it followed from the highly selective reading of Saussure, the loose application of his various heuristic principles, and the failure to engage with other (e.g. Fregean) accounts of the sense/reference distinction which might have pointed a way beyond the structuralist prison-house of language. Althusser was quick to diagnose this tendency, as one can see from some remarks about 'the slogan of interdisciplinarity' that he offers here as a useful example of the difference between science (or theoretical practice) and ideology. Thus 'it is clear that something like interdisciplinarity corresponds to an objective and well-founded necessity when there exists a "command" that requires the co-operation of specialists from several branches of the division of labour' (84). But there is also a widespread use of this idea – especially in literary studies and the humanistic disciplines – where it becomes just a fashionable 'slogan', or a means of evading the rigorous *theoretical* efforts required to sort out genuine advances in knowledge from forms of ideological mystification. And nowhere is this more evident – so Althusser argues – than in the turn towards various linguistic analogues and quasi-philosophical ideas as a basis for novel departures in the 'human sciences'.

Thus it is often the case, as with structuralism, that 'when disciplines are in search of a universal "method", we may wager that they are a little too anxious to demonstrate their scientific credentials really to have earned them ... True sciences never need to let the world know that they have found the key to becoming sciences' (96). And again, more pointedly:

> it is only because they themselves realize the dominant ideology that the human sciences can exploit philosophy or the other disciplines that stand in for philosophy (thus linguistics and psychoanalysis function increasingly as 'philosophies' for literary history, semiology etc). In all this to-ing and fro-ing something appears, if we are willing to see it, as

an absence, a lack – the very thing which the sciences need if they are to deserve the name of a science: a recognition of their theoretical base (96-7).

What is wrong with such ideas when carried over from structural linguistics into other disciplines – especially those with 'philosophical' pretensions – is that theory thus becomes, *on its own submission*, a 'discourse' captive to the meanings and concepts that happen to predominate at any given time. And the way is then open for postmodernists, neo-pragmatists and 'end of ideology' ideologues to claim that 'theory' was always a hopelessly misguided endeavour, since it thought to criticise existing relations of power-knowledge in terms that could only make sense in accordance with some likewise presently-existing 'discourse' or intellectual paradigm.[7] In which case structuralism can be seen to have effectively dug its own grave by invoking a suspect (uncritical) notion of science – more specifically, the regional 'science' of structural linguistics – and thus giving rise to insoluble antimonies which subsequent thinkers (Baudrillard among them) were more than willing to exploit.

The above-quoted passages are taken from the title-essay of this volume, 'Philosophy and the Spontaneous Philosophy of the Scientists', reconstructed from some lectures that Althusser delivered at the Ecole Normale Supérieure in 1967. His main interest here is in the shifting relation between science, philosophy and criticism (*Ideologiekritik*) at times of epistemological crisis when those relations can become exceedingly confused. On the one hand he hopes to persuade his audience – a good number of (presumably sceptical) scientists among them – that philosophy has something useful to contribute to the critique of those various dominant ideologies, especially forms of religious prejudice, that had stood in the way of scientific progress down through the ages. On the other he acknowledges that philosophers have often been ready to 'exploit' science by erecting all manner of half-baked metaphysical doctrines on the basis of a spurious 'scientific' appeal. Thus:

> if it is to be able to serve scientific practice, a materialist philosophy must be prepared to combat all the forms of the idealist exploitation of the sciences; and if it is to be able to wage this combat *en connaissance de cause*, this philosophy must be capable of *mastering through knowledge and criticism* the organic link that binds it to the practical ideologies on which it, like any other philosophy, depends (142).

Althusser goes on to give substance to this argument by examining various instances where philosophers have either traded on their dubious scientific credentials in order to promote some mystified creed (Teilhard de Chardin), or aligned themselves squarely with the scientific cause while conserving certain elements of non-scientific (that is to say, pre-critical or ideological) thought. Such would be the case of those eighteenth-century materialist thinkers for whom science was indeed the sole source of truth, but whose concept of truth was so closely tied to the putative self-evidence of reason and empirical observation that it left no room for self-critical reflection on their own governing motives and interests. For the *philosophes*, in short, 'the conviction that scientific truth is omnipotent is closely bound up with something other than the sciences themselves: with the juridical, moral and political "consciousness" of the *intellectuals* of a rising class which is confident that it can take power thanks to the obviousness of Truth and Reason, and which has already put Truth in power' (138). Such passages are often reminiscent of Habermas – especially of his early works like *Knowledge and Human Interests*[8] – despite what has since come to seem the well-nigh unbridgeable gulf between the French and German (i.e. Frankfurt) traditions of critical theory.

So the scientists have some reason to mistrust the philosophers, especially where philosophy presumes to instruct them in matters of fundamental ontology, or in the 'deep' metaphysical presuppositions that inform their day-to-day scientific practice. After all, 'what scientist has not felt the very particular impression created by philosophy in its relation to the sciences ... the impression of blackmail and exploitation?' (129). At such points, typically, an 'inversion' occurs, a gesture of compensatory self-aggrandisement whereby 'philosophical discourse transforms its act of submission to the sciences and situates itself, as "philosophy", above the sciences, assuming power over them' (244). But there are also instances where this relationship is reversed, and where philosophy is able to point out forms of covert ideological investment on the part of scientists who otherwise maintain a strict regard for the determinate (theoretico-material) conditions of production that constitute their own specialised domain of knowledge. This latter is perhaps the most interesting type of case since it enables Althusser to explain with some precision what distinguishes the realms of 'philosophy' and 'theory', or – as he now conceives that relation – what allows philosophy at certain times to practise a form of self-critical reflection on the 'spontaneous philosophy of the scientists'. That is to say, science may not be best placed to understand those elements in its own 'world-view' that derive from some specific *ideology* of truth and method, while apparently correcting other ('philosophical') distortions of its wider social and ethical import. Such would be the kind of Marxist 'theoretical practice' which criticised not only the false pretensions of philosophy but also those cases where science fell in with some mystified (e.g. positivist) view of its role *vis-à-vis* the intellectual division of labour or the social production of knowledge.

II THE SPINOZIST TURN: SCIENCE, TRUTH, IDEOLOGY

Althusser's test-case here is the work of the molecular biologist Jacques Monod, a 'philosophy of science' – as expounded in his book *Chance and Necessity* – that seemingly eschews all forms of metaphysical elaboration, which opposes any attempt (like Teilhard's) to enlist science in the name of some ersatz quasi-religious creed, but which also reveals an underlying commitment to theses that belong with the history of practical ideologies, and not with 'science' as defined on his own (properly exacting) terms. The result, as Althusser describes it, is

> simple but very important: two irradiating nuclei, centres of opposed tendencies – a *materialist tendency* radiating from the material-objective nucleus of scientific practice and science itself; and an *idealist tendency* radiating from Monod's ideological position in the face of 'values' implied by the socio-political-ideological problems that divide the modern world (165).

This is not to say – as anyone will know who has read Althusser's work – that we should therefore think of Monod's 'ideology' as a matter of false consciousness, of a world-view that totally ignores, conceals or distorts the conditions of actual scientific practice. For it is one (indeed the major) thesis of Althusserian Marxism that ideology is *not* – as the vulgar account would have it – a product of merely delusory beliefs which bear no relation to practical (lived) experience. On the contrary: it reveals the truth of such experience, but reveals it in the guise (or under the aspect) of a generalised world-view which claims something more than the status of first-hand experiential knowledge. Thus 'ideology is so much present in all the acts and deeds of individuals that it is *indistinguishable from their "lived experience"*, and every unmediated analysis of the "lived" is profoundly marked by the themes of ideological obviousness' (24; italics in original). And again: 'an ideological proposition is [one] which, whilst it is the symptom of a reality other than that of which it speaks, is a false proposition to the extent that it concerns the object of which it speaks' (84). This argument again takes us back to Spinoza and his cardinal distinction between 'knowledge of imagination' (i.e., that which appears self-evident from the standpoint of commonsense or everyday human perception), and the order of 'adequate ideas' where such 'obvious' (pre-critical) truths of experience are subject to a process of assessment and critique.[10]

For Althusser, as indeed for Spinoza, any genuine advance in the scientific, political or philosophic spheres can only come about through such a rigorous questioning of naive sense-certainty or spontaneous belief. But they are also at one in rejecting the (equally deluded) scientistic or rationalist view that criticism could ever succeed altogether in breaking the hold of commonsense awareness, or the partial understanding *inevitably* imposed by our experience as subjects inscribed within this or that order of socio-political relations. Thus:

> in its social function science cannot replace ideology, contrary to what the *philosophes* of the Enlightenment believed, seeing only illusion (or error) in ideology without seeing its *allusion* to the real, without seeing in it the social function of the initially disconcerting – but essential – couple: *illusion* and *allusion*, recognition and misrecognition (29-30).

So it is that a thinker like Monod can on the one hand articulate a cogent critique of philosophies that 'exploit' science to some quasi-religious or ideological end, while on the other express a 'world-view' that undoubtedly derives from the social and material conditions of his own scientific practice, but which nonetheless constitutes an *ideology* of science, albeit one with impressive credentials at the level of specialised (intra-disciplinary) research. At this point, Althusser argues, 'Monod's theoretical theses enter into contradiction with the way he has *situated* his WV [world-view] *vis-à-vis* the religious and Marxist WVs' (164). His outlook is a version of the rationalist faith that ideas (or the diffusion of scientific knowledge) can clear away those sources of confused understanding that in turn give rise to conflicts at the level of social, ethical and political belief. Thus it appears self-evident to Monod that 'in the modern world, science is the basis of history, that the activity of the scientist weaves the modern world, and that its salvation lies in a scientific ethics' (161-2). But this leads him to adopt an idealist stance which ignores the specific *material* constraints – the socialised conditions of knowledge-production – that remain operative in scientific practice even where that practice shows itself capable (as with Monod) of resisting the more blatantly manipulative forms of ideological thought.

'A specific moral doctrine, but a moral doctrine all the same, from which he expects political effects – including, if I understand him correctly, the hope of the advent of socialism' (162). For the point on which Althusser takes issue with Monod is *neither* his appeal to science as a means of criticising bankrupt (religious or metaphysical) views, *nor* his belief that such criticism may lead to a better, more progressive or enlightened form of socio-political dispensation. Rather, it is Monod's conviction that there exists an ethics or morality of scientific truth that can itself give rise to such wished-for effects, and which thus excludes any suspicion that science – or the current self-image of science – may harbour forms of 'spontaneous ideology' resistant to its own (discipline-specific) protocols of validating method. Again, Althusser is not contesting these ideas in their *practical* role as a source of powerful arguments against the kinds of irrationalist pseudo-science that Monod is out to undermine. For it is here – so he argues – that philosophy is (or ought to be) most closely allied with science in criticising those forms of ideological investment that exploit scientific 'evidence' to various mystificatory ends. But with Monod this alignment is rendered less effective by the resort to an ethos (that of science-as-politics or science-as-morality) which makes it impossible for philosophy to perform any function other than the 'spontaneous' endorsement of current scientific values and priorities. In short,

> [w]hat separates Monod from the religious WV, which he combats so resolutely, does not call into question the value of *morality* as the motor of history; it is simply that the morality he proposes is not a religious morality but an atheist morality centred on the spontaneous ethics of scientific knowledge ... [Whereas] for Marxism ... it is the class struggle that is the motor of history, not morality – even an atheist, ascetic morality, a pure and disinterested morality of the most disinterested of intellectuals, scientists (163).

All of which goes to make Althusser's point – again following Spinoza – that 'theoretical practice' can be effective only insofar as it achieves a precise understanding of its role in relation to science, ideology and the 'world-views' that subtend the various forms of socialised knowledge-production.

It also helps to show – as I have suggested already – how badly Althusser has been served by those standard accounts of 'structuralism' and its aftermath that take him as one more illustrative figure in the familiar roll-call of names and episodes. For it is clear from this essay that Althusser never subscribed to the central proposition of structuralist theory, namely that doctrinaire form of linguistic *a priori* that denied all access to knowledge, reality or truth except by way of the 'discourses' or structures of 'representation' that supposedly determine the limits of intelligible sense. On the contrary, he argues: theory is *impossible* – inherently condemned to the closed circle of specular self-confirmation – unless it can prove itself capable of breaking with the currency of received (commonsense) ideas and beliefs. Moreover, such changes don't come about through some radical but wholly inexplicable paradigm-shift (or mutation in the order of 'signifying practices') that just happens to occur from one epoch to the next, but which otherwise – as with so much writing inspired by Foucault's 'genealogies' of power-knowledge – eludes any form of rational accountability. Here again, one reads the signs of a drastically selective or short-term cultural memory, an approach that plays up the extreme relativist implications of Foucault's later work, while forgetting how much the structuralist enterprise owed to Bachelard's far more rigorous theory of 'epistemological breaks' within the discourse of science and critical philosophy.[11] To re-write the history of recent French thought with this influence in mind would be to take a very different view of post-structuralism and subsequent (e.g. postmodernist) varieties of all-out epistemological scepticism. Certainly it would complicate the received picture of an enterprise that only discovered its 'radical' potential by abandoning all notions of theory, method or truth and pursuing the linguistic turn to the point of a full-scale 'textualist' revolution. For it can then be seen that Althusser's work represents an alternative (albeit currently unfashionable) mode of thought, one that points back to Bachelard – and Spinoza – by way of countering those idealist tendencies at work within the structuralist project.

This point is made in a strikingly Spinozist passage from his essay in this collection 'On Theoretical Work: Difficulties and Resources', originally published in 1967. There is a particular problem, Althusser writes, when we attempt to make adequate sense of texts (e.g. those of Marx) that not only propound revolutionary theses, but do so in a language requiring some effort of conceptual re-definition. Thus:

> [w]e have seen what threatens the *words* used by a theoretical discourse: a rapid reading may construe them as having the same meaning they would possess in everyday life, when they actually have an entirely different meaning – that of *theoretical concepts*. We have seen what threatens the object of a theoretical discourse in the strong sense: a rapid reading can take this object as a real-concrete object, when it actually possesses an entirely different nature – that of a formal-abstract object. In these two cases, the specificity of theoretical language (terminology) and of the theoretical object is reduced and destroyed by the intervention of familiar 'obvious facts': those of 'everyday' ideology – i.e., of empiricist ideology (55).

Such an argument would have to be accounted strictly nonsensical from a structuralist standpoint, or indeed by the lights of any kindred ideology that took language – or the signifying structures of discourse – to constitute the limits of intelligibility in this or that context of debate. For if this were the case then clearly there could be no question of language taking on the distinctive *theoretical* character that Althusser describes, or of readers learning – through a similar process of conceptual clarification – to distinguish between words in their 'everyday', familiar usage and words whose sense had been reworked or refined for some specific theoretical purpose. And indeed, the only assumption on which this argument *can* make sense is the Spinozist doctrine that language is inherently, in its natural state, a source of 'confused' or 'inadequate' ideas, but that these can be corrected – rendered more perspicuous – through just such a process of conceptual critique.

Thus Spinoza takes account of all the manifold causative factors – perceptual, psychological, socio-historical, verbal-associative and so forth – whose influence combines in varying degree to create those figments of illusory belief (or 'knowledge of imagination') which sometimes affect even the best-regulated minds.[12] Like Althusser, he acknowledges their 'obviousness', their *reality* as a matter of immediate or 'lived' experience, and hence the impossible nature of any undertaking – like that of the later eighteenth-century enlightened *philosophes* – that aimed to remove them altogether, and thus to create a daylight realm of perfectly intelligible motives, meanings and ideas. But he likewise shares Althusser's more positive conviction: namely, that criticism (or 'theoretical practice') can so work upon the given materials of ideology as to produce what can rightly be called a *knowledge* – a discourse of adequately theorised concepts – with regard to ideology and its modes of operation.

> Yes, philosophy does act by modifying words and their order. But they are theoretical words, and it is this difference between words that allows something *new* in reality ... to appear and be seen. The new expressions do not reproduce the older ones: they bring to light a contradictory couple, a *philosophical* couple. The sciences are sciences: they are not philosophy. Theoretical ideologies are theoretical ideologies: they are not reducible to philosophy. But 'the scientific' and 'the ideological' are *philosophical* categories and the contradictory couple they form is brought to light by philosophy (107).

Hence the constant emphasis in Althusser's work on this need to distinguish between kinds and levels of intellectual production. For it is on Spinozist grounds, as well as in keeping with Bachelard's philosophy of science, that Althusser can advance his three most controversial theses: (1) that ideology in a certain sense 'has no history' (since its effects are structural to the order of pre-given subject-positions that constitute the realm of lived experience for each individual); (2) that these effects include the process by which subjects are 'recruited' into the dominant order of social, ethical and juridico-political relations; and (3) that we can nonetheless obtain a knowledge (even a 'scientific' knowledge) of the way this process works by elaborating concepts – Spinoza's 'adequate ideas' – that show up the limits of everyday (commonsense) perception and experience. For otherwise philosophy would have no option but to follow the path – obligingly flagged by Richard Rorty[13] – whose end-point is the post-modern-pragmatist doctrine that treats all truth-claims (including those of science) as so many plausible fictions in the service of this or that consensus ideology.

Hence Althusser's fixed opposition to movements in the *soi-disant* 'human sciences' (structuralism chief among them) that promoted this ethos of wholesale scepticism by their turn toward language – or a certain philosophically inadequate theory of language – as a model or paradigm for all such activities. It is impossible to read these essays with any care and still think of 'structural Marxism' as an offshoot of that same broad movement, or as sharing the attributes that more or less assured its rapid supersession by other, avowedly anti-theoretical or cultural-relativist doctrines. In fact they are remarkably prescient in tracking the course of French intellectual fashion over the twenty-year period since the earliest of them first appeared in print. Above all, they register an acute sense that the probity and intellectual strength of Marxist thought are inseparable from a strong set of philosophic claims regarding the science/ideology distinction, the relative autonomy of Marxist theoretical practice, and the need to distinguish this latter activity from other modes of cultural production, among them (and especially) linguistics and literary criticism. For, as Althusser remarks in his doctoral defence,

> demonstration and proof are the product of definite and specific material and theoretical apparatuses and procedures, internal to each science ... [T]here again, it is the relative autonomy of theory which was at stake, not this time in opposition to theoretical idealism but in opposition to the pragmatic and empiricist lack of discrimination which made it impossible to distinguish practices from one another, like the cows in the Hegelian night (209).

Structuralism prepared the way for this confusion of realms through its promotion of an undifferentiating semiotic model which left no room for such 'internal' (i.e. discipline-specific) criteria of method and truth.[14] Post-structuralism then compounded the error by blithely declaring that all talk of truth – or all attempts to hold criticism answerable to standards of theoretical consistency and rigour – must henceforth be seen as mere 'logocentric' ploys in the service of an omnipresent bourgeois ideology of meaning and representation. What price 'relative autonomy', 'theoretical practice', determination 'in the last instance', etc. at a time when *texts* were the main (indeed the only) site of struggle and revolutions were best thought of – if at all – in terms of subverting the Symbolic Order (Lacan/Kristeva), the cultural codes (Barthes), or the 'phrase-regimes' (Lyotard) that constituted 'reality' so far as we could possibly know it?

From this point of view the structuralist enterprise figured as one last symptomatic episode in the history of 'totalising' thought-systems which had now led up to this belated recognition of its own inescapably textual predicament. The retreat from grand theory – or from any kind of theory that claimed the least degree of critical or emancipatory power – went along with the retreat from political positions that counted for nothing at a time of widespread cynical disenchantment on the left. Thus it remained for postmodernist thinkers like Baudrillard to push right on and renounce every vestige of that old 'enlightenment' discourse that once strove to separate truth from falsehood, reason from unreason, fact from fiction, or the order of reality from the order of ubiquitous mass-media simulation that passes for reality with those attuned to this heady new dispensation.[15] So it is hardly surprising that Althusserian Marxism – or the structuralist reading thereof – should nowadays be offered as a case-study in the failure of 'theory' to produce anything more than a knowledge of its own chronic obsolescence when faced with the 'postmodern condition' announced by Lyotard, Baudrillard *et al*. And its demise seemed all the more inevitable given the course of events in Eastern Europe – not to mention electoral trends nearer home – and the agreement among media pundits that this was indeed the 'end of socialism', or of any politics (even more: any cogent political philosophy) answering to socialist aims and principles.

Already at the time of his doctoral defence Althusser could clearly count on provoking some resistance with his high claims for the status of Marxist theoretical practice. But he is nonetheless firm in maintaining those claims against any version of the pragmatist line that would ignore Spinoza's single most important lesson: namely, that the *truth* of certain cardinal theses is the precondition for our grasping their significance or their operative sense within this or that discourse, rather than the other way around (as the structuralists would have it). Thus:

> I argued that 'theory is a practice', and proposed the category of theoretical practice, a scandalous proposal in some people's eyes. Now this thesis, like every thesis, has to be considered in terms of its effect in drawing a demarcation line. Its first effect was, *in opposition to all forms of pragmatism*, to justify the thesis of the relative autonomy of theory and thus the right of Marxist theory not to be treated as a slave to tactical political decisions, but to be allowed to develop, in alliance with political and other practices, without betraying its own need ... I was able to cite Lenin, who put forward this provocative thesis (among many others):

'Marx's theory is all-powerful because it is true' (it is not because it is verified by its successes and failures that it is true, but because it is true that it is verifiable by its successes and failures) (208-9).

Among post-modernists, neo-pragmatists and other such arbiters of current intellectual fashion this passage would count as just one more (albeit fairly extravagant) instance of what goes wrong when theory gets above itself and starts making strictly impossible claims. No doubt it would serve as a prize specimen of that obsolescent mind-set which Stanley Fish has dubbed 'theory-hope', i.e. the hopelessly deluded idea that theorising can ever make the least difference to our in-place beliefs, principles or values as members of some existing 'interpretive community' which sets all the relevant terms for debate.[16] Nothing could appear more absurd, to this way of thinking, than the claim that Marxism might actually be *true*, and be so moreover in virtue of arguments (theoretical arguments) that possess this attribute in and of themselves, and not – as the pragmatist wisdom would have it – just insofar as they happen to accord with what is currently 'good in the way of belief'.

For Althusser, on the contrary, the passage states a series of 'provocative' but none the less *self-evident* theses that are basic not only to Marxist theory but to any theoretical enterprise that would claim to do more than simply reproduce the ideological self-images of the age. That is to say, there is no means of assessing arguments or truth-claims one against another unless it is acknowledged firstly that theory has its own distinct standards ('internal criteria') of validating method, and secondly that these must be arrived at through a process of rigorous immanent critique. Here again it is the Spinozist theory of knowledge – the doctrine of adequate ideas – that provides Althusser with his grounding rationale for this apparently circular sequence of arguments.

What does Spinoza in fact mean when he writes, in a famous phrase, '*Habemus enim veram ideam ...*'? That we have a true idea? No: the weight of the phrase lies on the '*enim*'. It is *in fact* because and only because we have a true idea that we can produce others, according to its norm. And it is *in fact* because and only because we have a true idea that we can know that it is true, because it is '*index sui*'. Where does this true idea come from? That is quite a different question. But it is a fact that we do have it (*habemus*), and whatever it may be that produces this result, it governs everything that can be said about it and derived from it. Thus Spinoza *in advance* makes every theory of knowledge, which reasons about the *justification* of knowledge, dependent on the *fact* of the knowledge which we already possess (224).

It might seem surprising, not to say extraordinary, that a Marxist like Althusser should rest his case on arguments that derive from the 'discourse' of seventeenth-century rationalist metaphysics. But this sense of incongruity is largely a product of the notion – put about by sundry historicist thinkers, Foucault among them – that what counts as 'truth' or valid reasoning at any given time is fixed entirely by the codes, conventions, paradigms, or language-games that currently provide consensual back-up for the truth-claims in questions.[17] What Althusser is suggesting (in common with 'analytical' philosophers like Donald Davidson) is that this gets the matter backward, since the main precondition for our being able to grasp any language – or any 'discourse' of elaborated meanings and concepts – is that we must first possess an adequate idea of what it is for a sentence to be true in that language, or to function in the paradigm linguistic case of a truth-bearing referential statement.[18] For otherwise we should lack any criteria for distinguishing between truth and falsehood, literal and figural expressions, fact and fiction, concepts and metaphors, or valid arguments and those that rest on erroneous, imaginary or 'ideological' grounds of assurance.

Of course it is an article of faith among post-modernists that this just *is* our current situation, like it or not, and that anyone who still tries to make such distinctions hasn't caught up with the latest rules of the game. But it is not hard to show that their pronouncements collapse into manifest nonsense as soon as one asks from what critical standpoint – or by appeal to what kinds of argument or evidence – they can offer this confidently terminal diagnosis of reason, truth and reality. The difference between Althusser and Baudrillard is the difference between consequent and confused thinking, and not – as postmodernism would have it – the result of our now having closed the last page of the last dull chapter in a volume entitled 'Enlightenment Meta-Narrative'. One great virtue of Althusser's work is that it offers an alternative to the path taken by those *Marxisant* post-structuralist ideologues and erstwhile proponents of a textual 'revolution of the word' whose subsequent political tergiversations are written all too plainly in the history of recent French thought. What that alternative involves – to repeat – is the refusal to treat language (or structural linguistics) as a pilot discipline for the human sciences at large, an insistence on the proper specificity and truth-claims of Marxist 'theoretical practice', and a due regard for the standards of conceptual cogency and rigour required of any self-respecting philosophic discourse.

III THE CLAIMS OF ANALYSIS

In this respect Althusser's work is much closer to elements in the modern Anglo-American reception of Marx's thought, especially the writings of analytically-minded commentators like Jon Elster and G.A. Cohen.[19] This is not to deny that these thinkers differ from Althusser at numerous points as regards those aspects of Marxist theory that lend themselves to a form of 'rational reconstruction' in the present-day analytic mode. Nevertheless, they are agreed on the three main principles: (1) that Marxism stands in need of a cogent *philosophical* analysis and critique; (2) that this requires a close attention to the logical functioning of Marxist concepts and categories; and (3) that any such process will involve a clarification – even, at times, a stipulative re-definition – of terms whose 'familiar' or 'everyday' meaning may not be adequate to the purpose. For otherwise, as Althusser observes, we shall run the risk of 'reduc[ing] the prodigious philosophical novelty of Marx's thought to existing, ordinary, "obvious" forms of thought – that is, to forms of the dominant theoretical ideology' (55). This places Althusser squarely in the company of those among the analytic school who reject the appeal to 'ordinary language' (or criteria derived from commonplace usage) as a bedrock source of philosophical wisdom, and who argue on the contrary – like Russell *contra* Austin and the later Wittgenstein – that one needs to take account of possible confusions arising from the discrepancy between language in its 'natural', everyday aspect and those structures of logical presupposition and entailment that subtend its surface grammatical forms. Indeed, his whole enterprise is best understood as an attempt to apply such analytical procedures, not (as in Russell) to the task of regimenting various set-piece protocol sentences, but rather to the process of grasping more adequately the kinds of far-reaching conceptual innovation that characterised the emergence of Marxist discourse in its 'mature' or fully elaborated form.

Thus for instance, Russell proposed his famous 'theory of descriptions' as a technique for sorting out the *logical form* of certain everyday referential phrases, and for showing how problems with (e.g.) fictive or imaginary referents could be avoided by providing a more elaborate paraphrase along logico-semantic lines.[20] In Althusser likewise,

> the meaning of words ... is not fixed by their ordinary usage but by the relation between theoretical concepts within a conceptual system. It is these relations that assign to words, designating concepts, their *theoretical meaning*. The peculiar difficulty of theoretical terminology pertains, then, to the fact that its *conceptual* meaning must always be discerned behind the usual meaning of the word, and is always different from the latter ... For example, everyone thinks they immediately know what Marx means when he uses so ordinary a word as 'labour'. Yet it requires a great effort to discern, behind the common (ideological) obviousness of this word, the Marxist *concept* of labour – or, better still, to see that the word 'labour' can designate *several* distinct concepts – the concepts of the labour process, labour power, concrete labour, abstract labour, etc (45).

I wouldn't want to push too far with this comparison, given the very different philosophical (as well as political) values and priorities that animate Russell's and Althusser's work. But it is worth noting their common admiration for Spinoza, and in particular that aspect of Spinoza's philosophy that identified the interests of conceptual critique – or the framing of adequate ideas – with the progress toward a more enlightened order of socio-political existence.[21] For each of these thinkers it is a manifest fact that the mind has to labour against sizable odds of ignorance, prejudice and deep-grained 'commonsense' belief, but also that there do exist standards of right reason – standards quite distinct from the ruling conventions of this or that culture-specific 'discourse' or 'interpretive community' – by which to adjudicate in matters of truth and falsehood.

In Russell's case this conviction went along with a sturdy contempt for any version of pragmatist doctrine, as also for movements – like the Oxford school of 'ordinary language' philosophy – which claimed to derive their most important insights from a study of the manifold nuances and subtleties enshrined in our everyday habits of usage. For, according to Russell, this attitude amounted to a kind of amateur folk-wisdom, a sedulous regard for 'commonsense' custom and belief which could offer no help in clearing away the confusions engendered by our ordinary (i.e. pre-philosophical) ways of thinking and speaking.[22] The only hope of getting straight on these problems was to offer some account of the underlying 'logical grammar' – the predicative structures, referential constraints, validity-conditions, etc – which often diverged quite sharply from the surface grammatical form, and which therefore lay beyond reach of the appeal to a sacrosanct 'ordinary language'. And there are numerous passages in Russell's work where he makes it clear that such debates in the province of 'technical' philosophy have an important bearing on the way one thinks about ethical, social and political questions. For at some point these questions will always come down to the issue that Althusser poses most sharply with his claims for the efficacy of Marxist 'theoretical practice', i.e. the extent to which critical reason can effect a break with the ideas and values that make up some presently-existing cultural consensus.

It is the same issue that divides Chomsky and Foucault in a little-known dialogue first broadcast on Dutch television where these thinkers discuss the relation between specialised intellectual work (e.g. on transformational-generative grammar or Foucauldian discourse-analysis) and the 'politics of knowledge' in its broader, institutional or socio-cultural context.[23] (See Chapter One, pp45-9 for a more detailed discussion of this exchange.) For Chomsky, like Russell, this relation has to do with the quest for a better, more adequate grasp of the underlying *structures of intelligibility* that characterise both our linguistic 'competence' and – as he sees it – our cognate capacity for exercising powers of enlightened judgment in the public (ethical and political) spheres.[24] For Foucault, on the contrary, 'enlightenment' is a part of the problem, not the solution, bound up as it is with that epistemic will-to-truth whose genealogy Nietzsche was the first to expose, and whose hold on our thinking can best be overcome by renouncing all such presumptuous habits of thought.[25] One could hardly wish for a clearer, more sharply polarised statement of the two main positions that have lately been adopted with regard to philosophy (or 'theoretical practice') and its role *vis-à-vis* the self-legitimising forms of state or institutional power.

This is why, as I have argued, Althusser belongs much more in the so-called 'analytical' tradition than in the line of thought that descends from Saussure, via 'classic' French structuralism to its various latter-day offshoots and derivatives. What these all have in common –

and what sets them so markedly at odds with Althusser's project – is the root persuasion that analysis *cannot do more* than bring to light those various 'discourses', 'language-games', 'signifying practices', 'structures of representation' and so forth that supposedly constitute the limits of cognition within this or that field of intellectual enquiry. From which it would follow of necessity that theorists like Althusser (as well as analytical philosophers like Russell) are practising a form of grandiose self-deception when they claim to have reasons – philosophical reasons – for not acknowledging those limits, or (what amounts to the same thing) for rejecting the widespread 'linguistic turn' as it affects their particular discipline. From the 'analytic' standpoint, on the contrary, such arguments would figure as just another symptom of the currently widespread pragmatist malaise, a style of inert consensus-ideology that ignores (or wilfully precludes) the possibility of critical-emancipatory thought.

There can be no doubt as to just where Althusser stands on this question. Thus '[t]he important thing to grasp', he writes,

> is that this operation of critical rectification is not imposed *from without* on the works of Marx and his successors, but results from the *application* of these works *to themselves*; very specifically, it results from the application of their more elaborated forms to their less elaborated forms – or, if one prefers, of their more elaborated concepts to their less elaborated concepts, or again, of their theoretical systems to certain terms of their discourse, etc. This operation reveals some 'blanks', 'plays on words', lacunae, inadequacies which rectification can then reduce. All this work proceeds concurrently: it is by bringing to light the most elaborated forms and concepts, the theoretical system to certain terms of their discourse, etc. This operation reveals some 'blanks', 'plays on words', lacunae, inadequacies which rectification can then reduce. All this work proceeds concurrently: it is by bringing to light the most elaborated forms and concepts, the theoretical system, that rectification can be carried out, and it is rectification that foregrounds forms, concepts and systems which determine its objects (61).

Passages like this – yet another clear instance of Althusser's Spinozist approach – underline the extent of his commitment to principles totally at odds with the currency of postmodern-pragmatist or counter-enlightenment thought. They should also remind us of the internal complexities and divisions that always marked the structuralist project, deriving as it did from a range of fairly disparate intellectual sources, some of them (like Bachelard's epistemology of science) very far from supporting any kind of cultural-relativist doctrine. Indeed, *Philosophy and the Spontaneous Philosophy of the Scientists* enables us to see just how partial and selective was the reading of Althusser – mainly among literary theorists – that played up the notionally 'structuralist' leanings of his work while ignoring these other, more precisely articulated aspects.

One thing that dropped out of sight in the process was Althusser's steady insistence – maintained despite various detailed shifts of theoretical alignment – that philosophy could serve no useful purpose unless it kept closely in touch with developments in the natural sciences. Here again, his approach is at the furthest possible remove from that levelling strain of neo-pragmatist thought (exemplified in the work of Richard Rorty) which treats science as just one more voice in the cultural 'conversation of mankind', and scientific truth-claims as so many privileged metaphors or 'final vocabularies', ways of thinking that enjoy great prestige for this or that culture-specific reason, but which otherwise possess no special authority or epistemic warrant. Thus it is naive – so Rorty argues – to think that Galileo in any sense *got things right* in his quarrel with the Catholic Church. It is just that his particular set of metaphors happened to catch on (along with various other successful candidates in the period of early modern science), and thus came to define what would henceforth count as a reputable theory, observation, or truth-claim. But there is no question of science so to speak 'cutting nature at the joints', or delivering truths that would somehow hold good for all times, all purposes or all communities of knowledge. Rather, we should think of science pretty much as we think of poetry, literary criticism or the 'human sciences' in general: that is to say, as an open-ended process of creative exchange where truths are invariably *made*, not found; where explanatory concepts always turn out to be poetic metaphors in disguise; and where theories are justified solely in terms of their imaginative yield, or the extent to which they happen to suit the self-image of some given cultural enterprise.[26]

Nor can it be said that Rorty is alone in maintaining this position of extreme cognitive scepticism with regard to science and its truth-claims. In fact he finds support – or at any rate signs of an allied tendency – in numerous present-day thinkers, among them post-modernist culture-critics, Wittgensteinians who talk about 'language-games', 'forms of life', etc, Nietzschean genealogists of knowledge like Foucault, 'post-analytical' philosophers (arguably including Quine and Davidson), Bloomian proponents of creative misprision or 'strong misreading', anarchistic philosophers of science (notably Feyerabend), and just about anyone who has entertained doubts as to the adequacy of an old-style logical-empiricist theory of knowledge and truth. But it is clear that the single most important contribution, as Rorty sees it, is the linguistic (or hermeneutic) turn across various disciplines that has taught us *not* to think of truths – or facts – as just waiting out there to be discovered, but to treat them rather as interpretive constructs out of this or that 'final vocabulary'. And it is precisely on account of this belated discovery that we need to deconstruct the hitherto privileged relation between *science* (as a source of objective truths about the world) and *philosophy* (as the discipline best qualified to explain how and why those truths hold good). For this relation will now come to seem nothing more than a product of wishful thinking, a desire among philosophers to emulate science (or bask in its reflected glory), while in fact science has itself turned out to have no special claims as a cognitive or truth-telling discipline.

It is not surprising that Rorty's ideas have found favour with those in the postmodern-pragmatist camp who likewise take the view – to paraphrase Nietzsche – that we won't get rid of 'truth' and enlightenment values until science has been knocked off its pedestal. Hence the almost ritual habit of alluding to a work like Thomas Kuhn's *The Structure of Scientific Revolutions*, a work that in fact goes nothing like so far in their own direction as these thinkers would fondly suppose.[27] One factor that has worked to encourage such misapprehensions is the widespread (almost *de rigueur*) belief among literary theorists that anyone with an interest in the history or sociology of science must necessarily subscribe to some form of wholesale anti-realist or ultra-conventionalist doctrine. Here again, they lose sight of the alternative (properly dialectical) relation between science and philosophy that Althusser regards as the precondition for philosophy's having anything useful to say. Let me offer one further lengthy quotation to bring out the extent of his difference with Rorty and others of a kindred persuasion. 'There are false ideas about science', he writes,

> not simply in the heads of philosophers but in the heads of scientists themselves: false 'obviousnesses' that, far from being means of making progress, are in reality 'epistemological obstacles' (Bachelard). They

must be criticised and dispelled by showing that the imaginary solutions they offer in fact conceal real problems ... A philosophy capable of discerning and criticising them can have the effect of drawing the attention of scientists to the existence and efficacy of the epistemological obstacle that this spontaneous scientific ideology represents: the representation that scientists have of their own practice, and of their relationship to their own practice. Here again philosophy does not substitute itself for science: it intervenes, in order to clear a path, to open a space in which a correct line may then be drawn (88).

Such passages are often cited as proof of Althusser's extreme 'theoreticist' position, his clinging to an outworn enlightenment paradigm that takes no account of more recent (anti-foundationalist) modes of thought. And indeed, some of the texts collected in this volume – especially his 1978 essay 'The Transformation of Philosophy' – show Althusser willing to modify certain of his earlier theses in light of subsequent discussions and political events. But there is never any question of his backing down on the most important points at issue, i.e. the crucial and continuing role of Marxist 'theoretical practice', the dialectical relation between science and philosophy (the latter standing in where necessary as the intellectual conscience of scientific-materialist thought), and the indispensability of *truth* – or adequate concepts – as the one criterion for distinguishing 'imaginary' (ideological) solutions from the 'real problems' they invariably serve to conceal. In short, Althusser remains unrepentantly a Spinozist in everything concerning both the philosophic status *and* the real-world political efficacy of Marxist thought. And he does so, moreover, with what now appears a shrewd foreknowledge of the way things would go when the structuralist paradigm at length gave way to those various successor-movements whose effect – or at any rate whose constant claim – has been to relegate Marxism to the history of dead ideas.

There are signs that philosophers of science (Roy Bhaskar among them) are again taking stock of Althusser's work in the context of a revived critical-realist project that would seek to expose the inbuilt aporias of postmodern-pragmatist thinking.[28] (I examine these developments at greater length in Chapter Four.) And this project goes along with a re-evaluation of Marxist concepts and categories, one that rejects the kind of cynical 'commonsense' wisdom embodied in once-again fashionable talk about the 'end of ideology' and the chronic obsolescence of enlightenment-emancipatory thought. Such arguments merit the closest attention at a time when so many commentators – not only right-wing ideologues but influential figures on the 'post-Marxist' left – are suggesting that the trend of world historical events can only signal the imminent demise of everything that belonged to that old, self-deluded Marxist meta-narrative. As against these claims it is worth pondering Althusser's consciously provocative (even scandalous) assertion: that Marxism is *true*, that is to say, borne out by the rigour and demonstrative force of its arguments, and thus *neither proven nor disproven* by its success (or lack of it) in falling square with the 'evidence' of short-term historical developments. Nor can it be said that Althusser maintained this 'theoreticist' position only through a stubborn disregard for the unpalatable facts of 'actually-existing' communism as exhibited in the Soviet Union and its satellites, or in the tortuous history of Western communist parties as they struggled to justify or accommodate those facts. For it was Althusser's signal merit, as Gregory Elliott notes in his foreword to this volume, that he not only criticised such flagrant distortions of fact, principle and practice, but did so from a standpoint of principled dissent within the French CP that was rigorously faithful to his own theoretical premises.

In short, there is much to be gained from a reading of Althusser that rejects the commonplace (structuralist-inspired) account of his work and its 'relevance', but which also seeks to understand that work in light of the present, much-publicised 'crisis' of socialist politics in general. For there are few thinkers – and certainly none among the current postmodernist crop – who have done as much to sustain the activity of genuine critical thought at a time when 'theory' is often just a catch-word for the latest variety of zany irrationalist doctrine.

NOTES

(All references to Althusser's *Philosophy and the Spontaneous Philosophy of the Scientists* are given by page-number only in the text.)

1. See for instance Ted Benton, *The Rise and Fall of Structural Marxism* (London: New Left Books, 1984) and Gregory Elliott, *Althusser: the Detour of Theory* (London: Verso, 1987).
2. See especially Althusser, 'Freud and Lacan', in *'Lenin and Philosophy' and other essays*, trans. Ben Brewster (London: New Left Books, 1971), pp177-202.
3. See Christopher Norris, *Spinoza and the Origins of Modern Critical Theory* (Oxford: Basil Blackwell, 1991) for a more extended treatment of Spinozist elements in the work of Althusser, Balibar, Macherey, Deleuze

and other recent French thinkers.

4. Althusser, *For Marx*, trans. Ben Brewster (London: Allen Lane, 1969); Althusser and Balibar, *Reading Capital*, trans. Brewster (London: New Left Books, 1970).
5. Roland Barthes, *S/Z*, trans. Richard Miller (London: Jonathan Cape, 1975).
6. See for instance Jean Baudrillard, *The Mirror of Production*, trans. Mark Poster (St Louis: Telos Press, 1975); *For a Critique of the Political Economy of the Sign*, trans. Charles Levin (St Louis: Telos Press, 1981).
7. For a series of ingenious arguments to this effect, see Stanley Fish, *Doing What Comes Naturally: Change, Rhetoric and the Practice of Theory in Literary and Legal Studies* (New York: Oxford University Press, 1989).
8. Jürgen Habermas, *Knowledge and Human Interests*, trans. Jeremy J. Shapiro (London: Heinemann, 1972).
9. Jacques Monod, *Chance and Necessity: an Essay on the Natural Philosophy of Modern Biology*, trans. A. Wainhouse (London: Collins, 1972).
10. See especially Spinoza, *On the Improvement of Understanding*, in *The Chief Works of Benedict de Spinoza*, ed. & trans. R.H.M. Elwes, Vol. II (New York: Dover, 1951), pp3-41.
11. As Gregory Elliott notes, 'in 1948 he [Althusser] had written a *diplôme* on *La notion de contenu dans la philosophie de Hegel* under the supervision of Bachelard' (Elliott, *The Detour of Theory, op cit*, p87n). See Gaston Bachelard *La Formation de l'esprit scientifique* (Paris: Vrin, 1938/1980) and the chapters on Bachelard in Dominique Lecourt, *Marxism and Epistemology* (London: New Left Books, 1969).
12. See Spinoza, *On the Improvement of Understanding (op cit)*; also *A Theologico-Political Treatise*, in Elwes, *The Chief Works (op cit)*, Vol. I, pp3-266.
13. See especially Richard Rorty, *Contingency, Irony, and Solidarity* (Cambridge: Cambridge University Press, 1989); 'Postmodern Bourgeois Liberalism', *The Journal of Philosophy*, Vol. LXXX (October, 1983), pp583-9; 'Habermas and Lyotard on Post-Modernisty', *Praxis International*, Vol. IV (April, 1984), pp32-44: 'Texts and Lumps', *New Literary History*, Vol. XVII (1985), pp1-15; *Objectivity, Relativism and Truth: philosophical papers*, vol. I (Cambridge: Cambridge University Press, 1989).
14. See Thomas F. Pavel, *The Feud of Language: a History of Structuralist Thought* (Oxford: Basil Blackwell, 1990) for a shrewd critique of these various philosophical shortcomings; also – from a broader comparative viewpoint – Ian Hacking, 'Two Kinds of "New Historicism" for Philosophers', *New Literary History*, Vol. XXI, No. 2 (Winter 1990), pp343-64.
15. See especially Jean Baudrillard, *Simulacra and Simulations*, trans. Paul Foss, Paul Patton and Philip Beitchman (New York: Semiotext(e), 1983); 'The Masses: the Implosion of the Social in the Media', trans. Marie MacLean, *New Literary History*, Vol. XVI, No. 3 (1985), pp577-89; *Seduction*, trans. Brian Singer (London: Macmillan, 1990).
16. See Fish, *Doing What Comes Naturally (op cit)*.
17. See especially Foucault, *The Order of Things: an Archaeology of the Human Sciences*, trans. Alan Sheridan-Smith (New York: Random House, 1979), and *Language, Counter-Memory, Practice: Selected Essays and*

Interviews, trans. Donald F. Bouchard and Sherry Simon (Ithaca: Cornell University Press, 1977).

18. Donald Davidson, 'On the Very Idea of a Conceptual Scheme', in *Inquiries into Truth and Interpretation* (Oxford: Oxford University Press, 1984), pp183-98. See also Christopher Norris, 'Reading Donald Davidson: truth, meaning and right interpretation', in *Deconstruction and the Interests of Theory* (London: Pinter Publishers, 1988), pp59-83.
19. See for instance G.A. Cohen, *Karl Marx's Theory of History* (Oxford: Clarendon Press, 1978) and Jon Elster, *Making Sense of Marx* (Cambridge: Cambridge University Press, 1982).
20. Bertrand Russell, 'On Denoting', *Mind*, Vol. XIV (1905), pp479-93; see also his *Logic and Knowledge* (London: Allen & Unwin, 1956).
21. For a detailed study of this relationship, see Kenneth Blackwell, *The Spinozistic Ethics of Bertrand Russell* (London: Allen & Unwin, 1985).
22. 2See the concluding chapter of Russell, *My Philosophical Development* (London: Allen & Unwin, 1959) for an account of his differences with Wittgenstein, Austin and the 'ordinary language' school.
23. Noam Chomsky and Michel Foucault, 'Human Nature: justice versus power', in Fons Elders (ed), *Reflexive Water: the Basic Concerns of Mankind* (London: Souvenir Press, 1974), pp133-97.
24. See for instance Chomsky, *Cartesian Linguistics: a Chapter in the History of Rationalist Thought* (New York: Harper & Row, 1966); *Language and Problems of Knowledge* (Cambridge, Mass.: MIT Press, 1988); *Language and Politics* (Montreal: Black Rose Books, 1988).
25. See for instance Foucault, 'The Intellectuals and Power', in *Language, Counter-Memory, Practice* (*op cit*), pp205-17.
26. See Rorty, *Contingency, Irony, Solidarity* (*op cit*).
27. Thomas S. Kuhn, *The Structure of Scientific Revolutions* (Chicago: Chicago University Press, 1970).
28. See Roy Bhaskar, *Scientific Realism and Human Emancipation* (London: Verso, 1986) and *Reclaiming Reality: a Critical Introduction to Contemporary Philosophy* (London: Verso, 1989).

4

TRUTH, SCIENCE AND THE GROWTH OF KNOWLEDGE: ON THE LIMITS OF CULTURAL RELATIVISM

I   INTRODUCTION: OF THEORIES AND THINGS

What is the status of scientific truth-claims? Can they purport to hold good for all time across vastly differing contexts of language, culture, and society? That is to say: is science in the business of providing valid explanations of physical objects, processes and events whose nature remains constant despite deep-laid shifts of cultural perspective? Or is it not rather the case – as currently argued by relativists, pragmatists, and 'strong' sociologists of knowledge – that those contexts provide the only means of understanding why science has taken such diverse forms (and come up with such a range of competing 'truths') throughout its history to date?[1]

These questions are of interest not only to philosophers and historians of science but also, increasingly, to cultural and critical theorists influenced by the widespread 'linguistic turn' across various disciplines of thought.[2] They are often linked with the issue of ontological relativity, that is, the argument – deriving principally from W.V. Quine's famous essay 'Two Dogmas of Empiricism' – that there exist as many ways of describing or explaining some given phenomenon as there exist ontological schemes or methods for redistributing predicates over the entire range of sentences held true at any particular time.[3] On this holistic account there is no means of drawing a firm, categorical line between synthetic and analytic propositions, or matters of factual (contingent) truth which might always be subject to revision in the light of further evidence, and on the other hand those so-called logical 'laws of thought' whose truth is assumed to be a matter of *a priori* necessity and hence – by definition – valid for all possible contexts of enquiry.[4] And with the collapse of this distinction, so Quine argues, we must also relinquish the idea that philosophy of science might yet come up with an adequate method for linking observation-sentences to theories (or vice versa) through a clear-cut set of logical procedures. For in a holist perspective those sentences can possess meaning – that is to say, be assigned determinate truth-values – only as a function of their role within the entire existing 'fabric' or 'web' of beliefs, or the entire set of truth-claims ('empirical' and 'logical' alike) that currently happen to command widespread assent. Which is really to say that there are no such determinate truth-values since theories are always at some point 'underdetermined' by the best evidence to hand, while that evidence is always 'theory-laden' – or committed to some prior ontological scheme – right down to the level of its basic data as given in first-hand observation-sentences. Thus for Quine it follows that one must apply a principle of strict ontological parity as between (for instance) Homer's gods, centaurs, numbers, set-theoretical classes, and brick houses on Elm Street. Any preference in the matter – and Quine admits readily that he has a whole range of such preferences – must in the end come down to one's particular choice of ontological scheme.[5]

II VARIETIES OF RELATIVISM

There are many other sources of this relativist trend in contemporary philosophy of science. They include Thomas Kuhn's highly influential account of the way that science alternates between periods of 'normal' and 'revolutionary' activity, the former characterised by broad agreement on what counts as a proper (constructive and disciplined) approach to certain well-defined problems, the latter by a sense of impending crisis – and an absence of agreement on even the most basic principles – which heralds the transition to a new epoch.[6] Here as with Quine it is taken for granted that all the components of a given scientific 'paradigm' – from observation-sentences to high-level theories – are intelligible only in terms of the prevailing consensus, or according to the overall framework of beliefs that provides its own (strictly immanent) criteria of truth, progress, theoretical consistency, evidential warrant and so forth. But it then becomes difficult – if not impossible – to explain how we could ever gain insight into scientific world-views other than our own, or again, how historians of science could ever claim to understand the *reasons* (i.e. the scientific grounds) for some decisive paradigm-shift, as distinct from the various short-term cultural, social or historical factors that may have played some part in bringing them about. Hence Quine's recourse to the idea of 'radical translation' as a means of (purportedly) bridging this otherwise insuperable gulf between different observation-languages or ontological schemes.[7] Hence also the difficulties that Kuhn confronted in his 1969 Postscript to *The Structure of Scientific Revolutions* when responding to his critics on the issue of relativism and its self-disabling consequences. For it is far from clear that these difficulties are in any way resolved by his Quinean (radical-empiricist) line in the face of such strong counter-arguments.[8]

The problem is yet more acute with those kinds of ultra-relativist position adopted by proponents of the present-day 'linguistic turn' in its full-fledged (postmodern) guise. Thus it is sometimes claimed – as for instance by Richard Rorty – that our best model for interpreting the process of scientific paradigm-change is what happens when poets and novelists come up with striking new 'metaphors we can live by', or again, when strong-revisionist literary critics interpret such metaphors after their own fashion.[9] Then again there are those – Paul Feyerabend chief among them – who espouse an anarchistic philosophy of science which rejects all appeals to truth, logic, reason, consistency, experimental proof, etc.[10] On this view the idea of scientific 'progress' is nothing more than a piece of bogus mythology, one that takes hold through our myopically equating 'truth' with what currently counts as such according to this or that (self-authorised) 'expert' community. Much better, Feyerabend thinks, to have done with this misplaced reverence for science and instead take account of the various factors – social, political, psychological, careerist and so forth – which have always played a decisive role in the history of scientific thought. For we can then see how mixed were the motives (and often how random or opportunist the methods) which gave rise to some so-called 'discovery' or 'advance' that is nowadays treated as a text-book example of its kind. And this will bring two great benefits, as Feyerabend sees it. First, it will help to demythologise science – to remove some of its false prestige – and thereby open it up to criticism from other (i.e., non-'expert' but socially and ethically more responsive) quarters. Second, it will encourage scientists to become more adventurous in framing risky conjectures or in pursuing novel and heterodox lines of thought.

There are various explanations that might be adduced for the current appeal of such ideas. One is the widely-held view that philosophy of science can no longer have recourse to any version of the logical positivist (or logical-empiricist) distinction between truths-of-observation on the one hand and self-evident (tautologous) truths of reason on the other.[11] There are similar problems – so it is argued – with the resort to nomological-deductive (or covering-law) theories, those that would seek to account for observational data by bringing them under some higher-level (metalinguistic) order of logical entailment-relations.[12] For here again the way is open for sceptics like Quine to argue that any such distinction will always be drawn according to some preferred ontological scheme, some language- or culture-specific set of descriptive or explanatory priorities. One alternative that has enjoyed wide favour, not least among practising scientists, is Karl Popper's hypothetico-deductive account whereby the measure of a theory's claim to genuine scientific status is not so much its truth as established by the best current methods of experimental testing but its openness to falsification by those same methods.[13] This account has the signal advantage of explaining how a great many scientific theories that once enjoyed widespread credence should eventually have turned out mistaken, or – as with Newton's conceptions of absolute space and time – 'true' only relative to a certain restricted spatio-temporal domain. It thus meets the criticism of those, like Feyerabend, who would exploit such evidence to the point of denying that notions of truth have any role to play in the history and philosophy of science.

But there are difficulties with Popper's position, among them its reliance on under-specified criteria of what should count as a decisive falsification (or as grounds for rejecting some candidate hypothesis) in any given case. In other words, the methodology of 'conjecture and refutation' – as Popper describes it – amounts to just a minor inverted variation on the positivist or logical-empiricist theme. Moreover, so his critics maintain, Popper has made illicit use of this dubious methodology in order to attack what he sees as the pseudo-scientific pretensions of Marxism and other such 'historicist' trends in the sociological, interpretive, or humanistic disciplines.[14] For if there is one type of argument that always draws fire from the present-day cultural relativists it is the idea that science should enjoy any privileged truth-telling status, any method or set of validity-conditions that would place it apart from those other (on its own terms) less rigorous

157

or rationally accountable modes of knowledge. Such is the distinction standardly drawn between the 'context of discovery' for scientific truth-claims and the 'context of justification' wherein those claims are subject to testing by the best available criteria of experimental warrant, theoretical consistency, causal-explanatory yield, and so forth.[15] But this distinction is rejected by those who maintain – whether on grounds of 'ontological relativity' or in pursuit of the so-called 'strong programme' in sociology of knowledge – that truth is just a product of localised beliefs whose origin should be sought in their cultural context or in the socio-biographical history (the professional interests, careerist motives, childhood experiences, religious convictions, etc) of the scientists who held them.[16]

The poet Auden nicely epitomised this genre in its vulgar form: 'A penny life will give you all the facts'. More sophisticated – but no less sophistical – variants would include Feyerabend's well-known claim that in the case of Galileo *versus* Cardinal Bellarmine and the Church authorities it wasn't so much an issue of truth – i.e. of the heliocentric as against the geocentric hypotheses – but simply a question of who had the better argument on rhetorical, social, or political grounds.[17] Thus if Bellarmine sought to promote the interests of communal stability and peace, while Galileo can be shown to have fudged certain details (observational data) in order to preserve his theory, then the Church comes off rather better on balance and – so Feyerabend advises – should even now stick to its doctrinal position and not lean over to accommodate the present-day scientific orthodoxy.[18] Other versions of this argument (if rarely pushed to such a provocative extreme) are often to be found in the current literature on history and sociology of science. What they all have in common is the nominalist persuasion that 'truth' is just a term honorifically attached to those items of belief that have managed to prevail – by whatever strategic or rhetorical means – in this contest for the high ground of scientific 'knowledge' and 'progress'. Other sources include the 'social construction of reality' thesis (taken up in philosophy of science by writers like Barry Barnes and David Bloor)[19]; the sceptical 'archaeology' of knowledge essayed across a wide range of disciplines by Michel Foucault[20]; and the argument of postmodernist thinkers such as Jean-François Lyotard that science is just one amongst a range of incommensurable language-games (cognitive, ethical, historical, political, etc) and no longer exerts any privileged claim in respect of knowledge or truth.[21]

III ONTOLOGY AND EPISTEMOLOGY

We have seen already how such scepticism extends to philosophies of science that invoke some form of deductive warrant from covering-law theories or hypotheses framed with a view to experimental proof or refutation. But the same sorts of objection have also been brought against inductivist arguments, i.e. those that take the opposite route, seeking to derive generalised descriptive or explanatory accounts from observed regularities in this or that physical domain. David Hume was of course the first to remark upon the problems that arise in offering any adequate (i.e. more than 'commonsense' or probabilistic) defence of inductive procedures.[22] As he saw it, our ideas of causality came down to just a matter of regular succession, contiguity, and 'constant conjunction', or our indurate belief that if one event normally follows another in the order of phenomenal experience then this must be due to some intrinsic causal nexus or relationship between them. This fallacy ('post hoc, propter hoc') was for Hume the product of a manifest non-sequitur, albeit one so deeply embedded in our everyday as well as scientific habits of thought as to leave little hope of effective reform. More recently the 'puzzle of induction' has been re-stated in various elaborate and ingenious guises, some of them due to the philosopher Nelson Goodman.[23] Even where not thus intended they have all served to reinforce the widespread trend toward sceptical or relativist philosophies of science which assimilate 'truth' to the shifting currency of in-place consensus belief.

However these arguments have not gone unopposed, as indeed one might expect given their strongly counter-intuitive character and our natural disposition – as Hume recognized – to attribute something more to scientific truth-claims then mere lazy-mindedness or force of habit.[24] The challenge has come from various quarters, among them the Critical Realist school of thought whose chief proponent is Roy Bhaskar, himself much influenced by the work of Rom Harré.[25] Central to their case is a 'stratified' conception of reality, knowledge and human interests where distinctions may be drawn between, on the one hand, a realm of 'intransitive' objects, processes and events – i.e. those that must be taken to exist independently of human conceptualisation – and on the other hand a 'transitive' realm of knowledge-constitutive interests which are properly subject to critical assessment in terms of their ethical and socio-political character. To conflate these realms – so Bhaskar argues – is the cardinal error of relativist philosophies and one that leads to disabling consequences in both spheres of enquiry. Thus it relativises 'truth' (in the natural and human sciences alike) to whatever form of discourse – or *de facto* regime of instituted power/knowledge – happens to prevail in some given discipline at some given time. And it also undermines any critical questioning of scientific projects, investigations or research-programmes that would argue in terms of their ethical implications or their consequences for human individual and collective well-being. Such criticism can have no purpose – no grounds or justification – if it fails to take adequate (realistic) account of what science can or might yet achieve on the basis of present knowledge and research.

So Bhaskar has a twofold reason for maintaining his 'transitive'/'intransitive' distinction. It is necessary, first, as a condition of possibility for science and also (*a fortiori*) for the history and philosophy of science. That is to say, these projects would be simply unintelligible in the absence of a presupposed object-domain which is *not* just a construct out of our various (e.g. linguistic, discursive, historical, or cultural) schemes. Where the relativists err is in confusing *ontological* and *epistemological* issues. Thus they take the sheer variety of truth-claims advanced (and very often subsequently abandoned) down through the history of scientific thought as evidence that no truth is to be had, and that nothing could justify such claims aside from their own 'internalist' perspective on issues of truth, realism, progress, adequate explanation, etc. To requote Wittgenstein: 'the limits of my language [for which read 'discourse', 'paradigm', 'conceptual scheme' or whatever] are the limits of my world'.[26] But this conclusion holds only on the mistaken premise – as Bhaskar sees it – that *ontology* (questions like 'what things exist?' 'what are their real attributes, structures, generative mechanisms, causal dispositions, etc?') is synonymous with *epistemology* ('how does such knowledge come about?', 'according to what criteria?', 'within what limits of human cognitive grasp or knowledge-constitutive interest?'). Whence his second main point against the relativists: that by confusing these questions they deprive criticism of any effective purchase on the way that science has actually developed to date and the extent to which – within practical limits – its potential may be harnessed for the communal good.

These objectives both find expression in the title of Bhaskar's best-known book *Scientific Realism and Human Emancipation* (1986). Here he argues that relativist (or anti-realist) doctrines may well start out with the laudable aim of opposing that narrowly positivist conception of science which excludes any concern with ethical issues by reducing truth to a matter of purely instrumental (or means-end) rationality. But their proposed alternative is not much better, amounting as it does to a species of cognitive scepticism devoid of critical content and lacking any basis for informed evaluative judgment. Thus it simply reproduces all the well-worn puzzles – like Hume's problem of induction – which result from a reified conception of the physical object-domain joined to a passive spectator-theory of knowledge. Nor is Bhaskar by any means alone among recent philosophers of science in arguing the case for a return to causal-explanatory modes of understanding. Wesley Salmon offers numerous convincing examples of advances that have come about through the achievement of a deeper, more adequate grasp of precisely such underlying causal mechanisms.[27] These advances would include (for instance) the capacity to define and measure heat in terms of the mean kinetic energy of molecules; the understanding of electrical conductivity in terms of the passage of free electrons; or the characterisation of the colour 'blue' as that which pertains to wavelengths within a given frequency-range (as distinct, say, from Plato's idea that blue objects were perceived as such on account of their participating in the Form or the Essence of blueness).

Thus the case for causal realism, in Nicholas Rescher's words, is that 'every objective property of a real thing has consequences of a dispositional order', even if – as he readily concedes – they 'cannot be surveyed *in toto*'.[28] For this latter is in fact not so much a concession as a further strong argument for the realist case. That is, our chief evidence for the mind-independent status of real-world objects is precisely their possession of attributes, properties, causal dispositions, etc. which may always turn out to be *not* what we expect according to our present state of knowledge. In which case, as Rescher shrewdly points out, the relativist 'argument from error' (i.e. that scientists have often been wrong in the past so could just as well be wrong all the time) is one that fails to stand up. It is not so much an argument against scientific realism as an argument against 'the ontological finality of science as we have it'.[29] Thus Caesar didn't know – could not have known – that the metal of his sword contained tungsten carbide and that this was an explanatory factor in its fitness for the purpose intended. Moreover we can now give additional reasons (chemical, molecular, microstructural, etc) for the fact that certain metals or metallic compounds possess certain well-tried physical qualities.

Nor are such claims in any way confounded by the high probability – indeed near-certainty – that future science will come up with yet further, more detailed or depth-ontological explanations. For this doesn't alter the knowledge we have that our current explanation is better (more adequate) than anything available to Caesar.[30] That is to say, we have rational warrant for supposing that the objects, theories and causal postulates involved in our own best constructions are closer to the truth than what Caesar (or the scientific experts of his time) might have counted an adequate hypothesis. And this despite the always open possibility that certain gaps or shortcomings in our present state of knowledge might yet be revealed by some further advance – some improvement in the means of observation or the powers of theoretical synthesis – which rendered that knowledge either obsolete or henceforth restricted in its range of application. The most obvious example is that of Newtonian physics in the wake of relativity-theory, where classical conceptions of gravity or of absolute space and time continue to play an explanatory role, albeit under certain limiting conditions or in certain specified regions of enquiry.

IV THE GROWTH OF KNOWLEDGE

Such instances are often adduced in support of the standard relativist claim, i.e. that there exist as many ways of construing the phenomena as there exist scientific theories, paradigms, ontologies, conceptual schemes and so forth. But this argument misses the point in two crucial respects. First, it fails to note that Einstein's Special Theory of Relativity itself has recourse to an absolute value – the speed of light – which then serves as an invariant measure for assigning all loci in the space-time continuum.[31] Thus it is wrong – little more than a play on words – to confuse 'relativity' in this well-defined sense with the kinds of all-out ontological or epistemic relativism which Einstein strenuously sought to avoid.[32] And second, such arguments ignore the extent to which past theories are often not so much discredited *en bloc* as conserved and refined through the ongoing process of scientific elaboration and critique.

Sometimes this occurs when previously well-established items of knowledge are shown to possess only a partial truth or a power of explanation that is no longer adequate for present purposes. Such would be the case with (for instance) those advances in the fields of particle physics or molecular biology which built upon the work of earlier physicists, chemists and biologists, but which reconfigured the object-domain by opening up new regions of depth-ontological enquiry. At other times this process may operate (so to speak) in reverse, starting out with some relatively abstract conjecture regarding the existence of as-yet unobservable entities, and then seeking to verify its claims through experiment or further research. Thus, as Newton-Smith notes, the term 'electron' was at first a 'predicate ... introduced [by Roentgen] with the intention of picking out a kind of constituent of matter, namely that responsible for the cathode-ray phenomenon'.[33] Thereafter it not only 'entered the vocabulary' of theoretical physics – as a Kuhnian relativist might choose to phrase it – but also attained the status of a necessary postulate and then (with Rutherford's pioneering work) that of an entity whose passage could be tracked and whose causal-explanatory role placed its existence beyond reasonable doubt. And the same is true of a range of other items – such as molecules, genes, DNA proteins, and viruses – which have likewise exhibited a power to explain what previously lacked any adequate account. This is the chief virtue of a realist approach, according to Rescher: that it pays due regard to the prior claims of a 'non-phenomenal order from which the phenomena themselves emerge through causal processes'.[34] For otherwise – lacking such grounds – we should have absolutely no reason to think that electrons (or molecules, genes, viruses, etc) exerted any greater claim upon our credence than phlogiston, magnetic effluxes, or the luminiferous ether.

At this point the relativist will answer – most likely with reference to Kuhn – that those grounds are indeed lacking since there is no guarantee of the meaning-invariance of terms from one theory to the next. For if it is the case (as Kuhn thinks, following Quine) that all terms are 'theory-laden', object-languages and observation-statements included, and moreover that theories are radically 'underdetermined' by the evidence, then it follows that scientists perceive different objects under different theoretical descriptions.[35] Thus – for instance – the ancient atomists were in no sense talking about the 'same' entities as those later physicists (from Dalton to the present) who have themselves come up with such a diverse range of models, metaphors, 'elementary' particles, etc, as to render their theories strictly 'incommensurable'. And again, to take one of Kuhn's best-known examples: Priestley and Lavoisier each laid claim to have discovered the chemical process involved in combustion, although the latter based his account – correctly as we now think – on the existence of a hitherto unknown element named 'oxygen', while the former adhered to the phlogiston-theory and produced experimental results which fully confirmed it. Thus where Lavoisier detected the existence of oxygen Priestley talked about 'dephlogistated air', along with a whole set of congruent hypotheses and reasonings on the evidence that amounted to a counterpart theory with similar explanatory scope. Kuhn offers many such examples, among them the difference of views between Aristotle and Galileo regarding what we now – after Galileo – perceive as the gravity-induced motion of a pendulum, but what Aristotle 'saw' as matter seeking out its rightful (cosmological) place in the order of the elements.

This is all taken by Kuhn's relativist followers (and arguably by Kuhn himself) to justify a stance of thoroughgoing cognitive scepticism *vis-à-vis* the issue of scientific truth and progress. But there are obvious problems with any strong version of the incommensurability-thesis. One is the straightforward logical point that we could be in no position to mount such a claim unless we were able to recognize the differences between two rival theories, or possessed at least some minimal ground of comparison on which they could be said to diverge. After all, as Andrew Collier remarks, 'nobody bothers to say that astrology is incompatible with monetarism or generative grammar with acupuncture'.[36] And there is also the fact – well-attested by numerous examples from the history of science – that knowledge accrues around certain topics *across and despite* the widest differences of theoretical framework, ontological scheme, investigative paradigm or whatever.[37] Thus it does make sense to think of modern (post-Dalton) atomic and particle physics as belonging to a line of descent from the ancient atomists, even though the latter may be said to have inhabited a different 'conceptual universe', and to have advanced their ideas on a purely speculative basis, devoid of genuine scientific warrant.[38] What enables us to draw this distinction is precisely our knowledge of the growth of knowledge, our ability to grasp those salient respects in which the current understanding of atomic or subatomic structures differs from – and has indeed advanced far beyond – the ancient atomists' conceptions.

Thus the Quinean/Kuhnian thesis of radical meaning-variance gives rise to some awkward, not to say nonsensical conclusions. It would require us to believe not only that the Greek atomists were talking about something completely different, but also that later physicists – such as Dalton, Rutherford, Einstein and Bohr – were themselves working on such disparate assumptions as to rule out any meaningful comparison between them.[39] One might perhaps be tempted to adopt this outlook in other, more extravagant cases, like Anaximander's idea of the earth as 'a slab-like object suspended in equilibrium at the centre of the cosmos'. (I take this example from Rescher.) But even here it can reasonably be argued that we have grounds for thinking Anaximander wrong – and subsequent thinkers right – with respect to a given planetary body (the earth) whose structure, properties and place in the universe are now much better understood. And the same would apply to a great deal of early science, including Aristotle's theory of matter as composed of a mixture, in various proportions, of the four 'elements' (earth, air, fire and water), along with the 'humours' supposedly produced by their manifold possible combinations. The trouble with such a theory is not that the evidence fails to bear it out but, on the contrary, that it is perfectly compatible with any kind of 'evidence' that might turn up. In Popper's terms it is so vaguely framed as to lack the falsification criteria – or the grounds for its own subsequent disproof – which mark the difference between science and pseudo-science.

V THE TEST OF PRACTICE

However there is a stronger argument that avoids the above-noted problems with Popper's account. This is the causal-realist theory according to which scientific explanations have to do chiefly with the properties of things themselves – with their structures, effects, 'transfactually efficacious' powers (Bhaskar), etc – rather than the various propositions or logics of enquiry that purport to account for them. Thus, in Bhaskar's words: 'if there is a *real reason*, located in the nature of the stuff, such as its molecular or atomic structure, then water *must* tend to boil when it is heated'.[40] It is worth noting that this proposed shift from a descriptive-analytic to a causal-explanatory approach is one that finds a parallel in recent philosophy of language, notably Saul Kripke's influential work *Naming and Necessity*.[41] In both cases it entails the argument that certain words – those denominating 'natural kinds' – possess reference by virtue of their capacity to pick out certain corresponding objects, substances, or real-world entities. These words ('proper names' in Kripke's non-standard usage of that term) are defined as such through a chain of transmission which at each stage relates them back to their referent, itself 'baptized' in a first (inaugural) act of naming and thereafter subject to various modifications or refinements in the light of newly-acquired scientific knowledge. Kripke's chief aim in all this is to avoid the kinds of problem that arise with descriptivist theories (like those advanced by Frege and Russell) which make truth-values a function of reference and reference – in turn – a function of those meanings (or senses) that attach to a given term. For it is then a short step to Quinean and other such forms of wholesale ontological relativism, arrived at by rejecting any clear-cut distinction between analytic (logically necessary) and synthetic (empirical or factual) propositions. For Kripke, conversely, there is an order of *a posteriori* necessary truths which have to do with the way things stand in reality and with our knowledge of them as expressed in the form of propositions about natural-kind terms.

Bhaskar again provides some pertinent examples from the scientific field. Thus: 'if there is something, such as the possession of the same atomic or electronic configuration, which graphite, black carbon and diamonds share, then chemists are rationally justified in classing them together – the reason is that structure'.[42] He also makes the point rather neatly with regard to the standard text-book instance of a deductive syllogism: 'All men are mortal. Socrates is a man. Therefore, Socrates is mortal.' On Bhaskar's causal-realist account this becomes: 'in virtue of his genetic constitution, if Socrates is a man, he must die'.[43] That is, we have grounds – experiential as well as scientific – for asserting the order of necessity here quite apart from the syllogistic structure that identifies a well-formed deductive inference. And the same would apply to propositions about other natural-kind terms, as for instance (to repeat) that *water* tends to boil when heated, that electrical *conductors* are characterised by the passage of free electrons when a current is applied, or that the *blueness* of an object consists in its reflecting or absorbing light of a certain wavelength. These are all cases of what Kripke would call *a posteriori* necessity. Their names denote precisely those sorts of occurrent phenomena – structures, qualities, causal dispositions, etc – which on the one hand require our having found out about them, through experience or scientific investigation, while on the other hand belonging to their intrinsic (necessary) character as *just* that kind of phenomenon. And, as Bhaskar would claim, it is just this kind of knowledge that enables us to make sense of science, along with the history and philosophy of science.

Of course there are always counter-examples which the sceptic can adduce by way of contending that science deals only with hypothetical entities or with constructs out of this or that preferred ontology, conceptual scheme, etc. Such doubts attach most often to objects (or quasi-objects) at the leading edge of current speculative thought, as with the various postulated items – from electrons to mesons and quarks – that have figured in the history of modern particle physics. There is also the question as to how far science may create (rather than 'discover') such putative realia through its own, ever more resourceful, techniques for manipulating the materials at its disposal. Examples might be drawn from the field of recombinant DNA technology, from the new range of particles observed (or produced) with the advent of high energy accelerator programmes, or from the filling-out of Mendeleev's periodic table with elements previously unknown in nature. Even so it is the case – as Ian Hacking remarks in his book *Representing and Intervening* – that such proteins, particles or elements are possessed of both structural and causal-explanatory attributes which define their role within an ongoing project of scientific research.[44] Thus some new particle may well start out as a purely speculative construct, an hypothesis required in order to balance the equations or to fill the gap in an otherwise attractive and powerful unifying theory. But its existence will remain matter for conjecture until that hypothesis can be proven, perhaps through the arrival of an electron-microscope with higher powers of resolution, or an accelerator capable of achieving the required velocity. In which case, as Hacking more succinctly concludes, 'if you can bounce electrons off it, it is real'.[45]

VI OF REALITY AND TRUTH IN AN EXTRA-DISCURSIVE SENSE

Such arguments would of course carry little weight with cultural or literary theorists for whom realism of any variety is an option scarcely to be thought of. In these quarters it has become an article of faith – whether derived from Saussure, Foucault, Rorty, or Lyotard – that 'truth' is a wholly linguistic or discursive construct, and 'science' just the name that attaches to one (currently prestigious) language-game or discourse. Hence their inordinate fondness for loose analogies with those branches of 'postmodern' science that may be thought to exhibit (in Lyotard's parlance) a sublime disregard for ideas and values like truth, rationality, or progress. This new kind of science, 'by concerning itself with such things as undecidables, the limits of precise control, conflicts characterised by incomplete information, 'fracta', catastrophes, and pragmatic paradoxes, is theorizing its own evolution as discontinuous, catastrophic, nonrectifiable, and paradoxical'.[46] And again: since 'the reserve of knowledge – language's reserve of possible utterances – is inexhaustible', therefore it is no longer a question of truth (of that which pertains to the cognitive or constative phrase-regimes), but rather a question of the sheer 'performativity', the power of suasive utterance, that enables scientists to pick up research-grants, plug into information-networks, and so forth. In so far as this 'increases the ability to produce proof', so likewise it 'increases the ability to be right'. Thus Lyotard comes out pretty much in agreement with Feyerabend. On his account the best (indeed the only) criterion for scientific 'progress' is that which seeks to multiply discursive differentials, to judge (so far as possible) 'without criteria', and thereby do away with all those authoritarian constraints imposed by notions of scientific 'truth' and 'method'.

With Foucault one can see yet more clearly what results from an ultra-nominalist stance coupled to a deep suspicion of science and all its works. In *The Order of Things* this approach takes the form of an 'archaeological' questing-back into the various discourses, 'epistemes' or structures of linguistic representation that have characterised the natural and the human sciences alike.[47] Their history is marked – so Foucault contends – by a series of ruptures, or 'epistemological breaks', which make it strictly impossible to compare them in point of scientific truth, accuracy, scope, or explanatory power. The only meaningful comparisons to be drawn are those that operate (in Saussurean terms) on a structural-synchronic axis, that is to say, between the various disciplines that constitute the field of accredited knowledge at any given time. Foucault's chief interest is in those ambivalent regions of enquiry – midway between the physical and the human sciences – where issues of truth are most deeply bound up with questions of an ideological, interpretive, or hermeneutic nature. Thus he tends to avoid the 'hard' disciplines of (e.g.) physics or chemistry in favour of those – like philology, economics, and biology – that can plausibly be treated as interpretative constructs out of this or that dominant (period-specific) 'discourse'.[48] So it is that Foucault's self-professed 'archaeology of the human sciences' can also lay claim to a generalised validity for branches of knowledge outside and beyond what would normally fall within that sphere.

The most famous passage from *The Order of Things* is also the passage that most vividly displays Foucault's extreme anti-realist, conventionalist or nominalist viewpoint. It is taken from one of Borges' riddling parabolic fictions, and purports to reproduce a Chinese enclopaedia entry wherein 'animals' are classified as follows: '(a) belonging to the Emperor, (b) embalmed, (c) tame, (d) sucking pigs, (e) sirens, (f) fabulous, (g) stray dogs, (h) included in the present classification, (i) frenzied, (j) innumerable, (k) drawn with a very fine camelhair brush, (l) *et cetera*, (m) having just broken the water pitcher, (n) that from a long way off look like flies'.[49] Foucault treats this as an object-lesson in the fact of ontological relativity, an index of the culture-bound, parochial character of even our most deep-laid concepts and categories. Thus '[i]n the wonderment of this taxonomy, the thing we apprehend in one great leap, the thing that, by means of the fable, is demonstrated as the exotic charm of another system of thought, is the limitation of our own, the stark impossibility of thinking *that*'.[50]

Three responses would seem to be in order here. First: the *possibility* of thinking such exotic thoughts is demonstrated clearly enough by the existence of Borges' fable, of Foucault's commentary on it, and of our (i.e. the readers') capacity to perceive it as just such an instance of wild or zany categorisation. But second: we do so on the understanding that this is, after all, a piece of fabulous contrivance, a fiction invented by Borges (and cited by Foucault) with the purpose of offering an 'exotic' slant on our naturalised habits of thought and perception. In which case (third): it is an error – a confusion everywhere manifest in *The Order of Things* – to argue from the mere possibility of thinking such starkly 'impossible' thoughts (whatever this might mean) to the idea that *all* our concepts, categories, ontological commitments and so forth are likewise fictive constructions out of one such 'arbitrary' discourse or another. But this is exactly the premise that underwrites Foucault's entire project, from his early structuralist-inspired 'archaeology' of knowledge to the Nietzschean-genealogical approach that characterized his post-1970 works.[51] It is perhaps best seen as a *reductio ad absurdum* of that anti-realist line of argument which begins by locating truth in propositions about things, rather than in the things themselves, and which ends up – as with Quine, Kuhn, Rorty, Lyotard *et al* – by holistically relativising 'truth' to whatever sorts of language-game happen to enjoy that title. In other words it presses right through with that rejection of *de re* in favour of *de dicto* necessity which then turns out to undermine the very grounds of science as a truth-seeking enterprise. This irony indeed finds pointed expression in the title of Foucault's book. For on his account there cannot exist any 'things' – any extra-discursive objects, entities, kinds or categories of thing – whose various 'orderings' by language or discourse would render his thesis intelligible.

VII MIXED GENEALOGIES: DUHEM, BACHELARD, SAUSSURE

It is worth noting that there may be a common source for some of these issues that have recently emerged in both French and Anglo-American philosophy of science. It is to be found in the work of Pierre Duhem (1861-1916), a thinker whom Quine has acknowledged as a major influence, and whose name is standardly coupled with his own in discussions of the Duhem-Quine thesis with regard to ontological relativity.[52] Duhem, it is worth recalling, was a physicist who specialised in thermodynamics, as well as a philosopher-historian of science and a practising Catholic.[53] Hence his belief that science was not in the business of providing ultimate explanations, but should rather confine itself to an instrumentalist outlook whereby 'truth' is construed as whatever holds good for present observational or practical purposes. In this way he could keep science from encroaching upon matters of ultimate metaphysical or religious faith. In France there is a clearly-marked line of descent which runs from Duhem, via Gaston Bachelard, to that structuralist 'revolution' across various disciplines which achieved its high point in the 1960s and 1970s. Structural linguistics was at this time seen as converging with that movement in philosophy of science, represented most notably by Bachelard, which likewise sought to define the conditions under which a discipline could properly assert some claim to theoretical validity.[54] But this is now treated as a byegone episode in the history of thought, a distant prelude to the dawning awareness that science – like philosophy – is just one 'discourse' among others, a language-game with its own favoured idioms and metaphors, but without any privilege in point of epistemological rigour or truth. And since these include (as in Wittgenstein) the 'language-game' of religious belief it may not be fanciful to trace the line back to Duhem's attempt at a negotiated truce between science and Catholic doctrine. (Incidentally this might also cast a revealing light on Feyerabend's treatment of the issue between Galileo and Cardinal Bellarmine).[55]

If Bachelard is remembered nowadays it is chiefly for works like *The Psychoanalysis of Fire*, his essays in reflection on those modes of metaphoric or creative reverie that stand, so to speak, at the opposite pole from the scientific language of concept and rational inference.[56] What is thereby forgotten – one might say repressed – is the fact that these writings were themselves a part of his larger epistemological project, his attempt to distinguish more clearly between the two realms of thought. It is a plain misreading of Bachelard's work to extract from it the modish doctrine that 'all truth-claims are fictions', 'all concepts just sublimated metaphors', or ' "science" merely the name we attach to some currently prestigious language-game'. On the contrary: Bachelard's aim was to prevent such promiscuous levelling of the difference – the more than contingent, linguistic or localised (culture-specific) difference – between scientific epistemologies on the one hand and poetic-metaphorical 'reverie' on the other. Thus what Bachelard meant by his term 'epistemological break' was a decisive rupture with pre-scientific modes of thought, one that marked the crucial stage of advance to an adequate conceptualisation of some given domain.[57] It retains this significance – if more problematically – in Louis Althusser's structural-Marxist account of the science/ideology distinction.[58] But with Foucault the idea of an 'epistemological break' has been relativised to the point where it means nothing more than a random shift in the prevailing (discursively produced) 'order of things'.

That Saussure should nowadays be routinely coopted by adherents of this ultra-relativist view is, to say the least, something of an irony given his methodological concerns and his desire to set linguistics on the path toward a genuine (structural-synchronic) science of language.[59] Such was indeed the main source of its appeal for that earlier generation of theorists who saw in it – as likewise in Bachelard's work – a means of articulating the difference between metaphor and concept, ideology and science, natural (everyday) language on the one hand and theoretical discourse on the other. But in both cases, Saussure and Bachelard, these claims were lost from view with the post-structuralist turn toward an out-and-out conventionalist theory of science, knowledge and representation which treated such ideas as merely a species of 'metalinguistic' delusion. Thus Bachelard was read – or standardly invoked – as arguing that all scientific concepts could in the end be traced back to their subliminal source in some privileged metaphor or image-cluster.[60] And Saussure's theoretical commitments counted for nothing in comparison with the prospects that were opened up by treating all theories (his own presumably among them) as 'constructed in' or 'relative to' some localised signifying practice. For it could then be maintained – without fear of contradiction on reasoned philosophical grounds – that literary critics were among the vanguard party in a coming 'revolution' of the instituted order of discourse, an event whose signs they were able to read through their knowledge that 'reality' was merely the figment of a naturalised (though in fact merely 'arbitrary') relation between signifier and signified.[61]

The problems with this doctrine are those that have bedevilled every version of the relativist argument from Protagoras down. That is to say, if we redefine 'true' as 'true relative to L' (where L is taken to denote some language, paradigm, conceptual scheme, 'interpretive community' or whatever) then there is no way of counting *any* belief false just so long as it can claim – or could once claim – some measure of communal assent.[62] From which it follows *ex hypothese* that all beliefs are true by their own cultural lights, or according to their own immanent criteria as manifest in this or that linguistically mediated 'form of life'. Every single truth-claim that was ever entertained by a community of like-minded knowers must count as valid when referred to the language-game, vocabulary, or belief-system then in place. Thus for instance it was once *true* – not just an artefact of limited knowledge or erroneous 'commonsense' perception – that the fixed planets were seven in number; that the Sun rotated about the Earth; that the process of combustion involved the release of a colourless, odourless, intangible substance called phlogiston, rather than the uptake of oxygen; and that no fixed-wing aircraft could possibly get off the ground since the necessary lift could be generated only by a bird-like flapping motion, or perhaps – as Leonardo was first to suggest – a rotary-blade arrangement of the helicopter type. In each case and numerous others besides – one could multiply examples at leisure – the belief in question is no less true, or no more demonstrably false, than those other beliefs that are nowadays widely (even universally) taken for matters of scientific fact. What counts is their suasive efficacy as measured by the current norms of 'science' as a going enterprise, a rhetorical activity where truth is defined in performative (not constative) terms, and where any distinction between concept and metaphor turns out to be merely – like the word 'concept' itself, not to mention the concept of 'metaphor' – a species of repressed or sublimated metaphor. From which it follows, supposedly, that all truth-talk – whether in the natural or the more theory-prone human sciences – comes down to a choice of the right sort of metaphor (or the optimum rhetorical strategy) for conjuring assent from others engaged in the same communal enterprise.

Scientists (and at least some philosophers of science) have understandably considered this an implausible account of how advances come about through the joint application of theory and empirical research. Hence – as I have argued – the recent emergence of anti-conventionalist or causal-realist approaches which offer a far better understanding of our knowledge of the growth of knowledge. After all, there would seem rather little to be said for a philosophy of science that effectively leaves itself nothing to explain by reducing 'science' to just another species of preferential language-game, rhetoric, discourse, conceptual scheme or whatever. The current revival of realist ontologies (along with the return to 'causal-realist' theories of reference) betokens a break with this whole – as it now appears – misdirected line of thought. In a longer purview it resumes the position attributed to Aristotle by his commentator Themistius: namely, the principle that 'that which exists does not conform to various opinions, but rather the correct opinions conform to that which exists'.[63]

NOTES

1. See for instance Barry Barnes, *About Science* (Oxford: Basil Blackwell, 1985); Peter L. Berger and Thomas Luckmann, *The Social Construction of Reality: a treatise on the sociology of knowledge* (Harmondsworth: Penguin, 1967); David Bloor, *Knowledge and Social Imagery* (London: Routledge & Kegan Paul, 1976); Steve Fuller, *Social Epistemology* (Bloomington: Indiana University Press, 1980) and *Philosophy of Science and its Discontents* (Boulder, Colorado: Westview Press, 1989); Steve Fuller, Marc de Mey, Terry Shinn and Steve Woolgar (eds), *The Cognitive Turn: sociological and psychological perspectives on science* (Dordrecht: D. Reidel, 1989); Karin D. Knorr-Cetina, *The Manufacture of Knowledge: an essay on the constructivist and contextual nature of knowledge* (Oxford: Pergamon Press, 1981); Bruno Latour, *Science in Action* (Milton Keynes: Open University Press, 1987); Bruno Latour and Steve Woolgar, *Laboratory Life: the social construction of scientific facts* (London: Sage, 1979); Steve Woolgar, *Science: the very idea* (London: Tavistock, 1988); Woolgar (ed), *Knowledge and Reflexivity: new frontiers in the sociology of knowledge* (London: Sage, 1988).

2. See especially Thomas Docherty (ed), *Postmodernism: a reader* (Hemel Hempstead: Harvester-Wheatsheaf, 1993); Clifford Geertz, *Local Knowledge: further essays on interpretive anthropology* (New York: Basic Books, 1983); Alan G. Gross, *The Rhetoric of Science* (Cambridge, Mass.: Harvard University Press, 1990); Richard Rorty (ed), *The Linguistic Turn* (Chicago: University of Chicago Press, 1967); Herbert W. Simons (ed), *The Rhetorical Turn: invention and persuasion in the conduct of inquiry* (Chicago: University of Chicago Press, 1990). For a recent challenge to this whole way of thinking, see Edward Pols, *Radical Realism: direct knowing in science and philosophy* (Ithaca, N.Y.: Cornell University Press, 1992).

3. W.V.O. Quine, 'Two Dogmas of Empiricism', in *From a Logical Point of View* (New York: Harper & Row, 1953), pp20-46. See also Quine, *Word and Object* (Cambridge, Mass.: MIT Press, 1960); *Theories and Things* (Cambridge, Mass.: Harvard University Press, 1981); with J.S. Ullian, *The Web of Belief* (New York: Random House, 1970).

4. For a critical survey of the field see Jerry Fodor and Ernest LePore, *Holism: a shopper's guide* (Oxford: Basil Blackwell, 1991); also Robert Barrett and Roger Gibson (eds), *Perspectives on Quine* (Oxford: Basil Blackwell, 1989); Donald Davidson and J. Hintikka (eds), *Words and Objections: essays on the work of W.V. Quine* (Dordrecht & Boston: D. Reidel, 1969).

5. Quine, 'Two Dogmas' (*op cit*). See also Sandra G. Harding, *Can Theories be Refuted? essays on the Duhem-Quine thesis* (Dordrecht: D. Reidel, 1976).

6. Thomas S. Kuhn, *The Structure of Scientific Revolutions*, 2nd edn. (revised) (Chicago: University of Chicago Press, 1970); also Kuhn, *The Essentian Tension: selected studies in scientific tradition and change* (University of Chicago Press, 1977); Gary Gutting, *Paradigms and Revolutions* (Notre Dame, Ind.: University of Notre Dame Press, 1980); Ian Hacking (ed), *Scientific Revolutions* (London: Oxford University Press, 1981); Mary Hesse, *Revolutions and Reconstructions in the Philosophy of Science* (Brighton: Harvester, 1980); John Krige, *Science, Revolution and Discontinuity* (Brighton: Harvester, 1980).

7. See Quine, *Word and Object* (*op cit*).

8. For further discussion see Larry Laudan, *Progress and its Problems* (Berkeley & Los Angeles: University of California Press, 1977) and *Science and Relativism: some key controversies in the philosophy of science* (Chicago: University of Chicago Press, 1990); also Martin Hollis and Steven Lukes (eds), *Rationality and Relativism* (Oxford: Basil Blackwell, 1982); Richard J. Bernstein, *Beyond Objectivism and Relativism: science, hermeneutics, and praxis* (Philadelphia, PA: University of Pennsylvania Press, 1983).

9. See especially Richard Rorty, 'Science as Solidarity' and 'Is Natural Science a Natural Kind?', in *Objectivity, Relativism, and Truth* (Cambridge: Cambridge University Press, 1991), pp35-45 and 46-62; also Rorty, *Philosophy and the Mirror of Nature* (Oxford: Basil Blackwell, 1980) and *Consequences of Pragmatism* (Brighton: Harvester, 1982).

reality (London: Routledge, 1994); Mary Hesse, *Models and Analogies in Science* (South Bend: University of Notre Dame Press, 1966); David Papineau, *Reality and Representation* (Oxford: Basil Blackwell, 1987).

46. Lyotard, *The Postmodern Condition* (*op cit*), p112.

47. Foucault, *The Order of Things* (*op cit*).

48. See Gutting, *Michel Foucault's Archaeology of Scientific Knowledge* (op cit).

49. Foucault, *The Order of Things* (*op cit*), pxv.

50. *Ibid*, pxv.

51. See for instance Foucault, *Language, Counter-Memory, Practice*, trans. D.F. Bouchard and S. Weber (Oxford: Basil Blackwell, 1977).

52. See Harding, *Can Theories be Refuted? essays on the Duhem-Quine thesis* (*op cit*).

53. Pierre Duhem, *The Aims and Structure of Physical Theory*, trans. Philip Wiener (Princeton, N.J.: Princeton University Press, 1954); *To Save the Phenomena: an essay on the idea of physical theory from Plato to Galileo*, trans. Edmund Dolan and Chaninah Maschler (Chicago: University of Chicago Press, 1969); *Premices Philosophiques*, ed. and intro. Stanley L. Jaki (Leiden: E.J. Brill, 1987); Stanley L. Jaki, *Uneasy Genius: the life and work of Pierre Duhem* (The Hague: Martinus Nijhoff, 1984).

54. See Dominique Lecourt, *Marxism and Epistemology: Bachelard, Canguilhem and Foucault* (London: New Left Books, 1975).

55. Feyerabend, *Against Method* (*op cit*) and *Farewell to Reason* (*op cit*).

56. Gaston Bachelard, *The Psychoanalysis of Fire*, trans. A.C.M. Ross (Boston: Beacon Press, 1964); *The Poetics of Space*, trans. M. Jolas (Boston: Beacon Press, 1969); *The Poetics of Reverie*, trans. Daniel Russell (Boston: Beacon Press, 1971).

57. Bachelard, *The Philosophy of No: a philosophy of the new scientific mind* (New York: Orion Press, 1968); *The New Scientific Spirit* (Boston: Beacon Press, 1984); *La Formation de l'esprit scientifique* (Paris: Corti, 1938). See also Lecourt, *Marxism and Epistemology* (*op cit*) and Mary Tiles, *Bachelard: science and objectivity* (Cambridge: Cambridge University Press, 1984).

58. See especially Louis Althusser, *Philosophy and the Spontaneous Philosophy of the Scientists and other essays*, trans. Gregory Elliott (London: Verso, 1990).

59. Thus Roy Harris notes that Saussure uses the words 'science' and 'scientifique' no less than thirteen times in the first chapter alone of his *Cours de linguistique générale*. See Harris, *Reading Saussure* (London: Duckworth, 1987), p4.

60. For a cogently argued critique of this reading, see Jacques Derrida, 'White Mythology: metaphor in the text of philosophy', in *Margins of Philosophy*, trans. Alan Bass (Chicago: University of Chicago Press, 1982), pp207-71.

61. This episode receives a more sympathetic treatment in John Mowitt, *Text; the genealogy of an antidisciplinary object* (Durham, N.C.: Duke University Press, 1993).

62. See for instance Hilary Putnam, *Realism and Reason* (Cambridge

10. See Paul K. Feyerabend, *Against Method* (London: New Left Books, 1975); *Science in a Free Society* (New Left Books, 1978); *Farewell to Reason* (London: Verso, 1987).

11. See Quine, 'Two Dogmas' (*op cit*).

12. C.G. Hempel, *Aspects of Scientific Explanation* (New York & London: Macmillan, 1965) and *Fundamentals of Concept Formation in Empirical Science* (Chicago: University of Chicago Press, 1972); also R.B. Braithwaite, *Scientific Explanation* (Cambridge: Cambridge University Press, 1953).

13. Karl R. Popper, *The Logic of Scientific Discovery* (New York: Harper & Row, 1934, 2nd edn. 1959). See also Popper, *Conjectures and Refutations* (Harper & Row, 1963) and *Objective Knowledge* (Oxford: Clarendon Press, 1972).

14. Popper, *The Poverty of Historicism* (New York: Harper & Row, 1957); *The Open Society and its Enemies*, Vols. I & 2 (5th edn., revised, London: Routledge & Kegan Paul, 1966).

15. See especially Hans Reichenbach, *Experience and Prediction* (Chicago: University of Chicago Press, 1938); also Wesley C. Salmon (ed), *Hans Reichenbach: logical empiricist* (Dordrecht: D. Reidel, 1979).

16. See entries for Note 1 (above); also – from a range of methodological viewpoints – Barry Barnes, *T.S. Kuhn and Social Science* (Oxford: Basil Blackwell, 1982): Augustine Brannigan, *The Social Basis of Scientific Discoveries* (Cambridge: Cambridge University Press, 1981); David Papineau, *For Science in the Social Sciences* (London: Macmillan, 1978); David L. Phillips, *Wittgenstein and Scientific Knowledge: a sociological perspective* (London: Macmillan, 1977); Richard Whitley, *The Social and Intellectual Organization of the Sciences* (London: Oxford University Press, 1986).

17. Feyerabend, *Against Method* (*op cit*).

18. Feyerabend, *Farewell to Reason* (*op cit*).

19. See Note 1 (above).

20. Michel Foucault, *The Archaeology of Knowledge*, trans. Alan Sheridan (London: Tavistock, 1972); *The Order of Things: an archaeology of the human sciences*, trans. Alan Sheridan (London: Tavistock, 1973); also Gary Gutting, *Michel Foucault's Archaeology of Scientific Reason* (Cambridge: Cambridge University Press, 1989).

21. Jean-François Lyotard, *The Postmodern Condition: a report on knowledge*, trans. Geoff Bennington and Brian Massumi (Minneapolis: University of Minnesota Press, 1984) and *The Differend: phrases in dispute*, trans. Georges van den Abbeele (Manchester: Manchester University Press, 1988).

22. David Hume, *A Treatise of Human Nature* (Oxford: Clarendon Press, 1984) and *An Enquiry Concerning Human Understanding* (Indianapolis: Bobbs-Merrill, 1955). For a reading that questions this commonplace account of Hume's scepticism with regard to causal explanations, see Galen Strawson, *The Secret Connexion* (Oxford: Clarendon Press, 1989); also J.L. Mackie, *The Cement of the Universe* (Oxford: Clarendon, 1974); John Wright, *The Sceptical Realism of David Hume* (Manchester:

Manchester University Press, 1983); and Simon Blackburn, 'Hume and Thick Connexions', in *Essays in Quasi-Realism* (London: Oxford University Press, 1993), pp94-107.

23. See especially Nelson Goodman, 'The New Riddle of Induction', in *Fact, Fiction, and Forecast* (Indianapolis: Bobbs-Merrill, 1955), pp59-83; also Simon Blackburn, *Reason and Prediction* (Cambridge: Cambridge University Press, 1973); L. Jonathan Cohen, *The Implications of Induction* (London: Methuen, 1970); Nicholas Rescher, *Induction* (Oxford: Basil Blackwell, 1980); G.H. von Wright, *The Logical Problem of Induction* (Blackwell, 1965).

24. See notably Mackie, *The Cement of the Universe (op cit)*; also Rom Harré and E.H. Madden, *Causal Powers* (Oxford: Blackwell, 1975); Bryan Skyrms, *Causal Necessity* (New Haven: Yale University Press, 1980).

25. Roy Bhaskar, *Scientific Realism and Human Emancipation* (London: Verso, 1986); *Reclaiming Reality: a critical introduction to contemporary philosophy* (London: Verso, 1989); *Dialectic: the pulse of freedom* (London: Verso, 1993); also Rom Harré, *The Philosophies of Science* (London: Oxford University Press, 1972) and *Varieties of Realism: a rationale for the social sciences* (Oxford: Basil Blackwell, 1986); Bhaskar (ed), *Harré and his Critics* (Oxford: Blackwell, 1990); Andrew Collier, *Scientific Realism and Socialist Thought* (Hemel Hempstead: Harvester, 1989) and *Critical Realism: an introduction to the work of Roy Bhaskar* (London: Verso, 1994).

26. For the consequences of this idea as applied to the philosophy, history, and sociology of science, see for instance Phillips, *Wittgenstein and Scientific Knowledge (op cit)*; also Peter Winch, *The Idea of a Social Science and its Relation to Philosophy* (London: Routledge & Kegan Paul, 1958) and David Bloor, *Wittgenstein: a social theory of knowledge* (New York: Columbia University Press, 1983).

27. See Wesley C. Salmon, *Scientific Explanation and the Causal Structure of the World* (Princeton, N.J.: Princeton University Press, 1984) and *Four Decades of Scientific Explanation* (Minneapolis: University of Minnesota Press, 1989); also Nicholas Rescher, *Scientific Realism: a critical reappraisal* (Dordrecht: D. Reidel, 1987); David Charles and Kathleen Lennon (eds), *Reduction, Explanation and Realism* (Oxford: Clarendon Press, 1992): J. Lepin (ed), *Scientific Realism* (Berkeley & Los Angeles: University of California Press, 1984); M. Tooley, *Causation: a realist approach* (London: Oxford University Press, 1988).

28. Rescher, *Scientific Realism (op cit)*, p116.

29. *Ibid*, p61.

30. See David-Hillel Ruben, *Explaining Explanation* (London: Routledge, 1992): Larry Laudan, *Progress and its Problems* (Berkeley & Los Angeles: University of California Press, 1977); Peter Lipton, *Inference to the Best Explanation* (London: Routledge, 1993); Peter Muntz, *Our Knowledge of the Growth of Knowledge* (London: Routledge & Kegan Paul, 1985); Nicholas Rescher, *Scientific Progress* (Oxford: Basil Blackwell, 1979); Peter J. Smith, *Realism and the Growth of Knowledge* (Cambridge: Cambridge University Press, 1981); J.M. Zimon, *Reliable Knowledge: an*

exploration of the grounds for belief in science (Cambridge: Cambridge University Press, 1978).

31. See especially J.R. Lucas, *A Treatise on Time and Space* (London: Oxford University Press, 1973); J.R. Lucas and P.E. Hodgson, *Spacetime and Electro-Magnetism* (Oxford University Press, 1990); Wesley C. Salmon, *Space, Time and Motion: a philosophical introduction* (Minneapolis: University of Minnesota Press, 1980); J.L. Mackie, 'Three Steps to Absolutism', in *Logic and Knowledge (Selected Papers)*, Vol. 1, Oxford: Clarendon Press, 1985), pp192-213; Christopher Ray, *Time, Space and Causality* (London: Routledge, 1991); Richard Swinburne (ed), *Time and Causality* (Dordrecht: D. Reidel, 1983).

32. See Arthur Fine, *The Shaky Game: Einstein, realism, and quantum* (Chicago: University of Chicago Press, 1986).

33. W.H. Newton-Smith, *The Rationality of Science* (London: Routledge & Kegan Paul, 1981), p173.

34. Rescher, *Scientific Realism (op cit)*, p51.

35. Kuhn, *The Structure of Scientific Revolutions (op cit)* and Quine, 'Two Dogmas of Empiricism' *(op cit)*; also Ian Hacking (ed), *Scientific Revolutions* (London: Oxford University Press, 1981).

36. Collier, *Critical Realism (op cit)*, p91.

37. See Muntz, *Our Knowledge of the Growth of Knowledge (op cit)*; Smith, *Realism and the Progress of Science (op cit)*.

38. See Robin Waterfield, *Before Eureka: the presocratics and their science* (Bristol: The Bristol Press, 1989).

39. On this topic see for instance Harold Brown, *Perception, Theory and Commitment: the new philosophy of science* (Chicago: University of Chicago Press, 1977); Hartry Field, 'Theory Change and Indeterminacy of Reference', *Journal of Philosophy*, Vol. 70 pp462-81 and 'Realism and Relativism', *Journal of Philosophy*, (1982), pp553-6; Donald Gillies, *The Philosophy of Science in the Twentieth Century: four central themes* (Oxford: Basil Blackwell, 1993); Michael E. Levin, 'On Theory-Change and Meaning-Change', *Philosophy of Science*, Vol. 46 (1979), pp407-24; Ernest Nagel, Sylvain Bromberger and Adolf Grünbaum, *Observation and Theory in Science* (Baltimore: Johns Hopkins University Press, 1971); David Papineau, *Theory and Meaning* (London: Oxford University Press, 1979); Frederick Suppe, *The Structure of Scientific Theories* (Chicago: University of Illinois, 1977).

40. Bhaskar, *Dialectic (op cit)*, p35.

41. Saul Kripke, *Naming and Necessity* (Oxford: Basil Blackwell, 1980); also Stephen Schwartz (ed), *Naming, Necessity, and Natural Kinds* (Ithaca, N.Y.: Cornell University Press, 1977); David Wiggins, *Sameness and Substance* (Oxford: Basil Blackwell, 1980).

42. Bhaskar, *Dialectic (op cit)*, p35.

43. *Ibid*, p35.

44. Ian Hacking, *Representing and Intervening* (Cambridge: Cambridge University Press, 1983).

45. See also James Robert Brown, *Smoke and Mirrors: how science*

University Press, 1983). Protagoras finds his most resourceful and spirited modern defender in Joseph Margolis, *The Truth About Relativism* (Oxford: Basil Blackwell, 1993).

63. Cited by Rescher, *Scientific Realism* (*op cit*), p131.

5

MARXISM AGAINST POSTMODERNISM, OR THE *EIGHTEENTH BRUMAIRE* REVISITED

I   REALITY THROUGH THE LOOKING-GLASS

Over the past fifteen years or so, Alex Callinicos has produced an impressive series of books, articles and reviews defending Marxism – 'classical' Marxism, what's more – against its various detractors, right and left.[1] As theoretician-in-chief of the Socialist Workers Party he has managed to combine this tactical role with a sustained and highly articulate account of issues in Marxist epistemology, ethics, aesthetics, and historiography. In *Against Postmodernism: a marxist critique*, he takes on current 'postmodernist' fashion and argues that the term is just a floating signifier, a word without a referent or concept, a name for whatever sort of zany irrationalist doctrine happens to grab the fancy of the chattering classes in these vaunted 'New Times' of proliferating junk-theory, regressive political attitudes, and claims to be 'post-' just about everything, from Marxism to modernism, structuralism, feminism, politics, theory, and history itself. This essay is an adapted version of a review-article I wrote for a US journal when the book first appeared. But if things have moved on since then they have hardly moved toward a better understanding of the issues that Callinicos raises. 'Postmodernism' is still the shorthand description for a range of philosophically confused and politically vacuous ideas whose endless recycling has become a growth-industry in the British and US academies. Unfortunately my arguments are still relevant.

Callinicos lays his cards on the table in the book's opening sentence. It is, he writes, an attempt to challenge the strange mixture of cultural and political pessimism and light-hearted playfulness with which – in a more than usually farcical reprise of the apocalyptic mood at the end of the last century – much of the contemporary Western intelligentsia apparently intends to greet our own *fin de siècle*. (pix).

The combative tone, here and elsewhere, shouldn't be taken as a sign that Callinicos is engaging in mere knockabout polemics, or descending to the level of showy rhetoric and unargued oracular pronouncement which typifies so much of his opponents' writing. In fact his book is a powerful piece of sustained philosophical argument, as well as a shrewdly diagnostic account of the various socio-historical factors that have lately given rise to this widespread mutation in the discourse of 'radical' intellectuals. One can well understand why Callinicos should sometimes – like Marx before him – adopt a more abrasive, edgily defensive, or downright contemptuous tone. After all, he is arguing a case which is nowadays liable to be treated by the 'posties' with a mixture of wry condescension and pitying fondness, or simply an attitude of blank disbelief that anyone should *want* to defend such a patently outmoded and discredited set of political ideas. No wonder that this makes him feel on occasion like Abdiel alone against the forces of night. But *Against Postmodernism* is much more than just a product of rattled Marxist sensibility; its arguments merit close attention from anyone concerned to make sense of the so-called 'postmodern condition' and its various cultural appendages.

Notwithstanding my own recent work in this field,[3] *Against Postmodernism* stands as by far the most trenchant and significant critique of post-modernism that I have come across. Nor can it easily be written off as just another piece of superannuated theorising in the bad old 'enlightenment' or 'grand narrative' tradition, a sure sign that Callinicos hasn't yet caught up with the latest rules of the game, or recognised the chronic obsolescence of any argument based on notions like *truth, critique, ideology* or other such items of self-endorsing rhetoric dressed up as theoretical concepts. For Callinicos has anticipated all these charges, examined their credentials in a spirit of open (if openly sceptical) debate, and found them not only politically undesirable – which of course wouldn't impress his opponents very much – but also philosophically naive, ill-informed, and blind to their own motivating interests.

His book pretty much demolishes postmodernism in its more

ambitious doctrinal form, as a wholesale anti-philosophy premised on counter-enlightenment values and linked to a revamped 'end-of-ideology' thesis familiar from the writings of Daniel Bell and other such purveyors of a kindred rhetoric with its own fairly blatant ideological agenda.[4] Callinicos is willing to admit that the term has a useful (if limited) application in describing certain recently emergent tendencies in fiction, poetry, architecture, painting, and the sphere of artistic production generally. But even here, he suggests, the periodisation is so vaguely defined – and the degree of overlap with 'modernist' techniques so evident in almost every case – that one had better give up the delusive quest for characterising features (or even Wittgensteinian 'family resemblances'), and acknowledge that the thing just *doesn't exist* except as a product of media hype or a self-induced fantasy on the part of various jaded ex-radicals, *soi-disant* 'post-Marxist' (i.e. post-68) intellectuals, and media pundits with an eye to the market for catchy slogans and novelty imports. Talk of 'postmodernism' becomes in the end just a handy pretext for not thinking hard about anything – art, language, history, philosophy, least of all politics – but simply latching on to a ready-made discourse whose terms recycle the stalest clichés of postwar 'consensus' ideology. Above all, it does great service to the interests of state and corporate power in diffusing the idea that there is *really no difference* between things as they seem, things as they are, and things as they might be according to the values of enlightened critique, increased social justice and a genuinely working participatory democracy. For it is only by maintaining a sense of these distinctions – common to every form of emancipatory thought from Kant, via Marx to Habermas and other present-day varieties of *Ideologiekritik* – that theory can lay any claim to possessing a transformative or ethico-political force.

Postmodernism effectively denies such claims through its attitude of out-and-out sceptical mistrust with regard to all truth-claims, normative standards, or efforts to distinguish veridical knowledge from what is currently and contingently 'good in the way of belief'. Thus it becomes quite impossible or merely pointless – as these thinkers would have it – to criticise existing consensus values in the name of some 'enlightened' principle of reason (or 'grand narrative' of progress, justice, and truth) in light of which those values could at last be shown up as mere 'commonsense' illusions, products of a mystified social imaginary constructed in the interests of a *falsified* consensus brought about by dominant power-interests.[5] For we have now lived

10. See Paul K. Feyerabend, *Against Method* (London: New Left Books, 1975); *Science in a Free Society* (New Left Books, 1978); *Farewell to Reason* (London: Verso, 1987).
11. See Quine, 'Two Dogmas' (*op cit*).
12. C.G. Hempel, *Aspects of Scientific Explanation* (New York & London: Macmillan, 1965) and *Fundamentals of Concept Formation in Empirical Science* (Chicago: University of Chicago Press, 1972); also R.B. Braithwaite, *Scientific Explanation* (Cambridge: Cambridge University Press, 1953).
13. Karl R. Popper, *The Logic of Scientific Discovery* (New York: Harper & Row, 1934, 2nd edn. 1959). See also Popper, *Conjectures and Refutations* (Harper & Row, 1963) and *Objective Knowledge* (Oxford: Clarendon Press, 1972).
14. Popper, *The Poverty of Historicism* (New York: Harper & Row, 1957); *The Open Society and its Enemies*, Vols. I & 2 (5th edn., revised, London: Routledge & Kegan Paul, 1966).
15. See especially Hans Reichenbach, *Experience and Prediction* (Chicago: University of Chicago Press, 1938); also Wesley C. Salmon (ed), *Hans Reichenbach: logical empiricist* (Dordrecht: D. Reidel, 1979).
16. See entries for Note 1 (above); also – from a range of methodological viewpoints – Barry Barnes, *T.S. Kuhn and Social Science* (Oxford: Basil Blackwell, 1982): Augustine Brannigan, *The Social Basis of Scientific Discoveries* (Cambridge: Cambridge University Press, 1981); David Papineau, *For Science in the Social Sciences* (London: Macmillan, 1978); David L. Phillips, *Wittgenstein and Scientific Knowledge: a sociological perspective* (London: Macmillan, 1977); Richard Whitley, *The Social and Intellectual Organization of the Sciences* (London: Oxford University Press, 1986).
17. Feyerabend, *Against Method* (*op cit*).
18. Feyerabend, *Farewell to Reason* (*op cit*).
19. See Note 1 (above).
20. Michel Foucault, *The Archaeology of Knowledge*, trans. Alan Sheridan (London: Tavistock, 1972); *The Order of Things: an archaeology of the human sciences*, trans. Alan Sheridan (London: Tavistock, 1973); also Gary Gutting, *Michel Foucault's Archaeology of Scientific Reason* (Cambridge: Cambridge University Press, 1989).
21. Jean-François Lyotard, *The Postmodern Condition: a report on knowledge*, trans. Geoff Bennington and Brian Massumi (Minneapolis: University of Minnesota Press, 1984) and *The Differend: phrases in dispute*, trans. Georges van den Abbeele (Manchester: Manchester University Press, 1988).
22. David Hume, *A Treatise of Human Nature* (Oxford: Clarendon Press, 1984) and *An Enquiry Concerning Human Understanding* (Indianapolis: Bobbs-Merrill, 1955). For a reading that questions this commonplace account of Hume's scepticism with regard to causal explanations, see Galen Strawson, *The Secret Connexion* (Oxford: Clarendon Press, 1989); also J.L. Mackie, *The Cement of the Universe* (Oxford: Clarendon, 1974); John Wright, *The Sceptical Realism of David Hume* (Manchester:

Manchester University Press, 1983); and Simon Blackburn, 'Hume and Thick Connexions', in *Essays in Quasi-Realism* (London: Oxford University Press, 1993), pp94-107.

23. See especially Nelson Goodman, 'The New Riddle of Induction', in *Fact, Fiction, and Forecast* (Indianapolis: Bobbs-Merrill, 1955), pp59-83; also Simon Blackburn, *Reason and Prediction* (Cambridge: Cambridge University Press, 1973); L. Jonathan Cohen, *The Implications of Induction* (London: Methuen, 1970); Nicholas Rescher, *Induction* (Oxford: Basil Blackwell, 1980); G.H. von Wright, *The Logical Problem of Induction* (Blackwell, 1965).

24. See notably Mackie, *The Cement of the Universe* (*op cit*); also Rom Harré and E.H. Madden, *Causal Powers* (Oxford: Blackwell, 1975); Bryan Skyrms, *Causal Necessity* (New Haven: Yale University Press, 1980).

25. Roy Bhaskar, *Scientific Realism and Human Emancipation* (London: Verso, 1986); *Reclaiming Reality: a critical introduction to contemporary philosophy* (London: Verso, 1989); *Dialectic: the pulse of freedom* (London: Verso, 1993); also Rom Harré, *The Philosophies of Science* (London: Oxford University Press, 1972) and *Varieties of Realism: a rationale for the social sciences* (Oxford: Basil Blackwell, 1986); Bhaskar (ed), *Harré and his Critics* (Oxford: Blackwell, 1990); Andrew Collier, *Scientific Realism and Socialist Thought* (Hemel Hempstead: Harvester, 1989) and *Critical Realism: an introduction to the work of Roy Bhaskar* (London: Verso, 1994).

26. For the consequences of this idea as applied to the philosophy, history, and sociology of science, see for instance Phillips, *Wittgenstein and Scientific Knowledge* (*op cit*); also Peter Winch, *The Idea of a Social Science and its Relation to Philosophy* (London: Routledge & Kegan Paul, 1958) and David Bloor, *Wittgenstein: a social theory of knowledge* (New York: Columbia University Press, 1983).

27. See Wesley C. Salmon, *Scientific Explanation and the Causal Structure of the World* (Princeton, N.J.: Princeton University Press, 1984) and *Four Decades of Scientific Explanation* (Minneapolis: University of Minnesota Press, 1989); also Nicholas Rescher, *Scientific Realism: a critical reappraisal* (Dordrecht: D. Reidel, 1987); David Charles and Kathleen Lennon (eds), *Reduction, Explanation and Realism* (Oxford: Clarendon Press, 1992): J. Lepin (ed), *Scientific Realism* (Berkeley & Los Angeles: University of California Press, 1984); M. Tooley, *Causation: a realist approach* (London: Oxford University Press, 1988).

28. Rescher, *Scientific Realism* (*op cit*), p116.

29. *Ibid*, p61.

30. See David-Hillel Ruben, *Explaining Explanation* (London: Routledge, 1992): Larry Laudan, *Progress and its Problems* (Berkeley & Los Angeles: University of California Press, 1977); Peter Lipton, *Inference to the Best Explanation* (London: Routledge, 1993); Peter Muntz, *Our Knowledge of the Growth of Knowledge* (London: Routledge & Kegan Paul, 1985); Nicholas Rescher, *Scientific Progress* (Oxford: Basil Blackwell, 1979); Peter J. Smith, *Realism and the Growth of Knowledge* (Cambridge: Cambridge University Press, 1981); J.M. Zimon, *Reliable Knowledge: an*

exploration of the grounds for belief in science (Cambridge: Cambridge University Press, 1978).

31. See especially J.R. Lucas, *A Treatise on Time and Space* (London: Oxford University Press, 1973); J.R. Lucas and P.E. Hodgson, *Spacetime and Electro-Magnetism* (Oxford University Press, 1990); Wesley C. Salmon, *Space, Time and Motion: a philosophical introduction* (Minneapolis: University of Minnesota Press, 1980); J.L. Mackie, 'Three Steps toward Absolutism', in *Logic and Knowledge (Selected Papers*, Vol. 1, Oxford: Clarendon Press, 1985), pp192-213; Christopher Ray, *Time, Space and Causality* (London: Routledge, 1991); Richard Swinburne (ed), *Space, Time and Causality* (Dordrecht: D. Reidel, 1983).

32. See Arthur Fine, *The Shaky Game: Einstein, realism, and quantum theory* (Chicago: University of Chicago Press, 1986).

33. W.H. Newton-Smith, *The Rationality of Science* (London: Routledge & Kegan Paul, 1981), p173.

34. Rescher, *Scientific Realism (op cit)*, p51.

35. Kuhn, *The Structure of Scientific Revolutions (op cit)* and Quine, 'Two Dogmas of Empiricism' *(op cit)*; also Ian Hacking (ed), *Scientific Revolutions* (London: Oxford University Press, 1981).

36. Collier, *Critical Realism (op cit)*, p91.

37. See Muntz, *Our Knowledge of the Growth of Knowledge (op cit)* and Smith, *Realism and the Progress of Science (op cit)*.

38. See Robin Waterfield, *Before Eureka: the presocratics and their science* (Bristol: The Bristol Press, 1989).

39. On this topic see for instance Harold Brown, *Perception, Theory, and Commitment: the new philosophy of science* (Chicago: University of Chicago Press, 1977); Hartry Field, 'Theory Change and the Indeterminacy of Reference', *Journal of Philosophy*, Vol. 70 (1973), pp462-81 and 'Realism and Relativism', *Journal of Philosophy*, Vol. 79 (1982), pp553-6; Donald Gillies, *The Philosophy of Science in the Twentieth Century: four central themes* (Oxford: Basil Blackwell, 1993); Michael E. Levin, 'On Theory-Change and Meaning-Change', *Philosophy of Science*, Vol. 46 (1979), pp407-24; Ernest Nagel, Sylvain Bromberger and Adolf Grünbaum, *Observation and Theory in Science* (Baltimore: Johns Hopkins University Press, 1971); David Papineau, *Theory and Meaning* (London: Oxford University Press, 1979); Frederick Suppé (ed), *The Structure of Scientific Theories* (Chicago: University of Illinois Press, 1977).

40. Bhaskar, *Dialectic (op cit)*, p35.

41. Saul Kripke, *Naming and Necessity* (Oxford: Basil Blackwell, 1980). See also Stephen Schwartz (ed), *Naming, Necessity, and Natural Kinds* (Ithaca, N.Y.: Cornell University Press, 1977); David Wiggins, *Sameness and Substance* (Oxford: Basil Blackwell, 1980).

42. Bhaskar, *Dialectic (op cit)*, p35.

43. *Ibid*, p35.

44. Ian Hacking, *Representing and Intervening* (Cambridge: Cambridge University Press, 1983).

45. See also James Robert Brown, *Smoke and Mirrors: how science reflects*

reality (London: Routledge, 1994); Mary Hesse, *Models and Analogies in Science* (South Bend: University of Notre Dame Press, 1966); David Papineau, *Reality and Representation* (Oxford: Basil Blackwell, 1987).

46. Lyotard, *The Postmodern Condition (op cit)*, p112.
47. Foucault, *The Order of Things (op cit)*.
48. See Gutting, *Michel Foucault's Archaeology of Scientific Knowledge* (op cit).
49. Foucault, *The Order of Things (op cit)*, pxv.
50. *Ibid*, pxv.
51. See for instance Foucault, *Language, Counter-Memory, Practice*, trans. D.F. Bouchard and S. Weber (Oxford: Basil Blackwell, 1977).
52. See Harding, *Can Theories be Refuted? essays on the Duhem-Quine thesis (op cit)*.
53. Pierre Duhem, *The Aims and Structure of Physical Theory*, trans. Philip Wiener (Princeton, N.J.: Princeton University Press, 1954); *To Save the Phenomena: an essay on the idea of physical theory from Plato to Galileo*, trans. Edmund Dolan and Chaninah Maschler (Chicago: University of Chicago Press, 1969); *Premices Philosophiques*, ed. and intro. Stanley L. Jaki (Leiden: E.J. Brill, 1987); Stanley L. Jaki, *Uneasy Genius: the life and work of Pierre Duhem* (The Hague: Martinus Nihjoff, 1984).
54. See Dominique Lecourt, *Marxism and Epistemology: Bachelard, Canguilhem and Foucault* (London: New Left Books, 1975).
55. Feyerabend, *Against Method (op cit)* and *Farewell to Reason (op cit)*.
56. Gaston Bachelard, *The Psychoanalysis of Fire*, trans. A.C.M. Ross (Boston: Beacon Press, 1964); *The Poetics of Space*, trans. M. Jolas (Boston: Beacon Press, 1969); *The Poetics of Reverie*, trans. Daniel Russell (Boston: Beacon Press, 1971).
57. Bachelard, *The Philosophy of No: a philosophy of the new scientific mind* (New York: Orion Press, 1968); *The New Scientific Spirit* (Boston: Beacon Press, 1984); *La Formation de l'esprit scientifique* (Paris: Corti, 1938). See also Lecourt, *Marxism and Epistemology (op cit)* and Mary Tiles, *Bachelard: science and objectivity* (Cambridge: Cambridge University Press, 1984).
58. See especially Louis Althusser, *Philosophy and the Spontaneous Philosophy of the Scientists and other essays*, trans. Gregory Elliott (London: Verso, 1990).
59. Thus Roy Harris notes that Saussure uses the words 'science' and 'scientifique' no less than thirteen times in the first chapter alone of his *Cours de linguistique générale*. See Harris, *Reading Saussure* (London: Duckworth, 1987), p4.
60. For a cogently argued critique of this reading, see Jacques Derrida, 'White Mythology: metaphor in the text of philosophy', in *Margins of Philosophy*, trans. Alan Bass (Chicago: University of Chicago Press, 1982), pp207-71.
61. This episode receives a more sympathetic treatment in John Mowitt, *Text; the genealogy of an antidisciplinary object* (Durham, N.C.: Duke University Press, 1993).
62. See for instance Hilary Putnam, *Realism and Reason* (Cambridge

University Press, 1983). Protagoras finds his most resourceful and spirited modern defender in Joseph Margolis, *The Truth About Relativism* (Oxford: Basil Blackwell, 1993).
63. Cited by Rescher, *Scientific Realism* (*op cit*), p131.

5

MARXISM AGAINST POSTMODERNISM, OR THE *EIGHTEENTH BRUMAIRE* REVISITED

I REALITY THROUGH THE LOOKING-GLASS

Over the past fifteen years or so, Alex Callinicos has produced an impressive series of books, articles and reviews defending Marxism – 'classical' Marxism, what's more – against its various detractors, right and left.[1] As theoretician-in-chief of the Socialist Workers Party he has managed to combine this tactical role with a sustained and highly articulate account of issues in Marxist epistemology, ethics, aesthetics, and historiography. In *Against Postmodernism: a marxist critique*, he takes on current 'postmodernist' fashion and argues that the term is just a floating signifier, a word without a referent or concept, a name for whatever sort of zany irrationalist doctrine happens to grab the fancy of the chattering classes in these vaunted 'New Times' of proliferating junk-theory, regressive political attitudes, and claims to be 'post-' just about everything, from Marxism to modernism, structuralism, feminism, politics, theory, and history itself. This essay is an adapted version of a review-article I wrote for a US journal when the book first appeared. But if things have moved on since then they have hardly moved toward a better understanding of the issues that Callinicos raises. 'Postmodernism' is still the shorthand description for a range of philosophically confused and politically vacuous ideas whose endless recycling has become a growth-industry in the British and US academies. Unfortunately my arguments are still relevant.

Callinicos lays his cards on the table in the book's opening sentence. It is, he writes, an attempt to challenge the strange mixture of cultural and political pessimism and light-hearted playfulness with which – in a more than usually farcical reprise of the apocalyptic mood at the end of the last century – much of the contemporary Western intelligentsia apparently intends to greet our own *fin de siècle*. (pix).

The combative tone, here and elsewhere, shouldn't be taken as a sign that Callinicos is engaging in mere knockabout polemics, or descending to the level of showy rhetoric and unargued oracular pronouncement which typifies so much of his opponents' writing. In fact his book is a powerful piece of sustained philosophical argument, as well as a shrewdly diagnostic account of the various socio-historical factors that have lately given rise to this widespread mutation in the discourse of 'radical' intellectuals. One can well understand why Callinicos should sometimes – like Marx before him – adopt a more abrasive, edgily defensive, or downright contemptuous tone. After all, he is arguing a case which is nowadays liable to be treated by the 'posties' with a mixture of wry condescension and pitying fondness, or simply an attitude of blank disbelief that anyone should *want* to defend such a patently outmoded and discredited set of political ideas. No wonder that this makes him feel on occasion like Abdiel alone against the forces of night. But *Against Postmodernism* is much more than just a product of rattled Marxist sensibility; its arguments merit close attention from anyone concerned to make sense of the so-called 'postmodern condition' and its various cultural appendages.

Notwithstanding my own recent work in this field,[3] *Against Postmodernism* stands as by far the most trenchant and significant critique of post-modernism that I have come across. Nor can it easily be written off as just another piece of superannuated theorising in the bad old 'enlightenment' or 'grand narrative' tradition, a sure sign that Callinicos hasn't yet caught up with the latest rules of the game, or recognised the chronic obsolescence of any argument based on notions like *truth, critique, ideology* or other such items of self-endorsing rhetoric dressed up as theoretical concepts. For Callinicos has anticipated all these charges, examined their credentials in a spirit of open (if openly sceptical) debate, and found them not only politically undesirable – which of course wouldn't impress his opponents very much – but also philosophically naive, ill-informed, and blind to their own motivating interests.

His book pretty much demolishes postmodernism in its more

ambitious doctrinal form, as a wholesale anti-philosophy premised on counter-enlightenment values and linked to a revamped 'end-of-ideology' thesis familiar from the writings of Daniel Bell and other such purveyors of a kindred rhetoric with its own fairly blatant ideological agenda.[4] Callinicos is willing to admit that the term has a useful (if limited) application in describing certain recently emergent tendencies in fiction, poetry, architecture, painting, and the sphere of artistic production generally. But even here, he suggests, the periodisation is so vaguely defined – and the degree of overlap with 'modernist' techniques so evident in almost every case – that one had better give up the delusive quest for characterising features (or even Wittgensteinian 'family resemblances'), and acknowledge that the thing just *doesn't exist* except as a product of media hype or a self-induced fantasy on the part of various jaded ex-radicals, *soi-disant* 'post-Marxist' (i.e. post-68) intellectuals, and media pundits with an eye to the market for catchy slogans and novelty imports. Talk of 'postmodernism' becomes in the end just a handy pretext for not thinking hard about anything – art, language, history, philosophy, least of all politics – but simply latching on to a ready-made discourse whose terms recycle the stalest clichés of postwar 'consensus' ideology. Above all, it does great service to the interests of state and corporate power in diffusing the idea that there is *really no difference* between things as they seem, things as they are, and things as they might be according to the values of enlightened critique, increased social justice and a genuinely working participatory democracy. For it is only by maintaining a sense of these distinctions – common to every form of emancipatory thought from Kant, via Marx to Habermas and other present-day varieties of *Ideologiekritik* – that theory can lay any claim to possessing a transformative or ethico-political force.

Postmodernism effectively denies such claims through its attitude of out-and-out sceptical mistrust with regard to all truth-claims, normative standards, or efforts to distinguish veridical knowledge from what is currently and contingently 'good in the way of belief'. Thus it becomes quite impossible or merely pointless – as these thinkers would have it – to criticise existing consensus values in the name of some 'enlightened' principle of reason (or 'grand narrative' of progress, justice, and truth) in light of which those values could at last be shown up as mere 'commonsense' illusions, products of a mystified social imaginary constructed in the interests of a *falsified* consensus brought about by dominant power-interests.[5] For we have now lived on (so the argument goes) into an epoch of all-embracing 'simulation' or 'hyperreality', a world where – quite simply – there is *no possibility* of distinguishing truth from falsehood, fact from fiction, or the order of genuine (veridical) knowledge from its various 'ideological' fantasy-substitutes. In which case we might as well dump all that useless epistemological baggage and learn to enjoy these heady New Times where what counts is no longer the appeal to truth – to some reality 'behind' ideological appearances – but rather the willingness to just get along, exploit the various forms of fantasy gratification, and no longer fret about whether or not they match up to some (henceforth non-existent) realm of 'real-world' interests, actions, or events.[6] Theorists who cling to the old ways of thinking – Marxists preeminent among them – are thereby manifesting their unfortunate failure to grasp just how far this process has gone and how absurd their efforts must appear in light of this epochal shift (as Baudrillard terms it) from a regime of truth to an order now defined by the absence of truth-values or validity-conditions in any shape or form. Quite simply, 'simulation' is the name of the game, and anyone who thinks to opt out – whether on political, ethical, or epistemological grounds – can only be treated with mild contempt as playing in accordance with the old rule-book.

What this amounts to, in Baudrillard's case, is a full-scale systematic inversion of all those concepts and categories that have organised the 'discourse' of Western philosophical reason right down from its ancient Greek origins. In Callinicos's words, citing Baudrillard at various points:

> Unlike the problematic of representation, which is concerned with the relationship (of reflection, distortion or whatever) between images and a 'basic reality', simulation 'bears no relation to any reality whatever: it is its own pure simulacrum'. The kinds of distinction drawn by theoretical enquiry since the Renaissance revival of Platonism – between essence and appearance, for example – no longer make sense in the era of the 'hyperreal', of *'that which is always already reproduced'*. Instead of a world more or less adequately represented in images, we have a world *of* images, of hallucinatory evocations of a non-existent real (p145).

But this argument collapses into manifest nonsense, as Callinicos remarks, if one asks *from what standpoint* – what critical perspective – Baudrillard can advance his sweeping pronouncements about the demise of truth, the eclipse of the real, the irrelevance of theory, the obsolescence of critique, the collapse of all distinctions between fact and falsehood, knowledge and ignorance, *episteme* and *doxa*, 'science' and 'ideology' etc, etc. For he then winds up in the familiar relativist impasse of a thinker who asserts it as a generalised truth – or at any rate a fact of our present situation – that no such generalised truths are to be had, or that factual appeals are beside the point since they rest on a hopelessly deluded ontology of 'real' *versus* 'simulated' experience. In short, 'how can Baudrillard – or anyone trapped within simulation, as presumably we all are – describe its nature, and outline the transition from the real to the hyperreal?' (p148).

On a close reading – something rarely attempted by Baudrillard's admirers – one can see how the rhetorical trick is pulled off by a habit of constantly shifting across between different modalities of discourse or orders of truth-claim. Thus postmodernity is a *fact* of our present situation (constative mode), but also an attitude we *ought* to take up (performatively speaking) if we are not to lose touch with these exciting New Times. Or again: it is an 'event' of recent occurrence – brought about by changes in the mass-media or the socio-cultural sphere – but *also* a 'condition' that goes right back through the history of Western thought and which always shows up whenever theorists (from Plato to Kant, Hegel, Marx and their present-day offspring) deludedly attempt to distinguish between truth and untruth, knowledge and belief, reality and appearance or whatever. But most suspect of all is Baudrillard's refusal – or downright inability – to distinguish between statements of a *diagnostic* type (i.e., observations of what has gone wrong with our current 'postmodern condition') and statements of a wholesale generalising type which treat it as simply and inevitably the way things are, and moreover the way they have always been except in the minds of those self-deceived 'enlightenment' thinkers who clung to notions of truth, objectivity, critique, 'real' human interests and so forth. For there is no denying that the word 'postmodern' *does* capture something (however ill-defined) about conditions of life in the late twentieth-century Western liberal pseudo-democracies. And Baudrillard is undoubtedly a sharp-eyed diagnostician, one who has made vivid the extent to which 'reality', as nowadays perceived and consumed, is so largely a product of the mass-media images, the opinion-poll feedback, the PR machinery and other such techniques for creating a passively compliant 'public opinion' such that questions of truth and falsehood (or 'real' *versus* 'simulated' human interests) are indeed pushed out of sight. But these arguments lose all their point – or fall back into a posture of cynical indifference – if one goes along with Baudrillard's further (and self-contradictory) claim: that the 'real' is nowadays what it always was, just a fantasy-projection dreamed up to compensate for the absence of anything, any adequate concept or referent, that could ever correspond to that empty rhetorical term.

II CONSENSUS AND CRITIQUE: HABERMAS, DAVIDSON, RORTY

There are, I think, two main reasons why Callinicos is well placed to criticise this present-day *trahison des clercs*. One is his strong and clearly-defined political stance, a point to which I shall return later. The other is the fact that he has already, in previous publications, gone a long way towards explaining what is wrong with the various (mainly post-structuralist) ideas about language, meaning and representation which are pretty much taken on faith by the arbiters of current intellectual fashion.[7] Among other things, he has shown that these theorists have been led into error by an over-reliance on Saussure's highly specialised project of structural-synchronic linguistics, and a consequent tendency to raise certain purely heuristic principles (like the 'arbitrary' nature of the sign, the idea of language as a system of differences 'without positive terms', etc.) into a high point of doctrine absurdly remote from the way that language actually functions in a real-world social and material context. (See Chapter One of this volume for a more detailed account of the 'linguistic turn' in its various philosophical and literary-critical forms.) The trouble with post-structuralism, Callinicos argues, is that it has grown up in damaging isolation from other, more adequate or philosophically sophisticated treatments of the same basic issues. Thus for instance, some acquaintance with Frege's canonical essay on the sense/reference distinction – or with Davidson's writings on the relation between meaning and truth-conditions in fixing the reference of various kinds of discourse – might have saved the post-structuralists from a deal of confused pseudo-radical talk about that favourite bugbear, the 'classic realist text', and its equally unreal utopian counterpart, the text that breaks altogether with the codes and conventions of 'bourgeois' realism.[8] Callinicos has a good working knowledge of philosophy – 'analytic' as well as 'continental' – and he puts this knowledge to regular use in exposing the more naive or parochial aspects of post-structuralist thought.

In *Against Postmodernism* he carries this project on a stage by showing how Baudrillard and others in the postmodernist camp are still captive to the same root delusion, namely the idea that linguistics, sociology, discourse-theory or literary criticism could dispense altogether with the referential 'moment' in language and thereby envisage a new dispensation, a realm of free-floating or open-ended 'textuality' destined to transform the very conditions of human social and communicative practice. This was always an absurd position – never more so than in the heady old days of *Tel Quel* – and it is depressing to find the same ideas turning up, as if new-minted, among the latest crop of Parisian gurus. At any rate the reader of Callinicos's book will learn that there are strong alternative candidates for an approach – if not a definitive answer – to the problem about meaning and reference, theories which avoid the inescapable aporias (as well as the untoward political effects) of a full-blown relativist or anticognitivist stance.

Habermas comes off much better in Callinicos's view, not least for his pinpoint diagnosis of what's wrong with postmodernism, and his insistence that the 'unfinished project of modernity' demands that we keep faith with enlightenment ideals, even if these need recasting in the form of a 'universal pragmatics' (or theory of 'communicative action') devoid of all foundationalist or epistemological truth-claims.[9] Nevertheless Callinicos finds fault with Habermas for his narrowly 'procedural' conception of ethical values and judgment, his tendency to equate existing social structures with the achieved 'public sphere' of enlightened rationality, his definition of truth in terms of an 'ideal consensus' (thus ignoring the obvious counter-argument that we might be wrong about something even under the best humanly-achievable conditions), and – above all – Habermas's failure to pay sufficient attention to the *material* factors of class-conflict, uneven development, contradiction between the forces and relations of production, etc, which scarcely figure in his quasi-Kantian regulative idea of an 'ideal speech-situation'. Thus:

> If Habermas's theory of communicative rationality is too thin to be able to resist the post-structuralist critique of reason, it is at the same time too strong an account of social modernity, tending to exaggerate the extent to which the Enlightenment project has been realised in

contemporary society. In both cases the source of the difficulty lies in a
conception of sociality as action oriented on agreement (p113).

In other words, Habermas is right to see post-structuralism (and its
postmodernist derivatives) as politically and philosophically retrograde; right to diagnose this tendency as a strain of latterday
Nietzschean irrationalism devoid of any adequate historical or
intellectual warrant; but wrong to take refuge in the generalised appeal
to a 'public sphere' of enlightened human interests and values which
must *either* be thought of as well on the way to attainment (in which
case his theory effectively endorses 'contemporary society', or
something very like it), *or* as a purely abstract regulative notion with
no relevance – no critical or diagnostic power – as applied to the
material complexities and conflicts of a presently-existing social order.
It is perhaps not surprising that Callinicos should raise these
objections, since he writes – after all – from a Marxist (indeed, a
'classical Marxist') position; the points on which he takes issue with
Habermas are precisely those where Habermas departs from the
Marxist approach to such questions. However, this is no mere
party-line polemic but a cogent and sustained piece of argument which
engages Habermas at a level of philosophic grasp and socio-historical
specificity unapproached by those detractors in the postmodern camp
– Lyotard chief among them – who simply trot out all the well-worn
end-of-enlightenment slogans and catchwords.

Callinicos, as we have seen, wants a stronger theory of truth than
anything that Habermas can provide with his notion of an 'ideal
consensus' arrived at by eliminating the various obstacles to free and
open debate. The most promising candidate, he thinks, is Davidson's
kind of 'epistemological naturalism', one that rejects all talk of
'conceptual schemes', paradigms, discourses, interpretive communities, etc, as strictly incoherent, and which proposes instead that we
regard truth – or the capacity for uttering and interpreting truthful
statements – as the paradigm case of linguistic performance and the
precondition for attaining any grasp of language in its other (e.g.
fictive, metaphorical, or otherwise 'deviant') uses.[10] Thus, as
Callinicos describes it, 'Davidson's philosophy of language … is both
holist – following Quine, he conceives language as a "fabric" of
interconnected sentences – and realist – the sense of an individual
sentence is given by its truth-conditions, truth is understood in
accordance with the classical definition, so that a sentence is true or

false in virtue of the state of the world' (p111). This is not to deny that Davidson's arguments are capable of another, radically opposed interpretation, one that stresses the holistic aspect – the idea that the truth-value of any given sentence is determined by the way it hangs together with other sentences currently taken as bearing a similar value – and which therefore has little use for 'truth' in any stronger sense of the term.[11] Such is Richard Rorty's neo-pragmatist reading of Davidson, a reading that Callinicos understandably (and rightly) rejects, since it goes clean against Davidson's argument that we couldn't make a start in interpreting language – any kind of language – without having grasped the paradigm conditions (or the operative standards) for what makes a statement true in the sense of referring to some factual or veridical state of affairs.[12] And of course – as Callinicos notes elsewhere – this all fits perfectly with Rorty's rejection of 'philosophy' as a constructive, problem-solving activity of thought, and his postmodernist view that it should henceforth take its place as just one more optional 'kind of writing', a discourse without any privileged claims to truth, and one that exists on a level with poetry, criticism, and the human sciences at large.

Hence, Callinicos suggests, Rorty's prominence during the 1980s as a thinker who managed to 'translate post-structuralist themes into an analytical idiom' (p169). For it then became possible to view philosophy as yet another 'discourse' that had given up its old delusions of epistemological grandeur, accepting its role as a participant voice in the ongoing cultural 'conversation of mankind', but no longer presuming to lay down standards for the proper (philosophically accountable) conduct of debate in its own or other disciplines. And along with this sharply reduced idea of philosophy's critical or adjudicative role goes a consensus-theory of truth ('what's good in the way of belief') that likewise cuts the discipline down to size by arguing that it *cannot possibly do more* than reflect the cultural self-image of the age, in this case an easygoing pluralist outlook identified – as Rorty beguilingly puts it – with current 'North Atlantic postmodern bourgeois liberal pragmatism'. Any radical critique of those values – especially from a Marxist standpoint – is thus ruled out as strictly unthinkable (since it wouldn't make sense by the lights of that same all-embracing liberal consensus), as well as on the grounds that (in Rorty's view) they are, quite simply, the best that we have yet come up with, at least for those professionals, academics, and generally well-placed members of society who can take full advantage of the benefits offered.[13]

One major strength of Callinicos's book is that it sets out to combat such ideas through a mixture of hard-pressed philosophical critique and shrewd sociological commentary. Thus he sees very well how a thinker like Rorty has gained such widespread acceptance for his arguments at a time when the values of truth and reason are increasingly under attack, when the myth of liberal-consensus politics is enjoying yet another periodic revival, when various thinkers are propounding new versions of the 'end-of-ideology' thesis, and when the vogue for 'interdisciplinary' exchange – as by breaking down the genre-distinction between philosophy and literature, or treating historical texts as just another subclass of fictional narrative – is likewise taken as a handy excuse for various kinds of free-wheeling hermeneutic romp. One way of countering these trends is to show – as Callinicos does most effectively – how they have emerged as a product of cultural and socio-economic forces which the thinkers concerned seem scarcely willing to recognise, let alone take account of in trying to understand their own motivating interests and values. Baudrillard is by far the worst offender here, with his constant (unremarked) switches of focus from a socio-pathology of everyday life to a high postmodernist rhetoric of epochal change which treats these symptoms as the ultimate *truth* of our current destitute condition. Thus on the one hand Baudrillard can state quite plainly that 'it was capital which was the first to feed throughout its history on the destruction of every referential, of every human goal, which shattered every ideal distinction between true and false, good and evil, in order to establish a radical law of equivalence and exchange, the iron law of its power' (cited by Callinicos, p145). But on the other he is completely unwilling to pursue the kind of detailed historical or socio-political analysis which is clearly required if these claims are to carry any genuine diagnostic force.

Indeed, Baudrillard argues himself into a position where any such analysis could only figure as a tedious irrelevance, a pointless move, or a throwback to those old ('enlightenment') ways of thinking when it still seemed possible to *criticise* existing society on the basis of arguments or value-judgments unbeholden to the current consensual status quo. In short, as Callinicos puts it.

> *Ideologiekritik* is no longer appropriate, since 'ideology corresponds to a betrayal of reality by signs; [whereas] simulation corresponds to a short-circuit of reality and its reduplication by signs'. Any conventional left strategy, whether of reform or revolution, no longer makes sense;

the only form of resistance left is that of the silence and apathy of the masses, their refusal to be incorporated, manipulated, or represented, even (or especially) by socialist parties (p145).

It is, to say the least, a pretty bleak outlook, and one that Callinicos firmly rejects on political and ethical grounds. But it is clearly not enough – not an adequate line of counter-argument – to say that this amounts to a depressing diagnosis, a virtual recipe for despair, and that therefore we had better look around for more hopeful alternatives. What is needed is proof (demonstrative argument) that thinkers like Baudrillard and Rorty are *wrong*, that they have failed to take account of real criticisms – whether of a philosophic or socio-political nature – that rise up against them at every point and call their whole project into question. Hence the two-pronged line of attack in Callinicos's book: concerned to show *both* that postmodernism rests on very shaky philosophical foundations (especially in matters of language, logic, meaning, truth, and representation) *and* that it thrives on an attitude of wholesale indifference toward the various material factors – or specific historical conditions of emergence – that have figured in its own brief history. And Callinicos would also want to claim that these approaches are strictly inseparable, since – as must be the case for any Marxist thinker – theoretical weaknesses are always bound up with some failure of grasp brought about by the blindness to specific ideological values or commitments.

III THE MIRROR OF CONSUMPTION: MARX 'AFTER' BAUDRILLARD

This is where one needs to take fuller account of Callinicos's own position as a figure on the 'far left', a member (and leading theoretician) of the Socialist Workers Party. His broadly Trotskyite affiliations place him at odds not only with mainstream (middle-ground Labour) socialist thinking but also with the British Communist Party (now reconstituted as Democratic Left), in its flirtation with postmodernist ideas and a programme of wholesale revisionist reform along 'Eurocommunist' lines. When Callinicos argues 'against postmodernism' he is also clearly arguing against that fashionable style of *soi-disant* 'post-Marxist' thought whose most popular organ was the oddly misnamed (and now defunct) journal *Marxism Today*, and whose agenda – roughly stated – was to place the greatest possible distance between its own up-to-the-minute theoretical discourse and the lingering rearguard of old-style Communist orthodoxy. (The more orthodox, and minority, groups within the old CP split off and the largest of these groups continues to produce the daily *Morning Star*, a paper which has no time for such arcane superstructural chitchat.) As a Trotskyist Callinicos is opposed to both the 'Eurocommunist' and orthodox wings of the communist tradition and has to steer a difficult path between the opposed temptations of hardline economic determinism and the Eurocommunists' postmodern outlook which swings so far in the opposite direction that it more or less abandons every last precept of 'classical' Marxist thought. It is a hard position to defend at present, with so many prominent ideologues, right and left, lining up to proclaim the obsolescence of traditional (class-based) socialist politics, and with 'radicals' of a New Times persuasion – among them many contributors to *Marxism Today* – quite willing to dump the whole conceptual baggage of dialectic materialism if they can thereby recapture the supposed high ground of current intellectual exchange.[14] For Callinicos the lines of engagement are drawn up clearly enough: thus 'not least among the purposes of this book is the reaffirmation of the revolutionary socialist tradition against the apostles of "New Times" ' (p7). And his point will not be lost on anyone who followed *Marxism Today* in its efforts to keep up with intellectual fashion over five years of intensive debate on the politics of postmodernism.

His basic position can be stated quite simply: that these theorists have pushed so far towards abandoning the economic-determinist (or base/superstructure) model that they have completely lost touch with the material factors that influence their own and every other form of cultural production. Baudrillard is again the most striking example, committed as he is to the following exorbitant theses: that 'reality' no longer exists, since the real is nothing more than a fantasy-projection, an alibi or means of imaginary escape from the endless circulation of unanchored, arbitrary signs; that Marx got it wrong from the start by setting up a whole series of likewise imaginary distinctions (e.g. between use-value and exchange-value, forces and relations of production, 'genuine' human needs and those brought about by 'artificial' consumer stimulus, etc); and that we have now lived on into an epoch when those distinctions lack any semblance of explanatory force, since Marxism (and the whole associated project of enlightenment critique) has collapsed into various aporias and ironies of its own unwitting creation.[15] Thus for Baudrillard it is now

> on the level of reproduction (fashion, media, publicity, information and communication networks), on the level of what Marx negligently called the nonessential sectors of capital (we can hereby take stock of the irony of history), that is to say in the sphere of simulacra and the code, that the global process of capital is founded (cited in Callinicos, p146).

But according to Callinicos this is nothing more than a piece of high mandarin mystification, an analysis that remains giddily fixated on the spectacle of late-capitalist commodity production, and which is thus predestined simply to reproduce – without in the least understanding – those phenomena that Marx so brilliantly analysed under the heading of commodity fetishism.

In short, what Baudrillard ignores in thus confining his analysis to the sphere of cultural consumption is the fact that such developments can only come about as a consequence of changes in the underlying structure of material and productive resources, a structure that is no less 'real' for producing such a range of exorbitant (or hitherto unknown) effects. For after all it is still the case, as Callinicos remarks, that

> the proliferation of [these] phenomena ... requires a vast expansion of material production; the greater circulation of images depends upon a variety of physical products – television sets, video recorders, satellite discs and the like ... More fundamentally, people do not live by MTV alone, but continue to have mundane needs for food, clothing and shelter, meeting which makes the organization and control of production still the major determinant of the nature of our societies (p148).

Postmodernism will of course have nothing to do with such vulgar dialectical-materialist talk, regarding it as just another variant of the old base/superstructure model, one that is still trading (incredibly enough) on a classical Marxist vocabulary of 'real foundations', 'forces and relations of production', 'ideology', 'false consciousness' and suchlike chimerical notions. What is more – as Callinicos duly notes – it can point to developments in recent (post-analytical or anti-foundationalist) philosophy by way of backing up this blanket assault on any theory that deludedly continues in the quest for a reality (or genuine knowledge thereof) beyond what is envisaged by the current consensus of knowledge-constitutive interests. This is why Callinicos thinks it important to engage postmodernism also through its philosophic mentors and fellow-travellers – Rorty chief among them – and draw attention to alternative (realist) schools of thought on these cardinal questions of truth, knowledge, language, meaning, reference, and representation. For it is clear that a thinker like Baudrillard represents just one – albeit the most extravagant – version of a widespread contemporary drift toward kindred forms of wholesale epistemological scepticism. And it is only in such a context, Callinicos argues, that left intellectuals could be carried along to the point of embracing a fashionable creed so completely devoid of substantive or critical content.

Thus it is no coincidence that Baudrillard's *The Mirror of Production* (1975) and Rorty's *Philosophy and the Mirror of Nature* (1980) should bear such strikingly similar titles. Both books are aimed squarely 'against theory', in Baudrillard's case against the Marxist claim to theorise economic and social structures, use-value *versus* exchange value, modes of cultural production etc, while Rorty takes on the entire tradition of Western epistemological thinking, from Plato to Descartes, Kant, Husserl and the modern analytical schools, where philosophy is treated as a privileged discourse, a language whose propositions should ideally deliver some ultimate truth at the end of enquiry. What Callinicos therefore needs to show – as against the proponents of 'New Times' and their allies in the postmodern-pragmatist camp – is that this whole anti-foundationalist drive results from an absurdly over-simplified view of how truth-claims function in the discourse of Marxist *Ideologiekritik*, or indeed in the work of those philosophers (like Kripke and Putnam) who have gone a completely different way around in arguing the case for a realist theory of meaning, truth and reference.[16] Where these thinkers break new ground, Callinicos argues,

> is [in] their refusal to base their accounts of reference on any notion of the subject with direct access even to the contents of its consciousness. Thus the moral of Putnam's work on 'natural-kind' terms ... is that 'meanings ain't in the head': the sense of these words is fixed by their reference, which in turn depends partly on the inner structure of their referent, partly on the 'linguistic division of labour' through which the community as a whole, not individual speakers, acquires knowledge of that structure (p81).

It is unfortunate that so many vanguard theorists of a (broadly) post-structuralist persuasion have absolutely no knowledge of these or any other developments in the 'other' (analytical) tradition. For the effect of this isolationist stance has been to promote the kind of wholesale epistemological scepticism which takes it for granted that 'truth' and 'reference' are manifestly obsolete notions; that they derive from a thoroughly discredited paradigm (that of the mind as 'mirror of nature', or locus of ideal, self-present knowledge and truth); and that the only significant line of descent in recent (post-Kantian) philosophy is one that leads, via Hegel and Nietzsche to Foucault, Rorty and other such debunkers of a typecast 'enlightenment' or 'modernist' outlook. For nowhere is this more evident – Callinicos argues – than in the rush among notionally left intellectuals to demonstrate their up-to-the-minute postmodern credentials by abandoning every last concept and category of 'classical' Marxism. That a thinker like Baudrillard could even get a hearing – let alone achieve such remarkable prominence – in 'radical' circles is a sure sign that theory and politics have entered a phase of drastically uneven development.

Callinicos might have pushed this argument a bit further by noting how the fortunes of Marxist theory over the past two decades have been closely tied up – at least for many British and US cultural theorists – with the rise and fall of Althusserian structural Marxism.[17] Indeed one could argue that the whole current mood of disenchantment with 'theory' and its grandiose truth-claims is the outcome of a process that began with the eclipse (or at any rate the perceived failure) of Althusser's project for a 'scientific' Marxism, a theoretical discourse rigorously purged of humanist or ideological residues.[18] But this failure – if such it was – can best be understood not so much as a terminal crisis of Marxist thought in general, but as the upshot of precisely those problems and aporias in the *structuralist* paradigm that came of its reliance on an inadequate model of language, ideology, and representation. That is to say, Althusser's disciples took on the utterly impossible task of articulating Marxist (or dialectical-materialist) thought with a theory whose major conceptual resource was the *idealist* model of linguistic analysis bequeathed by Saussure. This was a model which programmatically – for heuristic purposes – eschewed all questions of historical or 'diachronic' import, which emphatically rejected any appeal to language in its referential aspect, and which could thus hardly fail to produce the kind of prison-house effect – the conceptual impasse or theoreticist dead-end – routinely diagnosed by commentators of a postmodern (or indeed 'post-Marxist') persuasion.[19] I have argued already (in Chapter Three) that his followers misconstrued some of the most important philosophical and political aspects of Althusser's work. They did so chiefly through a failure to grasp its intensive engagement with a complex history of thought – from Spinoza, Kant and Hegel to philosophers of science such as Bachelard and Canguilhem – whose particular import counted for little in the all-levelling post-structuralist scheme of things. Thus when the tide of fashion receded, Althusserian Marxism appeared as just a washed-up relic of that old 'scientistic' paradigm which had once exerted such a powerful hold upon those who now penned its obituaries. If his influence lingered despite all this it was only through the strain of theoretical anti-humanism which post-structuralists took over with not the least regard for its original – precisely articulated – role in Althusser's critical reading of Marxist ontology, epistemology, and ethics. Otherwise there was little interest in his work save as a pretext for mock-rueful commentary on that bygone decade of high political hopes and high theoreticist delusions. This is just another (all too typical) case of self-induced cultural myopia, of short-term localised symptoms mistaken for a long-term epochal decline, or of thinkers absurdly over-willing to extrapolate from their own limited perspective – their experience of 'theory' as a god that failed – to world-historical pronouncements about the 'postmodern condition', the collapse of 'grand narratives', the obsolescence of truth, and other such polemical slogans masquerading as arguments. My point is that these ideas have only enjoyed such widespread credence because the theorists most eager to embrace them have little (if any) acquaintance with arguments, thinkers or traditions of debate outside the charmed circle – or elective genealogy – of current intellectual fashion. For otherwise they would not be so inclined to fall in with a style of thinking (the phrase seems appropriate) which perfectly reflects the debased conditions of present-day political and social life while steadfastly refusing to subject those conditions to any kind of reasoned theoretical critique.

Callinicos makes the most important point – here as in previous books – when he links this political failure of nerve with the ascendance of doctrines (whether post-structuralist, postmodernist, neo-pragmatist or whatever) that regard truth as nothing more than a product of consensus belief. He does a good job of sketching the alternative critical-realist terrain, although inevitably he ignores (or has to pass over) some significant bodies of work that might have been given at least a mention by way of strengthening the case. Perhaps most surprising is the absence of Roy Bhaskar, whose writings on the history and philosophy of science have offered a powerful defence of realist arguments joined to a Marxist account of the knowledge-constitutive interests that shape the various prevailing ideologies of past and present scientific thought.[20] (See Chapter Four of the present volume for a fuller discussion of critical realism and kindred developments in recent philosophy of science.) Elsewhere one suspects that differences of political outlook have led Callinicos to disregard work that might have provided useful argumentative support. No doubt he finds much to disagree with in the project of those current revisionist thinkers (Jon Elster and G.A. Cohen among them) who have attempted a 'rational reconstruction' of Marxist theory by analysing crucial terms and concepts – forces and relations of production, the labour-theory of value, base and superstructure, etc – through the kind of detailed conceptual exegesis or logico-semantic critique developed over the past few decades of Anglo-American analytical philosophy.[21] He is, after all, committed to defending a much stronger version of 'classical' Marxism – or a version that conserves far more of its practical or mobilising force – than can easily be salvaged from the writings of Elster or Cohen. But their work does offer a cogent set of arguments for *not* going along with the prevailing postmodernist drift, that is to say, the idea that since concepts are constructed entirely in and through language (or 'discourse'), therefore it is a hopeless and delusory endeavour to elucidate or criticise those concepts as if they possessed some truth-value beyond the mere fact of their being inscribed within this or that culture-bound signifying system or contingent textual economy. Here again, postmodernism jumps clean across from a thoroughly inadequate (structuralist) theory of language, meaning and representation to the yet more extravagant (textualist) thesis: that reality and truth – or our concepts thereof – are nothing more than figments of a social imaginary which we could never begin to articulate or criticise since its limits are those of language itself, and the limits of language (in Wittgenstein's phrase) are also, ineluctably, the 'limits of our world'.

IV 'TRANSCENDENTAL ILLUSIONS': KANT AND LYOTARD

Of course these are deep and genuine puzzles, none the less so for thinkers in the 'enlightenment' tradition – whether Kantian, Marxist, or modern analytic – who have attempted the impossible (as Rorty sees it) and tried to come up with 'constructive' answers that would offer some exit from the prison-house of language, the snares of ideology, or the toils of speculative reason. What is wrong with postmodernism is not that it discovers problems where no real problems exist but that it treats them in a spirit of casual disdain which assumes *in advance* that the problems are beyond reach of constructive treatment, arising as they do from an old dispensation of reason, truth and enlightenment critique whose 'discourse' no longer makes any kind of sense in these brave New Times of free-floating radical chic. Theory – Marxist theory especially – becomes just a tedious irrelevance when (in Baudrillard's words) 'there is no longer any critical or speculative distance between the real and the rational' (cited by Callinicos, p147). And to this extent postmodernism cannot help but reproduce all the fads and gimmicks, all the forms of consumerist fashion-mongering, thrown up by a mode of late-capitalist cultural production that needs to find work – or at any rate some kind of harmless distracting activity – for the current generation of post-68 thinkers bred up on the idea of socialist revolution as an impossible dream, an illusion discredited by all the evidence of recent events. What emerges is a classic post-revolutionary syndrome, a case of intellectuals – many with a record of previous activist commitment – cheerfully bidding farewell to all that and embracing the current consensus-view of what is good (i.e. 'relevant') in the way of commodified junk-theory or varieties of pseudo-radical discourse.

Thus a thinker like Lyotard – erstwhile Trotskyist militant and latterly high postmodernist guru – can take it pretty much for granted that those events have demolished every last claim of enlightened or emancipatory reason, every effort to envisage a transformed social order through the radical critique of existing institutions. In Lyotard's words:

> the names which are those of 'our history' oppose counterexamples to their claim. – Everything real is rational, everything rational is real: 'Auschwitz' refutes speculative doctrine. This crime at least, which is

real, is not rational. – Everything proletarian is communist, everything communist is proletarian: 'Berlin 1953, Budapest 1956, Czechoslovakia 1968, Poland 1980' (I could mention others) refute the doctrine of historical materialism: the workers rose up against the Party – Everything democratic is by and for the people, and vice versa: 'May 1968' refutes the doctrine of parliamentary liberalism. The social in its everydayness puts representative institutions in check ...[22]

I have quoted this melancholy passage at length because it brings out not only the mood of deep 'post-historical' disenchantment but also the regular transition, in Lyotard's writing, from a *de facto* record of failed revolutions, socialist or left-liberal hopes that never materialised, to a *de jure* language of doctrinaire refusal to credit any version of those 'old' arguments that once pinned their faith to the values of enlightenment critique. From this he draws the lesson – expounded most fully in *The Differend* – that the only hope for securing any kind of social justice is by multiplying language-games (or 'phrase-regimes') to the maximum possible extent, resisting the tendency of certain such games (e.g. the scientific, theoretical, or ethico-juridical) to impose their authority on other, less prestigious genres, and refusing to credit any discourse that claims normative or truth-telling status over and above the existing 'dissensus' of manifold rival views. What these proposals amount to is a kind of anarchic recycling of Wittgenstein's language-game philosophy joined to variations on a whole current range of Nietzschean, Foucauldian, post-structuralist and other such arguments, all committed to an outlook of extreme cultural and epistemological scepticism. For it is Lyotard's conviction – arrived at in light of those cautionary episodes catalogued in the passage above – that the only safe employment for 'committed' intellectuals in our time is to bear witness to those 'phrases' (place-names and dates) that signal the collapse of revolutionary hopes, and thus prevent theorists or ideologues of whatever colour from investing any longer in the same false hopes.

Thus three main elements can be seen to combine in Lyotard's diagnosis of the 'postmodern condition'. One is the sense of chronic historical belatedness, of having lived on into an epoch of failed aspirations when nothing could any longer *count* as an argument (least of all an argument on theoretical or principled grounds) for criticising current consensus-values in the name of some better alternative. That Lyotard enjoins us to maximise 'dissensus', rather than cultivate 'consensus', might seem to place him rather firmly apart from neo-pragmatists like Rorty and Stanley Fish, thinkers whose appeal to prevailing norms of communal judgement and belief is more obviously geared to a conservative (or at any rate conformist) political agenda.[23] But this distinction will not seem so crucial if we consider the second of Lyotard's postmodernist premises: namely, his argument that no one 'phrase-regime' should set up to criticise any other, since it will thereby arrogate authority to itself – to its own distinct set of argumentative or evaluative criteria – and thus commit the very worst kind of social injustice, the kind that consists in ignoring or suppressing the irreducible *differences* of truth-claim, value-judgement, cultural world-view, etc, which characterise the discourse of rival litigants. For all its radical-libertarian rhetoric, this argument in fact amounts to nothing more than a minor variation on the Fish-Rorty line, one that proclaims the ultimate good of multiplying language-games, maximising differences, etc, but which identifies that wished-for condition – exactly as they do – with the range of options as currently defined by a postmodern-liberal consensus whose operative values (or whose differential terms of membership) are placed beyond reach of argued critique.

One can easily imagine what short work Fish would make of the supposed distinction between his and Lyotard's ethico-political stance on these matters. For he could simply point out – in good pragmatist fashion – that this is a difference that makes no difference; that to register the force of Lyotard's appeal to 'dissensus' as a measure of social justice is already to be a member of the cultural interest-group (or 'interpretive community') whose values such language expresses; and therefore that the bottom line of appeal, whatever one's political standpoint, is always to a presently-existing *con*sensus of in-place attitudes and beliefs. The pluralist rhetoric would then be just a sign that the community in question was one that could recognise something of its own self-image in precisely that appeal to an open-ended dialogue (Rorty's 'cultural conversation of mankind') where truth-claims have at last dropped out of the picture, along with all notions of 'enlightened' critique, ideological 'false consciousness' and so forth. For it is clear from Lyotard's pronouncements in *The Differend* that 'dissensus' cannot be construed as a matter of actually *debating or contesting* rival arguments, since any such debate would of course presuppose the possibility of one party turning out to have the stronger argumentative position, and thus imposing its own set of values – its own 'language-game' or 'phrase regime' – at the expense of some other (*ipso facto* disadvantaged) party to the same dispute. Hence what I take to be Lyotard's third main thesis: a variety of extreme nominalist doctrine which locates the highest good of communal existence in a realm of free-floating discourses or speech-acts devoid of all referential constraints, all notions of 'truth at the end of enquiry', or attachments to the old (deluded) regime of enlightened truth-seeking argument.

From this point of view there can be no greater injustice than the kind that Callinicos regularly commits when he claims to demonstrate the hidden agenda, the motivating interests or the 'real' (material) conditions that have thrown up this currently fashionable line of postmodernist talk. For his criticisms are clearly not intended as just one more voice in the ongoing medley, a Marxist 'intervention' with its own pet themes, its own 'final vocabulary' or whatever, but without any warrant – as Lyotard would have it – for explaining or critiquing that line of talk from a standpoint of superior theoretical and historical grasp. On the contrary: he sets out to demonstrate *conclusively* that the self-understanding of postmodernist thinkers like Baudrillard and Lyotard is a species of ideological misrecognition, that their arguments reduce to *manifest nonsense* when judged by other (more adequate) standards of theoretical accountability, and that the best – indeed the *only* – means of comprehending their current widespread appeal is a Marxist approach which takes full account of the material determinants (or the socio-historical conditions of emergence) that have characterised the past two decades of increasingly desperate revisionist manoeuvring on the intellectual left. Thus, for Callinicos – to take just one symptomatic instance – 'the observations of the twentieth anniversary of 1968 were remarkable chiefly for the disillusioned retrospects of former student leaders ... *Marxism Today*, which had made a marketing strategy out of the progressive abandonment of anything resembling socialist principle, was especially strident in its renunciation of revolutionary hopes which it had never shared' (p165). This is a partial description – but by no means a caricature – of the line *Marxism Today* pursued in response to the supposed hegemony of Thatcherite values, the collapse of East European communist regimes, and the lack (until recently) of credible alternatives on the British parliamentary left. (When I wrote this last sentence in 1989 the parenthesis seemed justified in view of Neil Kinnock's electoral prospects and at least some of his policy commitments. I let it stand now – as Tony Blair and his cohorts set about dumping every last item of socialist principle – so as not to falsify the melancholy record.) It is understandable, therefore, that Callinicos's arguments should often take on a sharply polemical edge. But this is no reason to regard his book simply as a product – a high-theoreticist offshoot – of the quarrel between 'classical' Marxism (or its self-appointed champions in the Socialist Workers Party) and those other, more currently 'marketable' ideas that march under the Eurocommunist banner and make a virtue of embracing every new fad, from postmodernism to post-Marxism. Certainly Callinicos is out to discredit what he sees as a case of massive self-deception on the part of these erstwhile left intellectuals. But he also sees that any adequate response will have to do more than adopt their own strategy – backed up by the appeal to Lyotardian 'language-games', 'narrative pragmatics' and other such rhetorical slogans – and argue its case on detailed philosophical and socio-historical grounds.

I have already said enough to give some idea of how Callinicos sets about the first of these tasks, i.e. reconstructing the basis for a Marxist theoretical approach to issues of language, truth, ideology and representation that would stand up philosophically and yield no hostages to current forms of anti-realist, neo-pragmatist or 'postmodern' thinking. But it is important to grasp how directly these arguments relate to his account of the specific historical background – more precisely, the conjuncture of social and economic forces – in terms of which this peculiar phenomenon can best be understood. For Lyotard, as we have seen, it is enough to give a roll-call of dolorous place-names and events – a litany of failed 'revolutions' from 1789 to 1968 and beyond – in order to discredit the very idea of political progress brought about through critique of existing social institutions. Callinicos rejects such counsels of despair not just because they offend his own, more optimistic sense of the prospects for revolutionary change, but because they rest on a false understanding of the relation between historical 'evidence' (i.e. the *facts* of successive setbacks, defeats and reversals on the post-war European left) and the longer-term crisis of a capitalist order whose containment of various challenges over the past three decades has resulted from a range of *contingent* factors, and not – as Lyotard chooses to believe – from some epochal breakdown of the 'grand narratives' that once lent heart to the revolutionary project.

After all, as Callinicos remarks,

the May-June events in France embraced not just student barricades in
the Latin Quarter and the occupation of the Sorbonne, but the greatest
general strike in European history. They were simply the most dramatic
episode in a crisis ... which produced a *generalized* upturn of class
struggle throughout Western capitalism which continued into, and was
initially exacerbated by the onset of World recession after the 1973 oil
crisis. This upturn – the greatest Western Europe had seen since the
aftermath of the Russian Revolution, comprised, alongside May-June
1968 in France, the Italian 'May in slow motion' which began in the
Autumn of 1969; the wave of strikes against the 1970-4 Heath
government, which culminated in Heath's overthrow by the miners; the
Portuguese Revolution of 1974-5; and the bitter industrial conflicts
which accompanied the death agonies of the Franco regime in Spain
during 1975 and 1976. While industrial militancy never reached anything
like this pitch in the US, the interaction of the antiwar movement, the
black ghetto risings, and the student revolt helped produce at the end of
the 1960s the worst American domestic political crisis perhaps since the
Civil War (p167).

It might be thought that the only real difference between this and the
passage from Lyotard that I cited above is the fact that Callinicos takes
an upbeat view – and selects his historical 'evidence' accordingly –
where Lyotard focuses on just those events that support his view of
revolutionary politics as a species of transcendental illusion, a failure to
distinguish the 'phrase-regime' of idealist-utopian imagining from that
other kind of discourse that properly has to do with events in the realm
of real-world practical experience. In which case the issue would
reduce to little more than a straightforward clash of political values or
ideological commitments. But what Lyotard manages to extract from
this quasi-Kantian argument is an attitude that effectively turns Kant
on his head by denying that it is any longer possible – on the evidence
of historical events so far – to entertain notions of a world political
order transformed in the light of those regulative values (Kant's 'ideas
of reason') which enable us to criticise existing forms of state or
institutional power. That is to say, he assumes – in common with
right-wing ideologues and Cold-War media pundits – that history has
somehow 'proved' the obsolescence of communism, socialism or any
such programme of jointly theoretical and practical endeavour. For
Lyotard, this is simply to confuse the language-game of speculative
reason with the phrase-regime of cognitive judgments as applied to

matters of phenomenal self-evidence or the witness of factual events. For the ideologues, more straightforwardly, it signals the advent of a 'new realism' premised on the defeat of socialist values, the bankruptcy of left-oppositional arguments, and the fact that so many communist regimes have either toppled or announced their belated conversion to 'market forces' and reforms in line with 'free-world' economic doctrine.

Hence the curious (not to say unholy) alliance between the kind of Western triumphalist rhetoric to be found in commentaries on events in Eastern Europe and the line of least resistance obligingly adopted by thinkers on the 'post-Marxist' left. As against these forms of cynical *post hoc* wisdom Callinicos argues that they each involve a highly partial understanding of the relation between localised historical episodes and longer-term patterns of socio-economic and political change, along with a failure – or a willed refusal – to analyse the specific material conditions that have produced *on the one hand* a series of undoubted setbacks to the project of revolutionary change, and *on the other* a variety of dead-end responses (postmodernism among them) which merely fall in with the received consensus wisdom. Thus:

> the failure of these struggles [i.e., those that Callinicos lists in the passage cited above] to make any inroads into the power of capital was a contingent one, reflecting not the immanent logic of the system but the dominance of the Western working-class movement by organizations and ideologies which, whether stemming from the social-democratic or the Stalinist traditions, were pledged to achieving partial reforms within a framework of class collaboration (p168).

Postmodernists like Lyotard are content to read the signs according to whatever 'language-game' or short-term swing of political sentiment happens to have captured the current high ground of advanced theoretical debate. Right-wing ideologues can exploit the same technique by instancing the various failed revolutions, the collapse of Soviet-style communist regimes, the abandonment of socialist principles by nominally socialist Western opposition parties, and the consequent near-global advance – as they see it – of 'market forces' thinking and other such all-purpose capitalist nostrums. But there are three main factors that these analyses necessarily leave out of account. One is the continuing crisis of the Western late-capitalist economic order, a crisis staved off by successive booms of short-term consumerist pseudo-prosperity, but none the less evident in what Galbraith diagnosed as the widening gap between 'private affluence' and 'public squalor'. The second is the fact – adroitly covered over by the globalising rhetoric of 'New Times' – that there still exist massive disparities of wealth and material wellbeing between First, Second and Third-World economies, differences which indeed reproduce, on a much larger scale, the class-divisions and modes of unequal distribution that continue to characterise our own societies. And lastly, there is the manifest failure on the part of these 'New Times' enthusiasts to reflect on the material conditions of emergence that have shaped their own discourse – their 'signifying practice' – as a welcome purveyor of consensus-values perfectly in keeping with the current self-image of Western liberal democracy.

Callinicos is often at his best when anatomising the various forms of muddled argument, intellectual bad faith and self-induced ideological mystification to be found among the proponents of this upbeat rhetoric. He connects it – as we have seen – with the symptomatic rise of a post-68 generation of disaffected ex-radicals, those who had entered early middle-age with 'all hope of socialist revolution gone', with a marked distaste for being reminded of their own youthful follies, and with attitudes shaped by the prevailing ethos of passive consensus-values and 'end-of-ideology' thinking. More specifically:

> most of them had by then come to occupy some sort of professional, managerial or administrative position, had become members of the new middle class, at a time when the overconsumptionist dynamic of Western capitalism offered this class rising living standards (a benefit often denied the rest of the workforce: hourly real wages in the US fell by 8.7 per cent between 1973 and 1986). This conjuncture ... provides the context for the proliferating talk of postmodernism (p168).

It is not hard to guess how Callinicos's opponents – the target-group of passages like this – would respond to his charges of political backsliding and self-ignorance with regard to their own motivating interests. They would no doubt remark (among other things) his adherence to a 'vulgar-Marxist' conception of class-society and its modes of material and ideological reproduction; his desperate clinging to a base/superstructure paradigm (or a distinction between 'real' forces and relations of production and their 'illusory' counterparts in the cultural sphere) which is now quite simply obsolescent; and finally, the fact that he speaks for a political tendency – the Trotskyist SWP – with its own very specific (and to them wholly irrelevant) programme of revolutionary aims and activities. To all of which Callinicos responds, once again, by a species of *tu quoque* argument: that these thinkers manifest a striking incapacity to recognise (let alone theorise) the specific material and socio-economic factors that have conspired to bring about this widespread retreat into attitudes of passive conformist zeal. In short,

> this stylization of existence (to borrow Foucault's phrase) is surely best understood against the background, not of 'New Times', but of good times for the new middle class, a class which found itself in the 1980s with more money in its pocket and easier access to credit, without the pressure to save to which the old petty bourgeoisie was subject (p169).

And if this seems – as perhaps it might – just a piece of revivalist old-left *ressentiment*, a throwback to the era of class-war slogans or the so-called 'politics of envy', then Callinicos can turn the argument around by asking what is supposed to have *changed* over the past ten years of 'pathological prosperity' achieved at the cost of mounting unemployment, inner-city decay, social welfare cutbacks, sweeping anti-union legislation and so forth. If postmodern intellectuals can afford to avert their gaze from this squalid panorama of waste and futility then they should at least acknowledge the massive gulf between their own cosy rhetoric of brave New Times and the realities of life outside the seminar-room or the pages of *Marxism Today*.

Callinicos borrows the phrase 'pathological prosperity' from the writings of Mike Davis, in particular his work on the inverse relation between service-sector or finance economies and the catastrophic run-down of closely adjacent urban or working-class environments.[24] Thus, according to Davis,

> the 'urban renaissance' of downtown Los Angeles reflects the 'hypertrophic expansion of the financial service sector', in which 'the transformation of a decayed precinct into a major financial and corporate-control node of the Pacific Rim economy has gone hand in hand with a precipitous deterioration of the general urban infrastructure and a new-wave immigration that has brought an estimated one million undocumented Asians, Mexicans and Central Americans into the Inner City (cited by Callinicos, p159).

And moreover, this relation is carried across into the styles of architecture and urban planning routinely praised by postmodernist critics as the expression of a new communal ethos, a break with the idea of administrative decisions taken 'from above', and thus (so it is argued) imposing their bureaucratic will on a local population whose tastes and values would otherwise achieve their own kind of healthy eclectic mix. On the contrary:

> the abandonment of urban reform is symbolized by the fortress-like character of the new buildings: John Portman's Bonaventure Hotel, treated by Jameson as the acme of postmodernism, rather marks, with its inclusion of 'pseudo-natural, pseudo-public spaces within the building itself', a 'systematic segregation from the great Hispanic-Asian city outside'. Similar patterns are repeated elsewhere: thus London, a key and expanding international finance sector, had in 1985 the largest concentration of unemployed in the industrialized world, and greater extremes of wealth and poverty than any other part of Britain. (Callinicos, p159)

In short, postmodernism – or its extrapolation into the realm of high cultural theory – amounts to little more than a pretext for ignoring the material, structural, and socio-economic factors that have produced this latest 'pathological' episode, one of whose symptoms (or most prominent forms of imaginary misrecognition) is precisely the discourse of postmodern theorists blind to its real-world character and consequences. What Callinicos seeks to do, in effect, is call the bluff of those theorists (notably Fredric Jameson) who maintain a kind of studious ambivalence, a commitment to Marxism that somehow finds room for all manner of accommodating postmodern gestures. Thus Callinicos would clearly give a much more emphatic and polemical edge to the title of Jameson's well-known essay 'Postmodernism, or the Cultural Logic of Late Capitalism'.[25] In fact he would regard it – unlike Jameson – as sufficient to remove any possible doubts as to the retrograde, complicitous, and self-deceiving character of postmodern discourse in general.

V ALTERNATIVE RESOURCES

It seems to me that Callinicos is right on all the main points. That is to say, he refutes the postmodernist case – such as it is – by providing copious evidence of its failure to meet the most basic requirements of argumentative consistency, political good faith, and (not least) social-documentary truth. That the thinkers in question – Baudrillard especially – would reject these criteria out of hand is no reason to view the whole debate as a stand-off between simply incommensurable viewpoints. For this would of course be to go right along with the familiar postmodernist line, namely the idea that any such appeal to truth, validity, argumentative warrant, etc, will constitute a form of speech-act oppression, a move to privilege one 'phrase-regime' (that of cognitive or truth-seeking statements) over all the others currently in play, thus evincing a blatant disregard for the rules of open-ended dialogical exchange that nowadays provide the only possible standard for the conduct of civilized debate. In fact this amounts to nothing more than a postmodern update of the time-honoured relativist position first enounced by Protagoras in Plato's dialogue of that name, and since then supplied with all manner of conceptual and terminological revisions in order to keep pace with what other ('constructive' or 'enlightened') thinkers were currently saying. Its present-day revival in a textualist form – as practised most adroitly by writers like Rorty and Fish – is not so much a sign of philosophical cogency (which in any case they are keen to disclaim) as an instance of one way that thinking can always go when it hits on a fashionable rhetoric of crisis with wide enough cultural resonance to give such ideas some measure of suasive appeal.

In short, there is a politics of anti-theory which has its own very definite agenda despite such avowals to contrary effect. This is why Callinicos refuses to separate the political issues (i.e. the relevance of truth-claims in the sphere of *Ideologiekritik*) from those other, seemingly more 'technical' issues that preoccupy present-day logicians, semanticists and philosophers of science. For it is clearly the case that any adequate response to postmodernism, post-Marxism or other kinds of fashionable 'New Times' thinking will need to do more than offer some alternative 'language-game', some rhetoric just as well suited to reflect the ideological self-image of the age. What is required is a defence of critical realism that takes full account of recent anti-foundationalist arguments but which sees no reason for pursuing those arguments in the direction of a thoroughgoing relativist outlook (or postmodern end-of-ideology rhetoric) which, in Baudrillard's words, refuses to acknowledge 'any critical or speculative distance between the real and the rational'. It is therefore understandable that Callinicos should look to developments in Anglo-American analytical philosophy, a tradition which – for all its manifest conservatism in other respects – has at least kept open the appeal to criteria of truth, valid argument, and constructive criticism. To see how these values have been persistently ignored – or written off as old hat – by thinkers of a 'New Times' persuasion is also to see just how narrow are the horizons set by this current line of talk. Postmodernism has thrived in the artificial hothouse climate of an intellectual culture – roughly speaking, that of the 'new' New Left – whose political trajectory was largely determined by events in the wake of 1968, and whose major philosophical points of reference are those established by French post-structuralism (that is to say, a combination of the 'linguistic turn' encouraged by excessive (uncritical) reliance on Saussure, with a Foucauldian 'genealogy' of power/knowledge whose Nietzschean sources marked it out clearly as a discourse opposed to any form of Marxist, enlightened or emancipatory thought.[26]) In which case, as Callinicos quite reasonably argues, we might do better to look elsewhere (i.e. to developments in the 'other', analytical tradition) by way of understanding what is wrong with postmodernism and its 'radical' credentials.

Thus one purpose of *Against Postmodernism* is precisely to remind us that such issues in the realm of language, logic and truth are always within reach of wider (socio-political) concerns. The point comes across with particular force in a passage on the Vienna Circle, which is part of an extended comparative survey of Viennese high-Modernist and present-day 'postmodern' culture. We should be wrong, Callinicos thinks, to regard this comparison as in any way indicating a clear-cut opposition between, on the one hand, modernism with its elitist cultural pretensions, its class of disaffected bourgeois intellectuals imposing their mandarin visions of order on a decadent *fin-de-siècle* society, and, on the other, postmodernism with its (supposedly) broad-based popular appeal, its cheerful stylistic eclecticism, and its desire to transgress all the boundaries set up by the old high-modernist paradigm. For this is to ignore that whole *critical* dimension of the modernist project – its elements of oblique social protest and its real (if relentlessly negative) relation to the prevailing values of its time – brought out in the analyses of theorists like T.W. Adorno, Marshall Berman and Peter Bürger.[27] Moreover, it manifests a similar naivety in taking the claims of postmodernism at face value and failing to recognise its conformist ethos, its lack of any genuine critical or emancipatory impulse, and the extent to which those claims implicitly endorse the 'cultural logic of late capitalism'. What is needed, in short, is a far more nuanced and discriminating treatment of both these episodes when viewed against the background of wider socio-political movements and events.

It is in this context, Callinicos argues, that we can best understand how specialised issues in the philosophy of language, logic and scientific method may always take on a political significance beyond their immediate sphere of application. Thus:

> [it is wrong] to regard *fin-de-siècle* Vienna as the site of a rebellion against the Enlightenment cult of reason. It is undoubtedly true that nowhere was a sense of the inadequacies of the kind of progress towards which the *philosophes* looked forward more vividly expressed than in Vienna between the 1890s and the 1930s. But there were other forces at work. Thus the Vienna Circle can be seen as not simply engaged in a technical philosophical exercise – the formulation of the epistemological and semantaic doctrines of logical positivism – but as a defence of the Enlightenment against the various forms of irrationalism that were only too visible a feature of postwar Vienna and which found expression in the clerical fascism of Dolfuss as well as in Nazism. Ernest Nagel, writing in 1936, described a lecture by Schlick, given 'in a city foundering economically, at a time when social reaction was in the saddle', as 'a potential intellectual explosive. I wondered how much longer such doctrines would be tolerated in Vienna.' Not for long, as Schlick's assassination showed, but the Vienna Circle's commitment to the defence of reason was continued ... (p46).

This passage brings out very clearly the three major points that need to be made in any adequate critique of postmodernism and its associated 'New Times' rhetoric. First, there is the fact that previous movements founded on the wholesale rejection of Enlightenment values have always gone along with a reactionary drive to deflect or discredit oppositional thinking by assimilating truth to what is (currently and contingently) 'good in the way of belief'. Second, it shows the close relation that exists between 'technical' questions of language, logic, veridical utterance, etc. and those other sorts of question that arise not only in the discourse of Marxist or left-wing theoreticians, but also – more urgently – in practical contexts where the dominant ethos is such as to discourage (or actively suppress) any notion of *Ideologiekritik* as a means of challenging dominant consensus-values. And third, it leaves no room for the argument that 'modernism' in philosophy, literature or the visual arts was nothing more than a symptom of terminal decline, a belated (if culturally vibrant) episode in that same 'dialectic of enlightenment' that had produced all the evils of latterday European history, from Auschwitz and the Gulag to high-rise blocks, urban ghettoes and a whole dreary catalogue of present-day woes. One need only compare Adorno's and Lyotard's writings on this topic to see how crassly reductive is the standard postmodernist line of approach. Thus 'to read the accounts of "New Times" in *Marxism Today* is to be confronted with an almost caricatured version of the kind of "expressive totality" criticised by Althusser, down to contrasted lists of the characteristics of "Modern Times" and "New Times" ' (p135). Hence no doubt the widespread appeal of postmodern attitudes and 'lifestyles' among thinkers of an erstwhile socialist or left-wing persuasion who have now given up any attempt to distinguish truth from falsehood, reason from rhetoric, or genuine argument from the various currencies of half-baked irrationalist dogma.

Callinicos makes out a strong case for regarding postmodernism as the transposition of this latest 'end of ideology' thesis into the realm of high cultural fashion, a realm where the last thing that is needed (or wanted) is serious thought about its own historical and material conditions of emergence. Hence Baudrillard's uncritical endorsement of a postmodern 'hyperreality' entirely given over to the simulating rhetoric – the images, slogans, PR campaigns, opinion-polls, advertising rituals and so forth – which he treats as a kind of intellectuals' consumer paradise, a realm where signs are blissfully detached from the 'real conditions' of material production, and where analysts may happily wander, provided only they play by the current rules of the game and agree not to raise those boring old Marxist questions. Here again, what is involved is a wholesale misreading of the signs, an argument that resolutely sticks with appearances – the giddy spectacle of Baudrillard's celebratory description – and refuses to consider how this spectacle might relate to a continuing and deepening crisis in the late-capitalist mode of production, a crisis whose symptoms are occasionally evident even to those whose job it is to pretend that no such problems exist. Thus Callinicos cites an analyst writing in the *Financial Times* shortly after the 'Black Monday' stock-market crash of 1987, and observing that 'governments around the world solved the immediate confidence crisis ... by throwing money at it, but have now added inflation to the problems of distorted payments balances and overstretched banks'. And again, with more striking postmodernist overtones: 'financial markets seem to have broken free from real-world constraints and ... are enjoying a heavenly dance of their own creation, [so that] even the hardened professionals are beginning to blanch' (p143). This may indeed be true of 'hardened professionals' since they – like the writer – have a good deal at stake in the continued functioning of a system that has so far managed to negotiate these periodic setbacks by developing ever more sophisticated forms of crisis-management, confidence boosting, and ways of bucking the market in a hyperreal economy increasingly prone to such symptoms of mass-induced stock market panic and hysterical disorder. Nor can their anxiety be cheerfully ignored by those other, more numerous members of society who have already found out what these symptoms mean when translated into the real-world terms of mass unemployment, social deprivation and the large-scale transfer of wealth and resources from manufacturing to finance or service-sector economies. In short, the only people with cause to celebrate are those, like Baudrillard, who have come out on the far side of all such vulgar-realist ontologies, all attempts to distinguish – in the old Marxist fashion – between use-value and exchange-value, or real human needs and the various modes of mass-induced fantasy fulfilment and substitute gratification.

For this whole grim scenario dissolves clean away if one views it as just another passing episode in the history of delusive representations, a hyperreal phase in that 'political economy of the sign' which previous thinkers – Marxists especially – were naive enough to treat as possessing some kind of objective, material reality. After such knowledge, what need for forgiveness? Postmodernism is the ultimate solvent of political bad faith since it denies that we could ever misread the signs, let alone come to recognise the fact of such misreading through any kind of socio-political analysis or *Ideologiekritik*. Small wonder that a journal like *Marxism Today* carried articles not only by assorted postmodernist gurus but also by conservative ideologues who evidently felt quite at home in its pages. For in the end there is not much to choose between a 'New Times' rhetoric that willingly abandons all the critical and ethical resources of socialist thinking and a New Right ideological agenda that wants nothing more than to broadcast the news of that same long-awaited demise. 'The discourse of postmodernism', Callinicos writes, is best seen as the product of a socially mobile intelligentsia in a climate dominated by the retreat of the Western labour movement and the 'overconsumptionist' dynamic of capitalism in the Reagan-Thatcher era. From this perspective the term 'postmodern' would seem to be a floating signifier by means of which this intelligentsia has sought to articulate its political disillusionment and its aspiration to a consumer-oriented lifestyle. The difficulties involved in identifying a referent for this term are therefore beside the point, since talk about postmodernism turns out to be less about the world than the expression of a particular generation's sense of an ending. (pp170-1).

Indeed, it might be argued that we have now reached the point where nominally left-wing cultural theorists are doing a lot more to prop up the 'discourse' of an ailing late-capitalist social order than those – like the *Financial Times* columnist cited above – whose material stake in the continuance of that order obliges them to adopt a more sharply diagnostic line. At any rate Callinicos is surely justified in viewing postmodernism – or the theories erected around it – as at best politically ambivalent, and at worst a species of disguised apologetics for a system whose increasingly erratic performance (quite aside from its massive and inbuilt structural injustice) would otherwise be apparent to all but the most obtuse or self-interested observers.

One can easily predict how these arguments will strike any well-versed apostle of the New Times creed or purveyor of the current postmodernist wisdom. They will no doubt be treated as a curious mixture of obsolete epistemological notions ('truth', 'critique', 'ideology' etc.) and an old-left moralism likewise carried over from the legacy of outworn 'enlightenment' values and beliefs. Or again, it might be said that Callinicos is writing – as indeed he is – from a definite party-political standpoint, a revolutionary socialist position that sets its own terms for what should properly count as 'informed' or 'adequate' debate on these matters. In which case (borrowing a handy line of argument from Fish, Rorty and other neo-pragmatists) we can safely ignore all the high theoretical talk – along with the show of documentary evidence and the appeal to principles of social justice, human emancipation, etc – and treat it as just another species of enabling rhetoric, a language-game adopted (as always) for short-term suasive or rhetorical purposes, and possessing no claims to validity or truth beyond what is currently 'good in the way of belief'.[28] For in the end, as Callinicos clearly perceives, there is nothing to prevent this kind of liberal-consensus ideology from leaning right over into that strain of irrationalist or anti-enlightenment thought which postmodernists like Baudrillard have carried to such a high point of sophistical refinement.

Hence what he sees as the necessary detour through issues in epistemology, philosophical semantics, Critical Theory (in the Frankfurt tradition) and other areas of specialised concern where these topics receive a more adequate treatment than anything to be found among the current proponents of *à la mode* textualist nihilism. After all, it has long been apparent – at least since Kant – that a good deal hangs, ethically and politically, on the way that one answers certain basic questions about the powers and limits of human understanding, the role of speculative reason, and the extent to which history (or contingent historical events) may be seen as comprising an intelligible order subject to judgment insofar as they display an enlightened (progressive) or reactive and retrograde character. Postmodernism wishfully treats all this as a closed chapter in the history of thought, an episode whose passing is variously marked by the collapse of foundationalist (or epistemological) paradigms in philosophy, the waning of those so-called 'grand narratives' that once characterised the discourse of modernity, and the supposed obsolescence of Marxist or left-oppositional thinking in any shape or form. But we shouldn't be overly impressed by such arguments if they turn out to rest – as Callinicos shows – on a series of sweeping generalisations about history, philosophy, and the 'postmodern condition' which scarcely begin to engage those issues at an adequate level of debate.

'The project of "radicalised Enlightenment" first outlined by Marx, for whom the contradictions of modernity could be resolved only by socialist revolution, still awaits realisation' (p171). This is, to be sure, a 'rhetorical' sentence, a speech-act whose meaning consists very largely in its will to bring about certain real-world transformative effects, or to persuade the reader that such effects are both possible and desirable. But it differs from the typical pronouncements of a thinker like Baudrillard – or the strain of all-purpose rhetorical 'deconstruction' practised by Rorty and Fish – in the fact that it follows from a sequence of arguments which *give good reason* for acknowledging the force of his ethico-political judgments. Of course it may be urged that this very idea of 'giving good reasons' is itself just another rhetorical ploy, a throwback to the old Enlightenment discourse whose truth-claims were likewise 'performative' through and through, a means of cashing in on those values and beliefs that happened to prevail among progressive intellectuals at a certain (irretrievably dated) stage in the history of European thought. Such is it any rate the consensus-view among those whose intellectual and political horizons are bounded by the postmodern-pragmatist reading of modernity and its discontents. This reading is staked on a resolutely partial – not to say myopic – understanding of the issues posed for philosophy and critical theory by events in the wake of those various failed revolutions which Lyotard and Baudrillard catalogue with such gloomy relish. It is also the perspective adopted more or less *de rigueur* by those who take their bearings on intellectual history since Kant from a line of counter-enlightenment polemic that begins with Nietzsche's sceptical assault on every kind of moral or epistemic truth-claim, and which issues in Foucault's Nietzschean genealogies of power/knowledge, along with other (less historically informed) varieties of ultra-relativist doctrine.

That these ideas have achieved near-hegemonic status among the partisans of recent 'superstructuralist' theory is yet another symptom of the tunnel-vision hindsight – or the failure to engage with arguments outside their own very narrow terms of reference – that has characterised so much of what nowadays passes as 'advanced' thinking in literary studies, cultural criticism and the human sciences at large.[29] For they could only have taken hold to this extent (as Callinicos shrewdly observes) at a time of widespread disenchantment or retreat on the intellectual left when theory itself has abandoned the ground of oppositional critique and assumed the role of a legitimising discourse with every motive for dissimulating its own material interests and conditions of emergence. In which case we would do better to drop all the glitzy self-promoting talk of 'postmodernism', 'New Times' etc, talk whose sole function – whether wittingly or not – is to offer an escape-route or convenient alibi for thinkers with a large (if unacknowledged) stake in the 'cultural logic of late capitalism'.

VI RETRIEVING MODERNITY: ADORNO AND JAMESON

Having noted the ambivalence in Jameson's treatment of this topic let me end by citing a passage from his 1990 book, *Late Capitalism: Adorno, or, the persistence of the dialectic*.[30] This is a passage that Callinicos would surely endorse despite all his express reservations with regard to Jameson's previous work. It comes towards the close of a strenuously argued sequence of chapters which address (among other things): the possibility of reading Adorno from a postmodernist standpoint; the relation between Frankfurt Critical Theory (in its negative-dialectical mode) and other, less philosophically and politically astute forms of socio-cultural analysis; and the prospects for a renovated Marxist criticism that would counter the vacuities and nihilist rhetoric of current intellectual fashion while also learning from Adorno's lessons in the deconstruction of totalising truth-claims, the vigilant practice of a philosophic *style* alert to every symptom of premature 'identity thinking', and, above all, the knowledge of philosophy's ethico-political obligations in light of that massive historical irony – the 'dialectic of enlightenment' – which has cut the ground from under any doctrinaire appeal to the values of truth, reason and critique.[31] In short, Jameson sees that there is a plausible case for regarding Adorno as a kind of postmodernist *malgré lui*, a thinker who desperately wanted to believe that theory could be turned back against itself, and thus preserve its critical or emancipatory force, but whose writings effectively subvert this claim through their relentless undoing of all theoretical concepts and categories.

And yet, as he shows, this reading falls short of the mark in so far as it ignores both the sheer dialectical cogency and rigour of Adorno's thought, and the way that his style manages to articulate those moments of aporia – of symptomatic blockage, contradiction or resistance – encountered in the passage from one sentence to the next. Nor can it be urged (as in Rorty's misreading of Derrida) that philosophy is, after all, just a collection of texts, or just one genre of writing among many others, with no special claim to argumentative validity or truth, so that really we should view Adorno's stylistic complications as nothing more than a novel way of making this 'textualist' point through various self-deconstructive tropes and devices.[32] For it is precisely the virtue of Adorno's 'style' that it renders such arguments strictly untenable by enacting *in itself* all the conflicts and tensions that philosophy has to negotiate when attempting to theorise the material conditions of late-capitalist cultural production.

The passage I now want to quote from Jameson is one that spells out the politics implicit in this agonized effort, on Adorno's part, to keep faith with enlightenment values and ideals while acknowledging the failures – even the catastrophes – brought about by a distorted 'dialectic of enlightenment' whose effects he and Horkheimer had anatomised in their book of that title.[33] It comes after several pages of commentary on the current world-political situation where Jameson concedes the obstacles posed to any 'classical' Marxist account, but also declares – as against a postmodernist reading of the signs – that Marxism is still the only adequate framework for grasping the logic of this same unfolding history. In Eastern Europe, he suggests,

> [w]hat follows the abdication by the Party of its ideological responsibilities to reinvent and project a vision of the socialist model is a vacuum in the state which is at once, but only provisionally, filled by the spectacle of intellectuals, or the intelligentsia itself, in power; some future Marx may outdo the analogous pages of the *Eighteenth Brumaire* in satirizing the euphoria with which this caste celebrates and seals the acquisition of its own professional guild-values ('freedom' of speech and 'free' elections) and then aimlessly confronts its own production crisis and begins to bicker, reuniting only to hold out a hand for money to the great ally and defender of 'freedom', a United States which, having benevolently neutralised the Soviet Union, goes on to reconquer Panama and to gear up for more such local 'defensive' operations around the world.[34]

Jameson's point is that the collapse of those communist regimes cannot be read as just another clinching instance of the bankruptcy of socialist ideals in general, or the terminal decline of a Marxist-dialectical schema which pinned its hopes to the delusive 'master-narrative' of progress, enlightenment, freedom, truth and other such emancipatory values. What the passage brings out with admirable force (in part via its shrewdly self-characterising reference to the *Eighteenth Brumaire*) is the fact that Marxism has descriptive and conceptual resources which enable it to interpret episodes of history which would seem to throw all its categories into disarray, but which in fact give hold for a diagnostic reading alive to every nuance of discrepant detail, every sign of history repeating itself, in Marx's famous phrase, 'the second time around as farce'.[35]

Jameson then goes on to assert the more positive lesson to be drawn from Adorno. This concerns the wider project of a Marxist criticism disabused of its more naive or over-confident teleological assumptions, but still quite capable of grasping such episodes – interpreting their *real* as distinct from their manifest or self-avowed political character – from a properly dialectical standpoint, one that enables thinking to resist the commodification of language and culture routinely endorsed by the celebrants of postmodernism. All of which suggests a very different reading of the current political and socio-economic signs. For, as Jameson says,

> None of [this] 'disproves' Marxism, which remains on the contrary the only current mode of thought intent on directing our attention to the economic consequences of the new 'Great Transformation', at the risk of throwing cold water on its superstructural illusions. Capital and labor (and their opposition) will not go away under the new dispensation; nor can there possibly exist in the future, any more than in the past, any viable 'third way' between capitalism and socialism, however tainted the rhetoric and conceptuality of this last may have become for people to whom bureaucrats fed it by rote ... Even a fully postmodernised First World society will not lack young people whose temperament and values are genuinely left ones and embrace visions of radical social change repressed by the norms of a business society. The dynamics of such commitment are derived not from the reading of the 'Marxist classics', but rather from the objective experience of social reality and the way in which one isolated cause or issue, one specific form of injustice, cannot be fulfilled or corrected without eventually drawing the whole web of interrelated social levels together into a totality, which then demands the intervention of a politics of social transformation ... Whether the word Marxism disappears or not, therefore, in the erasure of the tapes in some new Dark Ages, the thing itself will inevitably reappear.[36]

I have risked citing these passages out of context because they argue the case against postmodernism with an eloquence and intellectual force derived as much from Jameson's theoretical commitments (sharpened by the reading of Adorno) as from his Marxist ethico-political stance on matters of human welfare and social justice. That their 'rhetoric' will no doubt sound oddly dated – even quaintly moralistic – to readers brought up on the latest style of post-everything cultural fashion is all the more reason to examine that style with an eye to its unspoken ideological agenda.

This is why Adorno's negative dialectics holds out in the end against any form of postmodernist recuperative strategy: because it leaves no room for the kinds of superstructural mystification that take 'language', 'discourse' or 'textuality' as their horizon for what counts as an intelligible truth-claim in this or that context of socio-historical debate. That is to say, it rejects the facile line of argument whose premise is the manifest failure of history to bear out the hopes once vested in the project of enlightenment thought, and whose conclusion is that we might as well junk those hopes – or treat them as so many fictive scenarios in search of a deconstructive reading – since they have produced nothing more than the 'hyperreal' spectacle of presently-existing late-capitalist and post-communist societies. There is no doubting the widespread appeal of such notions at a time when the talk of 'crisis' endemic on the intellectual left is more often applied to the supposed breakdown of its own theoretical resources – its means of conceptualising history, ideology, material and cultural modes of production, etc – than to anything in the nature of that real-world crisis brought about by the increasingly dysfunctional workings of the system against which those same resources were once energetically directed. In this sense postmodernism is best viewed as a classic case of the symptom mistaken for a cure, a discourse whose sole purpose – or motivating interest – is to eke out the currency of 'radical' talk among those numerous *déclassé* intellectuals on the ex-Marxist left whose lack of any genuine political alignment would otherwise be all too plain. As Callinicos notes, '[t]he kind of ironic distance from the world which was so important a feature of the great works of modernism has become routinised, even trivialised, as it becomes a way of negotiating a still unreconciled reality which one no longer believes can be changed' (p170). His book – along with Jameson's – should figure high on the list of required reading for anyone who wants to see through and beyond this current superstructuralist charade.

NOTES

1. See for instance Alex Callinicos, *Is There a Future for Marxism?* (London: Macmillan, 1982); *Marxism and Philosophy* (Oxford: Clarendon Press, 1983); *Making History* (Cambridge: Polity Press, 1987).
2. Callinicos, *Against Postmodernism: a Marxist critique* (Cambridge: Polity Press, 1989). All further references given by the page-number in the text.
3. See for instance, Christopher Norris, *What's Wrong with Postmodernism: critical theory and the ends of philosophy* (Hemel Hempstead: Harvester & Baltimore: Johns Hopkins University Press, 1990) and *Uncritical Theory*.
4. Daniel Bell, *The End of Ideology* (Glencoe, Ill.: University of Illinois Press, 1960). For a postmodern update on this well-worn theme see also Francis Fukuyama, *The End of History and the Last Man* (London:

Hamish Hamilton, 1991).
5. See especially Jean-François Lyotard, *The Postmodern Condition: a report on knowledge*, trans. Geoff Bennington and Brian Massumi (Manchester: Manchester University Press, 1983).
6. See for instance Jean Baudrillard, *Selected Writings*, Mark Poster (ed) (Cambridge: Polity Press, 1988); also *Revenge of the Crystal: a Baudrillard Reader* (London: Pluto Press, 1990) and *Fatal Strategies* (Pluto, 1989).
7. See Callinicos, *Is There a Future for Marxism* (*op cit*) and *Marxism and Philosophy* (*op cit*).
8. See Gottlob Frege, 'On Sense and Reference', in *Translations from the Philosophical Writings of Gottlob Frege*, Max Black and P.T. Geach (eds) (Oxford: Basil Blackwell, 1952), pp56-78; Donald Davidson, 'On the Very Idea of a Conceptual Scheme', in *Inquiries into Truth and Interpretation* (London: Oxford University Press, 1984), pp183-98; Roland Barthes, *S/Z*, trans. Richard Miller (London: Jonathan Cape, 1975).
9. Jürgen Habermas, *The Philosophical Discourse of Modernity: twelve lectures*, trans. Frederick Lawrence (Cambridge: Polity Press, 1987).
10. Davidson, *Inquiries into Truth and Interpretation* (*op cit*).
11. See for instance S. Pradhan, 'Minimalist Semantics: Davidson and Derrida on meaning, use, and convention', *Diacritics*, Vol. XVI (Spring 1986), pp66-77; also Samuel C. Wheeler, 'Indeterminacy of French Translation: Derrida and Davidson', in Ernest LePore (ed), *Truth and Interpretation: perspectives on the philosophy of Donald Davidson* (Oxford: Basil Blackwell, 1986), pp477-94 and J.E. Malpas, *Donald Davidson and the Mirror of Meaning* (Cambridge: Cambridge University Press, 1992).
12. Richard Rorty, *Philosophy and the Mirror of Nature* (Oxford: Basil Blackwell, 1980) and *Consequences of Pragmatism* (Minneapolis: University of Minnesota Press, 1982). See also Christopher Norris, 'Reading Donald Davidson: truth, meaning and right interpretation', in Norris, *Deconstruction and the Interests of Theory* (London: Pinter Publishers & Norman, Okl.: Oklahoma University Press, 1988), pp59-83.
13. For a lively critique of this current postmodern/neopragmatist line, see Terry Eagleton, *Ideology: an introduction* (London: Verso, 1991).
14. See for instance the essays collected in Stuart Hall and Martin Jacques (eds), *New Times: the changing face of politics in the 1990s* (London: Lawrence & Wishart, 1990); also my essay 'Old Themes for New Times: postmodernism, theory and cultural politics', *New Formations*, No. 18 (Winter 1992), pp1-24.
15. See especially Baudrillard, *The Mirror of Production*, trans. Mark Poster (St. Louis: Telos Press, 1975) and *For a Critique of the Political Economy of the Sign*, trans. Charles Levin (St. Louis: Telos Press, 1981).
16. Saul Kripke, *Naming and Necessity* (Oxford: Basil Blackwell, 1980); Hilary Putnam, *Reason, Truth and History* (Cambridge: Cambridge University Press, 1981) and *Realism and Reason* (Cambridge, 1983). See also Roy Bhaskar, *Reclaiming Reality: a critical introduction to modern philosophy* (London: Verso, 1989); Gerald Vision, *Modern Anti-Realism*

and Manufactured Truth (London: Routledge, 1988).

17. See Ted Benton, *The Rise and Fall of Structural Marxism* (London: Macmillan, 1984); Gregory Elliot, *Althusser: the detour of theory* (London: Verso, 1987); E. Ann Kaplan and Michael Sprinker (eds), *The Althusserian Legacy* (London: Verso, 1993).
18. Louis Althusser, *For Marx*, trans. Ben Brewster (London: Allen Lane, 1969).
19. For a shrewd diagnostic account of these trends, see Perry Anderson, *In the Tracks of Historical Materialism* (London: Verso, 1983); also – from a more philosophical standpoint – Thomas A. Pavel, *The Feud of Language: a history of structuralist thought* (Oxford: Blackwell, 1989).
20. See Bhaskar, *Reclaiming Reality* (*op cit*); also *Scientific Realism and Human Emancipation* (London: Verso, 1986) and his near book-length critique of Richard Rorty in *Philosophy and the Idea of Freedom* (Oxford: Basil Blackwell, 1991).
21. Jon Elster, *Making Sense of Marx* (Cambridge: Cambridge University Press, 1982); G.A. Cohen, *Karl Marx's Theory of History* (Oxford: Clarendon Press, 1978).
22. Jean-François Lyotard, *The Differend: phrases in dispute*, trans. Georges Van Den Abbeele (Manchester: Manchester University Press, 1988), p179.
23. See Rorty, *Contingency, Irony, and Solidarity* (Cambridge: Cambridge University Press, 1989) and *Objectivity, Relativism, and Truth* (Cambridge, 1991); also Stanley Fish, *Doing What Comes Naturally: change, rhetoric, and the practice of theory in literary and legal studies* (Oxford: Clarendon Press, 1989).
24. Mike Davis, *Prisoners of the American Dream: politics and economy in the history of the US working class* (London: New Left Books, 1986).
25. Now incorporated into his book of the same title: Fredric Jameson, *Postmodernism, or, the Cultural Logic of Late Capitalism* (London: Verso, 1991). The essay was originally published in *New Left Review*, No. 146 (1984), pp53-92.
26. See especially Michel Foucault, *Power/Knowledge: selected interviews and other writings, 1972-77*, Colin Gordon (ed) (Brighton: Harvester, 1980) and *Language, Counter-Memory, Practice*, D.F. Bouchard and S. Simon (eds) (Oxford: Basil Blackwell, 1977).
27. See for instance T.W. Adorno, *Aesthetic Theory*, trans. C. Lenhardt (London: Routledge & Kegan Paul, 1984); Marshall Berman, *All That Is Solid Melts Into Air* (London: New Left Books, 1983); Peter Bürger, *Theory of the Avant-garde*, trans. Michael Shaw (Manchester: Manchester University Press, 1984).
28. See Fish, *Doing What Comes Naturally* (*op cit*).
29. I borrow this usefully capacious term from Richard Harland's book *Superstructuralism* (London: Methuen, 1987).
30. Fredric Jameson, *Late Capitalism: Adorno, or, the persistence of the dialectic* (London: Verso, 1990).
31. See especially T.W. Adorno, *Negative Dialectics*, trans. E.B. Ashton (London: Routledge & Kegan Paul, 1973).
32. Rorty, 'Philosophy as a Kind of Writing', in *Consequences of Pragmatism*

(*op cit*), pp90-109.
33. T.W. Adorno and Max Horkheimer, *Dialectic of Enlightenment*, trans. J. Cumming (London: Allen Lane, 1972).
34. Jameson, *Late Capitalism* (*op cit*), p250.
35. Karl Marx, *The Eighteenth Brumaire of Louis Napoleon*, in Karl Marx and Friedrich Engels, *Collected Works*, Vol. II (London: Lawrence & Wishart, 1979), pp103-97.
36. Jameson, *Late Capitalism* (*op cit*), p251.

6

OF AN APOPLECTIC TONE RECENTLY ADOPTED IN PHILOSOPHY

I TEN SLOGANS IN SEARCH OF AN AUTHOR

The rumpus during the early 1990s at Cambridge over Derrida's honorary degree was on the whole such a lamentable episode – such a display of petty resentment and unthinking 'philosophical' prejudice – that one's first response was to count the whole affair best forgotten as quickly as possible.[1] Derrida was unlikely to have lost much sleep over the intended snub, having known pretty well what to make of it from previous experience with the US professional network.[2] All this inclined me not to comment any further on that outbreak of professional *ressentiment* raised to a high point of principle by academics who lacked both the will and the competence to understand his work at anything like an adequate level of philosophic grasp.

But to let it go at that would perhaps be unwise, given the extent to which the anti-Derrida faction managed to impose their views on a duly scandalised (or easily diverted) public. In this article I shall therefore run through just a few of the idiotic slogans that were canvassed under the name of 'deconstruction' by those who (in virtue of their academic calling, not to mention the common intellectual and moral decencies) should have known better; then I aim to show just how wrong these characterisations are, and to offer some corrective remarks for those in need of guidance through the minefield of obfuscating *idées recues*.

Slogan 1: 'All reading is misreading, all interpretation misinterpretation, all truths merely modes of error' (etc). This idea has most often been imputed to Derrida by literary critics – sympathetic or hostile – who have little interest in philosophy and suppose that deconstruction is just another name for the 'anything goes' style of hermeneutic licence that rejects all standards of interpretative truth or rational accountability. It bears no relation to Derrida's work, as should be plain to anyone who has read (for instance) his two early books on Husserl, his essay on Plato (in *Dissemination*), or the emphatic disavowals of any such creed to be found, for example, in *Of Grammatology*.[3] Thus: 'To recognize and respect all [the] classical exigencies is not easy and requires all the instruments of traditional criticism. Without this recognition and this respect, critical production would risk developing in any direction at all and authorise itself to say almost anything'.[4] Which is not of course to deny that textual close-reading of the kind that Derrida practises may often go against the intentionalist grain – or against what the author *consciously and explicitly* wanted to say – in response to anomalous or discrepant details which have hitherto escaped notice. So far as the appeal to intentions is concerned, 'this indispensable guardrail has always only *protected*, it has never *opened*, a reading'. And again, in perhaps his most succinct formulation: '[a deconstructive reading] must always aim at a certain relationship, unperceived by the writer, between what he commands and what he does not command of the patterns of the language that he uses'.[5]

Of course these might be taken as mere passing gestures toward a high-toned ethic of 'respect' and 'recognition' which is elsewhere belied by Derrida's practice in the reading of philosophical or literary texts. After all (Slogan 2), everyone knows that, according to Derrida, philosophy is just another 'kind of writing', on a par with poems, novels, literary criticism, or any other sort of text you care to name. No matter that this phrase actually comes from the title of an essay by Richard Rorty who makes no bones about his own lack of interest in the more 'philosophical' aspects of Derrida's work, and his desire to speed up the imminent demise of philosophy as an academic discipline by playing off 'bad nephew Jacques' against 'honest uncle Kant' and all those other earnestly deluded seekers-after-truth.[6] Deconstruction thus figures as the sophist's revenge, as a handy set of rhetorical tricks for deflating philosophy's grandiose self-image, or again – in less provocative style – as a sensible adjustment to the pragmatist view of what's good in the way of belief. For Rorty indeed there can be no obligation to interpret Derrida aright, since notions like truth, right reading, argumentative rigour, etc, are merely so many hung-over symptoms of that same (now obsolete) 'foundationalist' paradigm that has long exerted such a powerful and delusory appeal. One can see why this 'strong revisionist' reading has enjoyed great favour with literary critics, few of whom possess much knowledge of philosophy beyond a vague sense of wounded self-esteem at having suffered an age-old history of arrogant put-downs, starting out with Socrates *versus* the poets, sophists and assorted rhetoricans, and carried on nowadays in numerous faculty disputes. More unfortunate is the fact that a good many philosophers have likewise given credit to the Rorty version, thus confirming all their preconceived ideas. For if this were anything like a fair rendition of Derrida's arguments then one could hardly blame the Cambridge Faculty of Philosophy for regarding him as a less than worthy recipient of its highest mark of esteem.

Hence (Slogans 3, 4 and 5) the widespread ideas that: deconstruction heralds the 'end of philosophy'; or, in any event, it heralds philosophy's demotion to the level of an undifferentiated textual 'freeplay' where literary critics can claim the upper hand since they – unlike the philosophers – have long been aware that 'all truths are fictions', that 'all concepts are metaphors'; and that interpretation (in Stanley Fish's phrase) goes 'all the way down'.[7] This message – or something very like it – has been doing the academic rounds for some time now, and was batted back and forth between journalists and philosophers during the Cambridge campaign. But even the most limited acquaintance with Derrida's work – for instance, with his essays in *Writing and Difference* or the superb deconstructive reading of Kant's third *Critique* – is enough to discountenance any such view of him as endorsing that facile 'end-of-philosophy' rhetoric that Rorty so assiduously seeks to promote.[8] On the contrary, Derrida has often insisted that deconstruction has nothing whatever in common with those fashionable trends (postmodernism, post-humanism, post-Marxism, etc) which naively presume to turn the page on so-called 'Western metaphysics' while failing to engage its problems and aporias with the requisite degree of analytical care.[9] One could multiply quotations to precisely this effect, all of them refuting the idea – the vulgar-deconstructionist doxa – that philosophy is *just* another 'kind of writing', a literary genre whose concepts and truth-claims are so many sublimated metaphors, and whose stylistic resources (or periodic shifts of 'final vocabulary') are its only contribution to the ongoing 'cultural conversation of mankind'. Such may be Rorty's view of the matter, one shared by more than a few literary theorists with reasons of their own for adopting it. Still there is no question of Derrida's subscribing to any such wholesale cultural relativist creed. See his classic essay 'White Mythology: metaphor in the text of philosophy' for a subtle and rigorous account of these issues that affords no excuse for the sloppy misreading put about by admirers and detractors alike.[10]

Slogan 6: 'If Derrida has anything worthwhile to say why say it in a style so wilfully obscure, cryptic, mandarin, prolix, self-indulgent, allusive, repetitious, rhetorical, "literary" (etc, etc)?' And again: 'why attempt to understand him if Derrida adopts such a range of sophistical techniques for baffling the good-willed reader?' On the rare occasions that this charge is backed up by reference to any specific text it is usually Derrida's notorious 'response' to John Searle on the topic of Austinian speech-act theory.[11] Otherwise it seems to express little more than a resentment of the fact that he manages to write so much and a failure to grasp that his writings are 'performative' in the sense of raising certain philosophic issues (e.g. the relation between concept and metaphor, or between constative and performative utterance) *in and through* the practice of a written style that self-consciously foregrounds those issues. One can see why such writing has caused great offence – if mainly through scandalised hearsay – to philosophers bred up on more ortho- dox ideas of what constitutes a decently intelligible style. But it is yet another sign of ingrown professionalism when these latter are treated as the hallmark of genuine, 'serious' philosophical work as opposed to mere 'literary' dilettantism.

Of course those who take this line will claim to be upholding the standards of argumentative rigour and truth against the blandishments of a pseudo-philosophical rhetoric which belongs (if anywhere) in departments of Comparative Literature, or maybe to some minor course-option in the history of ideas. Clear thought and fancy writing just don't mix, least of all the kind of writing that exploits certain fictive (as well as figural) devices by way of questioning the 'law of genre' that would keep them firmly apart. What is thus ruled out – despite all the manifold counter-examples from Plato to Wittgenstein, Austin, Kripke, or Parfitt – is any notion that philosophy might stand to gain (to sharpen and refine its analytical insights) through a speculative but none the less rigorous reflection on the realms of metaphorical and fictive possibility. Otherwise there is simply no accounting for the view that Derrida's 'style' goes beyond all the limits of genuine, competent or good-faith philosophical debate. For instances to the contrary see for example 'Plato's Pharmacy', 'The Double Session', 'The Law of Genre' and – most strikingly – his essays on the tangled relationship between philos- ophy, fiction and psychoanalysis: 'Coming Into One's Own' and 'To speculate – on "Freud"'.[12]

Slogan 7: 'How can Derrida see fit to complain that his work has been traduced, his texts misread, his arguments ignored or vulgarised, etc, when he himself makes a regular practice of doing just this with whatever he reads?' Or, in similar *tu quoque* fashion: 'why bother even trying to get Derrida right if, according to him, textuality rules and there is no appeal to the old ("logocentric") constraints of right reason, interpretive truth, authorial intention (etc)?'[13] Again, this is just the kind of reflex response that 'deconstruction' provokes among those who have avoided any contact with Derrida's work beyond a mere handful of phrases taken out of context and a firm conviction – on the authority of other non-readers – that the whole thing amounts to just a species of sophistical wordplay. It is hard to know what it would take to dislodge this deep-laid prejudice, backed up as it is by the guild mentality that equates 'serious' philosophy with work in the Anglo-American analytical tradition, and which views the other ('Continental') line of descent after Kant as fit for consumption only by muddle-headed literary theorists. So the point needs making with maximum emphasis: that Derrida is an exemplary close-reader of philosophic texts whose keen eye for the marginal, the discrepant or the anomalous goes along with an equally exigent sense of the prime obligation – the ethical imperative – to respect what is written and not let interpretation develop 'in any direction at all'. And this despite the fact – well attested in the latest round of polemics – that such reading may produce results which are counter-canonical (or counter-intuitive) to a degree that provokes outrage among mainstream commentators. But blanket dismissals are of course no substitute for what has so far been altogether lacking, that is to say, a critique of Derrida's claims that would engage them at anything like their own level of detailed textual exegesis. If he is able to run rings around an opponent like John Searle it is because Searle reads always with a view to confirming his own preconceptions, and thus fails to register the logical (as well as rhetorical) complications of Austin's, Derrida's and – not least – his own writing.[14]

Of course this is hugely annoying for Searle, as for others with the same understandable desire to ignore such bother-headed 'textualist' puzzles and get straight on with the business of expounding a clear-cut, coherent and pragmatically useful speech-act theory. Hence (slogan 8) the idea of deconstruction as a set of geared-up sophistical techniques for 'doing things with texts'. But it remains the case – as I have argued at length elsewhere – that Derrida is by far the more attentive, scrupulous, and faithfully *Austinian* exponent of Austin's *How To Do Things With Words*.[15] Above all he is alert to those signs of categorical confusion which begin with the attempt to distinguish clearly between constative and performative speech-act modes, and which then create problems (or, in Austin's phrase, 'play old Harry') with the effort to sort out 'serious' from 'non-serious' instances, good-faith promises from promises uttered in jest, real-life from fictive or set-piece examples, 'authentic' from 'deviant' ('parasitical') cases, and so forth.[16] What is at issue is the relation between constative *theory* and performative *practice*, a relation which Searle thinks unproblematic – provided one adopts an orderly and disciplined approach – but which Derrida (and Austin) find subject to all manner of destabilising ironies, doubts and complications. There are two crucial points to be made here, as against the standard view (standard at least in the Anglo-American 'analytic' community) that Searle won the argument hands down and exposed Derrida as a charlatan intent upon creating deconstructive mischief. One is that Austin, had he lived to witness this exchange, would surely have acknowledged more affinity – more sense of a kindred philosophical spirit – with Derrida's 'playful' than with Searle's ultra-'serious' way of reading his work. That is, he would have seen it as much more in keeping with his own willingness to suspend the requirements of 'constative' system and method when confronted with examples (jokes, anecdotes, 'deviant' performatives, awkward bits of written or oral evidence) which failed to support his larger philosophical claims. And the second point – following from this – is that Austin, like Derrida, perceived no merit in the standard (implicitly ethical) equation between truth, seriousness, and the drive to assimilate marginal or non-standard cases. What unites these thinkers – and sets them at odds with a theorist like Searle – is an openness to the sheer variety of human needs, satisfactions, and sense-making gambits, and also a knowledge of the violence that can often be masked behind doctrinaire systematising habits of thought.

That Derrida to some extent reads Austin against the grain is not – as Searle would have it – a wilful misprision or an act of hermeneutic violence on his part. Rather, it signals an awareness of the deep ambivalence in Austin's project, on the one hand his striving to articulate a systematic theory of (proper, authentic) speech-acts, and on the other his sense of the difficulties that arise to frustrate that ambition at every turn. A good deal has been written lately about the 'ethics of deconstruction', some of it (for example by Geoffrey Galt Harpham and Simon Critchley) very much to the point while some (for example by J. Hillis Miller) gives plentiful scope for those who would maintain – slogan 9 – that deconstruction celebrates the 'death of the author', the dissolution of the subject (the knowing, willing, and judging subject) into so many radically 'decentred' discourses or language-games, and hence the demise of any 'ethics' worthy the name.[17] There are, I should allow, some few isolated passages in Derrida's (mostly early) work that lend themselves to a reading in this late-1960s Nietzschean apocalyptic mode. They include the much-cited paragraph from 'Structure, Sign and Play' where Derrida writes of the two 'interpretations of interpretation', the one turned back nostalgically toward a Rousseauist ethos of origins, truth and presence, the other opening itself up to 'the joyous affirmation of the play of the world and of the innocence of becoming, the affirmation of a world of signs without fault, without truth, and without origin which is offered to an active interpretation'.[18] One can see – just about – why readers looking sharply for evidence of Derrida's profligate ways should have jumped at these seemingly extravagant pronouncements and felt themselves justified in avoiding any closer acquaintance with his work.

But such passages must always be read in context, like Derrida's equally notorious dictum that 'there is nothing outside the text' (more accurately rendered, 'no "outside" to the text').[19] This statement has similarly been bandied about – Slogan 10 – as proof that deconstruction is just a species of textual solipsism, a post-modern variant of the sceptic's refusal to acknowledge any reality beyond the prison-house of ideas, sense-data, private imaginings or whatever. But when restored to its original context in his reading of Rousseau the passage turns out to have no such dire or self-disabling implications. Derrida's point – familiar enough at least since Kant – is that we cannot have *direct or unmediated* access to the real, since our knowledge thereof is ineluctably structured by the forms of our sensory, perceptual, cognitive or linguistic grasp. To suppose otherwise is to confuse ontological with epistemological issues, and hence to find oneself driven – like Hume – into all sorts of fargone sceptical doubt. Textuality (or 'writing', in Derrida's extended sense of that term) is best construed as a deconstructive metonym for the various culturally mediated structures of thought, knowledge and representation which alone make understanding possible. Thus it is nearer the mark to see Kant, not Hume, as the thinker who anticipates some of Derrida's most characteristic turns of argument.

Of course, one has to take account of the difference between Kant's transcendental (or strong universalist) claims as regards the *a priori* powers and limits of human understanding, and Derrida's much greater allowance for the various (culture-specific) constraints that play a role in thus establishing the 'conditions of possibility' for thought and experience in general. Indeed, as Rodolphe Gasché has argued most convincingly, it is often with Derrida a matter of ascertaining the precise conditions of *im*possibility for anything like a Kantian transcendental deduction from first principles.[20] But these issues are raised – or these aporias located – through an enquiry into the structure, the logic and the grounding suppositions of Kantian thought which respects Kant's critical imperative to take nothing on trust but always to question what is offered in the name of self-evident (received, commonsense, or authoritative) belief. As with Austin, so here: Derrida's reading is more properly and rigorously 'Kantian' than those orthodox accounts (or unswervingly 'faithful' exegeses) that equate fidelity with a fideist acceptance of the standard interpretative line.

This is not to say of deconstruction (as Paul Ricoeur once remarked about structuralism) that it amounts to nothing more than 'Kantianism minus the transcendental subject', or a replay of nineteenth-century idealist themes in an updated linguistic-textualist idiom.[21] Where such arguments all too easily wind up – as with Rorty – is by sinking the difference between philosophy and literature, viewing all texts (Kant's included) as so many optional 'kinds of writing', and thus presenting the pragmatist upshot as an issue out of all our philosophical afflictions.[22] In fact Derrida's relation to Kant is both closer and more complicated than anything allowed for by Rorty's easygoing pragmatist approach. One has only to read an essay like 'Parergon' (in *The Truth in Painting*) to appreciate how Derrida questions the 'unthought axiomatics', i.e. the strictly unwarranted assumptions, pre-critical residues, *de jure* stipulations passed off as *de facto* truths, etc, which continue to characterise Kant's argument at certain crucial and problematic junctures throughout the three *Critiques*.[23] But this is – I repeat – no mere display of wire-drawn 'textualist' ingenuity, or perverse demonstration of the pleasures to be had by pursuing out-of-the-way details (or odd turns of metaphor) with a view to undermining the entire edifice of Kantian critical thought. On the contrary, Derrida argues his case with meticulous attention to the logic (as well as the rhetoric) of Kant's text, despite what emerges in the course of his reading as the difficulty of maintaining any such clear-cut distinction. On one point at least his opponents are right: that deconstruction raises issues (or discovers complications) which are simply not there according to the mainstream interpretive view. Certainly one's reading of an essay like 'Parergon' does nothing to facilitate – and much to problematise – one's reading of the three *Critiques*. Hence no doubt the quite extraordinary degree of resistance (including the downright refusal to read) which Derrida's texts have typically provoked among scholars of a more orthodox mind.

II THE LOGIC OF DECONSTRUCTION: DERRIDA ON PLATO, ROUSSEAU, KANT, AND HUSSERL

It is well to be clear what the charge amounts to if Derrida is to be counted a mischief-maker – or perverter of reason and truth – on the grounds that his writing presents such a challenge to received ideas of how Kant should properly be read. On this view it is the task of responsible commentary first so far as possible to elicit Kant's intentions, argumentative purposes, large-scale ('architectonic') designs, etc; second, to relate these back at every point to the detailed exegesis of particular passages in his work; and third – where necessary – to adopt a principle of charity and apply certain techniques of 'rational reconstruction' in order that his arguments be seen to comply with current (more refined or adequate) criteria of logic, consistency and truth. Such has been the standard approach of philosophers in the present-day analytic tradition. Undoubtedly it has yielded some impressive results and done much to elucidate matters of structure and detail. Moreover it is a project perfectly in keeping with the Kantian ethico-critical imperative, that which on the one hand enjoins a due respect for authorial intention (since otherwise one is at risk of treating texts, like persons, as a means to one's own interpretive end), but on the other upholds the right of philosophy to question doxastic truth-claims and beliefs in the interest of a better, more enlightened understanding. Thus the prime obligation is to *get things right*, whether right in the sense 'warranted by appeal to the text in hand' or right as construed in keeping with alternative (currently prevailing) criteria of reason and truth.

Such commentary can of course take various forms according to the degree of interpretive latitude, or – more often – the commentator's sense of what presently counts as a valid, cogent, or philosophically defensible reading. In some cases – as with Strawson's overtly revisionist approach – the aim is not so much to reconstruct Kant's intentions with maximum fidelity, nor yet to vindicate every detail of his argument, but rather to present a scaled-down ('descriptive' as opposed to 'prescriptive') version of Kantian metaphysics which answers more readily to current ideas about philosophy's legitimate scope and limits.[24] All the same there are certain features that characterise the 'analytic' approach despite and across these differences of view. They include a firm commitment to the principle of reason, a stress on the virtues of detailed and clear-headed conceptual exegesis, an acceptance of logical ground-rules (like the law of non-contradiction) whose abandonment would clearly spell the end of this enterprise, and – most importantly – a Kantian ethos that equates philosophical probity and truth with the quest for rational consensus on matters of shared disciplinary concern. Another main item, prominent in varying degrees, is the mistrust of writings that trade too much on their stylistic (or 'literary') brilliance, and which thus – so it is argued – make a disreputable bid to sidestep the requirements of adequate professional scrutiny or informed peer-group review.[25] For there is simply no engaging in serious, constructive debate with philosophers who raise idiosyncracies of style to a high point of obscurantist principle which can then serve as guard against any kind of reasoned counter-argument. In short there are certain minimal requirements – good faith, clarity, conceptual precision, the avoidance of wilful misreadings, verbal imprecision, logical blunders, category-mistakes, etc – in the absence of which philosophy might as well yield up its every last argument, principle, or truth-claim.

It should be clear from what I have said above that Derrida is far from rejecting this approach in the name of some postmodern-textualist appeal to the infinitised 'freeplay' of writing. Thus he acknowledges both the claims of authorial intent (that 'indispensable guardrail', as he puts it, which prevents interpretation from running off 'in my direction at all') and the critical requirement that reading should proceed in accordance with the best, most exacting criteria of logical accountability. It is simply a mistake – a polemical convenience – to suppose that 'deconstruction' and 'reconstruction' are flatly antithetical terms. But where Derrida *does* part company with commentators in the analytic school is by refusing to privilege those aspects of the Kantian text that conform most readily – or that offer least resistance – to a reading based on certain foregone assumptions about Kant's mode of argument, his philosophical priorities, conceptual resources, 'transcendental' (as opposed to 'metaphysical') claims, and so forth. What this amounts to is a *rigorous and principled* insistence that one read with an eye to certain 'marginal' details – metaphors, footnotes, analogical devices, parenthetical remarks – which in fact play a more-than-marginal role in Kant's developing structure of argument. That such details scarcely register on other, more orthodox readings of the Kantian corpus – and that Kant may himself have had motives for according them a strictly ancillary status – is all the more reason to keep an open mind as to their possible function and significance. For in each case it is only natural, so to speak, that the devices in question will be marginalised – or treated as merely 'parergonal' – in so far as they act (in Rodolphe Gasché's phrase) as 'conditions of '*im*possibility', that is, as enabling yet problematic grounds for the entire Kantian enterprise.

Small wonder that Kant scholarship has so far evinced a massive indifference to Derrida's reading, as also to other deconstructive essays (such as Paul de Man's 'Phenomenality and Materiality in Kant') which likewise raise issues undreamt-of on the orthodox view.[26] But again I should wish to stress that the dividing-line here is *not* drawn up between (on the one hand) faithful, attentive, analytical readers of Kant who respect his argumentative purposes and (on the other) super-subtle deconstructors who despise those old-fashioned virtues. It is not just that Derrida reads with a fine (indeed unequalled) sensitivity to matters of textual detail. For this could still leave him open to the charge of exploiting such nuances for all they are worth, subjecting philosophy to the alien techniques of 'literary' (i.e. rhetorical) exegesis, and thus – as Jürgen Habermas puts it – promiscuously levelling the 'genre-distinction' between these two realms of discourse.[27] If such objections have a certain *prima facie* plausibility it no doubt results from Derrida's use of terms like 'freeplay', 'undecidability' and 'dissemination', terms which suggest – on a cursory acquaintance – that to deconstruct a text is a matter of lifting all the usual normative criteria (logical, hermeneutic, historical, contextual or whatever), and extracting the maximum semantic yield without regard for those irksome constraints. And there are, to be sure, a good few literary critics – ranged on both sides of the current debate – who share this view of Derrida's work as a geared-up extension of the 'old' New Criticism which merely substitutes its own, more adventurous rhetoric for the previous (rather homespun and routine) talk of 'ambiguity', 'irony', 'paradox' and the rest. They are joined, as we have seen, by those ex- or anti-philosophers (Rorty chief among them) who find him a useful ally in the cause of cutting that discipline down to size by treating it as just another language-game, 'final vocabulary', 'kind of writing', etc. In so far as Derrida is to blame for his own reception-history one would have to agree with Habermas and the Cambridge opponents: that deconstruction is nothing more than a handy pretext for literary critics who want to romp freely over the philosophers' hitherto well-guarded textual preserve.

These confusions have been worse confounded by the fact that Derrida's writings were first borne in upon the US literary scene by the same mid-1970s wave of Francophile cultural fashion that heralded the advent of post-structuralist works like Roland Barthes's *S/Z*. What thus got around, very often in Derrida's name, was the notion – the strictly unintelligible notion – of a writing ('textuality' or *écriture*) that would throw off the bourgeois-realist constraints of truth, reference, origins, authorship etc, and henceforth revel in the prospects opened up by this utopian 'freeplay' of the sign.[28] Then of course there was Derrida's well-known talk of 'logocentrism' and the Western 'metaphysics of presence', phrases which – cited out of context – acquired a kind of malign potency among zealots of the new textual dispensation. And so it came about that deconstruction suffered the kind of *deformation professionel* that has often been the fate of philosophical ideas when taken up by literary critics. If Derrida's writings offered no resistance, no counter-arguments or conceptual resources against this appropriative reading of his work, then philosophers would surely be justified in dismissing deconstruction as just another import from the wilder fringes of literary academe. But they do so resist, and most firmly with regard to the idea of deconstruction as a species of all-out hermeneutic licence, a practice much akin to those modes of literary criticism that exploit the techniques of rhetorical close-reading in order to multiply semantic possibilities while showing no concern with language in its logical, propositional, or truth-functional aspect. Such ideas are completely wide of the mark, as Derrida has often had cause to complain.[29] For one thing they ignore his reiterated point that deconstruction has to do with the conceptual grammar (or logical syntax) of certain elements in the text, and not – as the commonplace account would have it – with the sheer multiplicity of meanings attached to this or that isolated key-word. Again, I wouldn't deny that his writings *can* be thus construed – or plausibly nudged in this direction – by literary critics (Geoffrey Hartman among them) or revisionists like Rorty keen to play down their philosophical content or significance.[30] But there does come a point with such readings – a point clearly signalled in Derrida's texts – where they overstep the limits of interpretive accountability and enter the realm of opportunist special pleading. It is all the more important that those limits be remarked when so many of the current misconceptions about Derrida's work derive from a hasty scanning of the secondary sources – most of them primers in literary theory – and a willingness to credit whatever is put around in the way of academic folk-wisdom.

There is no room here for an adequate address to this issue of truth-claims in deconstruction and the relation between logic, grammar and rhetoric as developed in Derrida's writing. All the same it is worth offering a few brief comments – with reference to the pertinent texts – since it is precisely on this question that opinion divides as to whether his work has any claim to philosophical standing or whether it is just a modish spin-off from the pseudo-discipline of literary theory. Some examples may help to clarify the issue. Take for instance his discussion of the word *pharmakon* (= 'poison' or 'cure') in Plato's *Phaedrus*, a term whose ambivalence – or whose undecidability in each of its manifold occurrences – is shown to result from its logico-grammatical underdetermination, rather than from any vague piling-up of semantic (associative) meanings.[31] To call this a 'literary' reading of the *Phaedrus* is fair comment if it is taken to signify a meticulous attention to matters of textual detail, a refusal to set aside complicating evidence in the interests of preserving the received (canonical) account, and an awareness of the conflicts that may always arise between, on the one hand, express philosophical truth-claims – in this case, claims about the relation between speech and writing, reason and rhetoric, philosophy and sophistics, spiritual and erotic love, paternal law and its bastard (unauthorised) offspring, etc – and on the other hand the way that those claims are called into question through a reading alert to the manifold signs of a different, counter-canonical logic at work. But it is *not* fair comment when applied – as it is more often – in a sense that opposes 'philosophy' and 'literature' (or 'concept' and 'metaphor') with the aim of discrediting Derrida's enterprise by association with the sophists and other purveyors of a false rhetorical wisdom. For the fact is – and I make no apologies for putting it like this – that Derrida is a better reader of Plato, a more rigorous and faithful reader, than those who assuredly know in advance what the *Phaedrus* means or how the dialogue is certain to turn out, and who thus reproduce the Platonic order of priorities without the least sense of those complicating factors. If this is a case of 'how to do things with texts' – the usual dismissive response – then what Derrida does with the *Phaedrus* is raise it to a level of philosophical interest and complexity unglimpsed by more orthodox commentators.

His reading of Rousseau in *Of Grammatology* is another impressive case in point. What Derrida locates is a curious and multiform 'logic of supplementarity', a pattern of repeated chiasmic reversals that compel Rousseau – against his own express intent – to question the priority that standardly elevates speech above writing, nature above culture, presence above absence, the innocence of origins above the bad effects of civilised (decadent) 'progress', and so forth. Again he is not simply discounting Rousseau's overt professions of intent, arguing (like the 'old' New Critics) that intentions are inscrutable and in any case beside the point for exegetical purposes, or – least of all – endorsing that modish post-structuralist line for which the 'death of the author' is a *fait accompli* and a cause for celebration among liberated readers. On the contrary: what Rousseau would wish to say (*voudrait dire*) is everywhere allowed due weight and prominence in Derrida's reading. But fidelity to the text doesn't stop at this point, since there is also a logic (more precisely: a chain of logico-grammatical-semantic entailment) that runs athwart Rousseau's overt statements of intent and generates aporias – moments of blindness to its own further-reaching implications – which cannot be resolved by a straightforward appeal to what Rousseau self-evidently meant. Thus: 'Rousseau's discourse lets itself be constrained by a complexity which always has the form of the supplement of or from the origin ... His declared intention is not annulled by this but rather *inscribed* within a system which it does not dominate'.[32] And again: '[Rousseau] *declares* what he *wishes to say*: that is, that articulation and writing are a post-originary malady of language; he says or *describes* that which he *does not wish to say*: articulation and therefore the space of writing operates at the origin of language'.[33]

Such is the 'dangerous supplement' – or logic of supplementarity – which comes into play whenever Rousseau attempts to argue, narrate or theorise the relation between a good (natural) and a bad (highly cultivated or civilized) order of existence. It emerges across the whole range of his manifold concerns, from social anthropology to the origins and history of language, from civil institutions to music criticism and a nascent ethno-musicology, from educational theory and practice to the quest for self-knowledge and authentic autobiographical truth pursued with such unprecedented zeal in Rousseau's *Confessions*. In each case, as Derrida convincingly shows, there is a tension – at times a flat contradiction – between the level of overt (thematic) statement and the level at which such statements are subject to a complicating logic which cannot but call Rousseau's premises into doubt. What distinguishes this from a 'literary reading' – in the usual (primarily interpretive) sense of that term – is its concern to articulate structures of logico-semantic entailment which characterise not only this or that passage, nor even some particular text of Rousseau, nor yet Rousseau's entire literary *oeuvre* treated as embodying distinctive attributes of consciousness, character, theme, or style. To be sure there is a sense – as Derrida acknowledges – in which *Grammatology* might well have been sub-titled 'The Age of Rousseau'. But this 'age' is more an epoch, one that is defined – from Plato to latterday self-professed Rousseauists like Saussure and Lévi-Strauss – by a set of deep-laid philosophical assumptions – call it 'logocentrism' or the Western 'metaphysics of presence' – which Rousseau both upholds in exemplary fashion and nevertheless (perhaps unwittingly) works to undermine. Such claims would be worthless – portentous variations on a stock Heideggerian theme – were they not backed up, in Derrida's case, by textual close-reading and conceptual exegesis of the highest analytical order.

Then again, there is Derrida's deconstructive reading of Husserlian phenomenology through the effects of *différance* ('differing' and 'deferral') as these impinge upon Husserl's attempted synthesis of the transcendental ego as source and guarantor of meaning.[34] Perhaps it is the case – as Derrida argues – that *différance* is not and cannot be a 'concept', since any attempt to specify its meaning, logical function, truth-conditions, etc must ignore what his reading has set out to demonstrate, namely the impossibility of assigning it a definite (fixed or punctual) place in Husserl's rigorously argued account of thought, language and time-consciousness. But this doesn't mean – as the literary theorists and philosophical opponents are apt to conclude – that *différance* is therefore some kind of free-floating signifier, open to just about any reading that suits the interpreter's fancy. What Derrida says of Husserl applies to his own work also: that the validity of a text, a reading or an argument is measured not so much by its adherence to preconceived (dogmatic) assumptions as by its readiness to acknowledge the problems that arise – the unlooked-for doubts and complications – in the process of detailed exegesis. Nor are these problems 'merely' textual in the sense that they exploit certain localised symptoms of semantic instability or 'freeplay' with a view to levelling the difference between philosophy and literature, reducing philosophy to just another 'kind of writing', or inverting the traditional (philosophic) order of priorities between logic and rhetoric. To deconstruct such differences and priorities is not simply to ignore, annul or even (in some notional Hegelian sense) to 'transcend' them, as I hope will be evident from what I have written so far.

There are indeed some few passages in Derrida's work on Husserl where he might appear to endorse such a reading. Thus at one point in 'Force and Signification' he invokes certain literary modernists (from Flaubert to Proust, Eliot and Woolf) as writers who implicitly questioned or problematised the axiomatics of Husserlian thought. These writers possessed what Derrida calls 'a sure and certain consciousness, although in principle not a clear and distinct one, since there is not intuition of a thing involved'.[35] And there is also – I should mention – the well-known passage in his introductory essay to Husserl's *The Origin of Geometry* where Derrida suggests that commentary confronts an ultimate choice between, on the one hand, a rigorous pursuit of essences, primordial intuitions, eidetic certainties, *a priori* concepts, univocal meanings etc, and on the other a 'literary' (Joycean) openness to the greatest range of semantic possibility.[36] One could – rather feebly – account for such flourishes by recalling that this was the period when a good many French intellectuals – Barthes among them – extolled *Finnegan's Wake* (by acquaintance or repute) as the 'writerly' text *par excellence*, one whose transgressions of the limits of bourgeois realism heralded an imminent 'revolution of the word'.[37] But this is to trivialise Derrida's long and intensive engagement with the question of philosophy and literature, one that started out with his abandoned doctoral thesis (on the 'ideality of the literary object'), and which continued through numerous subsequent texts.[38] It was focused most sharply in his writings on Husserl since here, more than anywhere, the issue arose as to how far philosophy – a rigorous philosophy that deployed and refined all the critical resources of logocentric reason from Plato to Kant – could hope to render adequate account of language in its 'literary' aspect. But what the term 'literature' signifies in this context is not, as might be supposed, a domain of specialised rhetorical figures ('ambiguity', 'polysemy', 'paradox', 'irony', the 'writerly' as opposed to the 'readerly' text, etc) where questions of truth, logic and reference simply don't obtrude.

Rather it is the name for whatever in language cannot be reduced to the Husserlian ideal of a pure, rigorously theorised yet unmediated *rapport-à-soi*, an 'intellectual intuition' – so to speak – whose attainment would thus mark the passage beyond all the vexing antinomies of post-Kantian philosophical thought.

Derrida shows with exemplary precision how Husserl cannot but fail in this attempt; how his language everywhere betrays the effects of a *différance* (a movement of differing-deferral) which prevents it from achieving that punctual correspondence between word and object, concept and intuition, or articulated meaning and professed intent. But there is no question of Derrida's simply dismissing the entire project of transcendental phenomenology as a pointless or misconceived enterprise, one whose failure consigns it – as Rorty would argue – to the history of obsolete ideas. Nor does he suggest (like Rorty again) that if we *must* continue reading the great dead philosophers then we should read them not for any truths to be had – any valid arguments that might yet be sifted from the rubble – but rather for the sake of their storytelling interest, their offbeat metaphors, fictive excursions, stylistic idiosyncracies, etc. Of course there are some texts of Derrida (late texts mostly, *La Carte Postale* chief among them) which appear to lend credence to this view of him as a 'literary' adept – brilliant or tedious according to taste – who couldn't care less about getting things right and who wishes only to frolic in the post-philosophical aftermath. So far as Rorty is concerned these are the writings that show Derrida at his best – as a gifted debunker of that boring old tradition – and which save one the trouble (the wasted effort) of engaging with his earlier, more 'serious' productions. But this gets the order of priorities exactly back-to-front. The 'Envois' section of *La Carte Postale* amounts to just a series of arcane, self-indulgent (and not very funny) jokes if one fails to perceive how it relates at every point to those various deconstructive topoi (speech/writing, presence/absence, Socrates/Plato, philosophy/literature and so forth) whose conceptual genealogy and structural logic are analysed with far greater depth and precision in works like *Margins of Philosophy* and *Of Grammatology*. This is, if you like, the 'performative' pay-off – the fictive or literary *mise-en-scène* – of a project whose credentials have already been established (or whose claims to serious attention adequately earned) by the 'considerable labour of conceptual exegesis' which makes up the bulk of Derrida's more analytical writings.

I borrow this phrase – slightly modified – from a remark of Paul de

Man's *à propos* the relation between constative and performative speech-act modalities in Nietzsche.[39] For it strikes me as yet more appropriate in Derrida's case, given his (decidedly un-Nietzschean) concern to remain faithful to the calling of philosophy – to its critical, pedagogical, and ethical imperatives – as against those varieties of postmodern scepticism which most often take Nietzsche as their tutelary spirit. And this despite Derrida's equal (but *not*, be it stressed, his opposed or contradictory) desire to question those grounding presuppositions – those 'unthought axiomatics' – which have structured the discourse of philosophical critique from Kant to Husserl. 'Who is more faithful to reason's call', he asks, 'who hears it with a keener ear ... the one who offers questions in return and tries to think through the possibility of that summons, or the one who does not want to hear any question about the principle of reason?'[40] It is not hard to guess whom Derrida might have had in mind when framing this rhetorical question. On the one hand it evokes that long history of dogmatic rationalist thinking which flatly refuses to entertain doubts as to its own authoritative status, its possession of ultimate justifying grounds (*a priori* concepts, axioms of logic, clear and distinct ideas, truths self-evident to reason) the acceptance of which defines what it means to be a serious, good-faith, competent philosopher. On the other – more directly – the passage takes aim at those opponents of deconstruction who denounce its 'irrationalist' or 'nihilist' character without the least knowledge of Derrida's work.

The above-cited passage occurs in an essay ('The Principle of Reason') whose genre is that of a dialogue – unmarked but everywhere implicit – between a voice that upholds the philosophic values of reason, critique and enlightened debate and another, less assertive, more tonally modulated voice whose role is to question those values in the name of a Heideggerian 'fundamental ontology'. To this extent the essay is indeed a 'literary' text, one that makes use of the dialogue form – along with various pronominal shifts, intertextual allusions, self-reflexive metaphors, passages of *oratio obliqua* and so forth – in order to maintain a certain calculated doubt with regard to the status (the enunciative modality) of its own statements and truth-claims. And there are other recent texts of Derrida – among them his *tour de force* in this mode, the essay 'Of an Apocalyptic Tone Lately Adopted in Philosophy' – which likewise go elaborate ways around to forestall any reading that would allocate truth to some single voice in the dialogue.[41] (See Chapter Three for a more detailed discussion of these and related issues.) All of which might seem to confirm the view that Derrida is a sophist, a wily rhetorician, or at best a canny 'dialectical' thinker who will always shift ground (or simply switch language-games) when confronted with a strong counter-argument. How can one engage in serious, constructive debate with a writer who perpetually exploits such devices with the sole purpose – so it seems – of denying responsibility for his own words and twisting the words of others into all kinds of strange (unintended) relation? On this account 'The Principle of Reason' would figure as a mere exercise in 'literary' ventriloquism, a text whose occasional obligatory nods in a Kantian (or Leibnizian) direction are just the sort of tactic that Derrida deploys in order to pass himself off as a 'philosopher' among readers of an ignorant or credulous disposition. Such was John Searle's exasperated response to Derrida, and such – with few exceptions – the Cambridge faculty line insofar as it achieved articulate form.

But this fails to take account of two main points, one with respect to Derrida's texts and the other concerning the role of 'literary' devices (narrative, dialogue, irony, indirect discourse, etc) in thinkers whose work is generally acknowledged as having some claim to serious philosophical attention. The first point is made in 'The Principle of Reason' by way of a sentence that evokes both the need for critique in the Kantian (enlightenment) sense and also for a thinking that would hold itself open to questions outside and beyond that philosophical domain. Such thinking requires, in Derrida's words, 'a double gesture, a double postulation: to ensure professional competence and the most serious tradition of the university even while going as far as possible, theoretically and practically, in the most directly underground thinking about the abyss beneath the university'.[42] One should not be misled by the obvious Heideggerian allusions – to the 'abyss' [*Abgrund*], the gulf that opens up beneath the 'principle of reason' – into counting this merely a piece of irrationalist rhetoric, a mystified 'jargon of authenticity' (in Adorno's telling phrase) which invalidates Derrida's dutiful talk of keeping faith with the values of enlightened critique. For, despite his indebtedness, in certain respects Derrida has always maintained a critical distance with regard to Heidegger's thinking, a distance that has become more explicit of late with the controversy surrounding Heidegger's allegiance to the politics of National Socialism.[43] His reserve is clearly marked in this essay by allowing the language of fundamental ontology to be questioned – summoned to account for itself – in the Kantian tribunal of reason. For in the end there is no dispensing with what Derrida calls the 'desire for vigilance, for the lucid vigil, for elucidation, for critique and truth'.[44]

Now of course it may be said that one displays great naivety by taking such statements on trust; that after all this passage is cited from his essay 'Of an Apocalyptic Tone', where nothing is what it seems since everything is subject to those invisible quote-marks which make it impossible to know for sure whether Derrida means what he says. But this leads on to my second point: that we shall misread Derrida if we take him to be merely playing off rival 'positions' through a mode of intertextual ('literary') writing that subjects all truth-claims to a generalised undecidability equated with language in its rhetorical or performative aspect. For philosophy has shown itself to be not without resources when it comes to interpreting other (more or less canonical) thinkers – from Plato to Hume, Kierkegaard, Wittgenstein and Austin – who have likewise utilised the dialogue form or various techniques of indirection by way of communicating truths unamenable to straightforward constative treatment. That Derrida presses yet further in this direction – that he raises issues undreamt of by most thinkers in the mainstream analytic tradition – should at any rate not be taken as evidence that his work scarcely warrants serious attention. For there is a sense in which philosophy has always been engaged in a dialogue with that which exceeds its present powers of adequate conceptualisation, its ability to offer reasons or justifying grounds on every question that is taken to fall within its proper remit. The history of philosophy is indeed in large part the history of just such unsettling encounters, from the 'Eleatic Stranger' of Plato's *Sophist* to the puzzles and perplexities which regularly surface to trouble the thoughts of a Wittgenstein, an Austin or – as Derrida notes in passing – a thinker like Gilbert Ryle.[45] Only on the narrowest disciplinary conception of what counts as 'competent' philosophical work – the professionalised ethos for which Searle is a prominent spokesman – could Derrida's writings be ruled out of court as not measuring up to the required (pre-established) standards.

Even then his critics would be missing the point in a manner inexcusable by their own professional lights. For with Derrida, as with Austin, that challenge takes the form of a constant readiness to question received ideas, among them the constative/performative distinction, the subordinate place of rhetoric (or 'literary' style) as a mere adjunct to logic, and the assumption that genuine (rigorous) argument can have nothing to do with such frivolous 'textualist' distractions. What they both bring out – Derrida more explicitly – is the extent to which the rigour of anything that calls itself 'linguistic philosophy' must be a matter of reflecting on its own performance, noting the occurrence of anomalous or problematic details, and not (like Searle) brushing these aside in the interests of defending a speech-act theory immune to any challenge not licensed by its own self-authorising precepts and principles. Thus:

> even from the point of view of classical theory and of its necessary idealization in the construction of conceptual models, I objected to the series of exclusions practised by Searle. Inasmuch as it does not integrate the *possibility* of borderline cases, the *essential* possibility of those cases called 'marginal', of accidents, anomalies, contaminations, parasitism, inasmuch as it does not account for how, *in* the ideal concept of a structure said to be 'normal', 'standard' etc (for example, that of the promise), such a divergence is *possible*, it may be said that the formation of a general theory or of an ideal concept remains insufficient, weak, or empirical. In such a case, the idealisation practised itself remains defective; it has not taken into account certain essential predicatees. It fails to render an account of that whose ideal concept it is seeking to construct.[46]

Again, this argument takes the Kantian form of an appeal to the *conditions of possibility* for any adequate (formalised) theory of speech-acts that would meet the requirement of covering all cases including– what Searle refuses to concede – those cases that deviate from the normative ideal, and which thus create problems for the standard account. More precisely, it involves a rigorous deduction of the conditions of *im*possibility that must apply to any such project (e.g., a generalised theory of performative utterance) insofar as there will always be problematic cases – 'accidents', 'anomalies', Austinian 'misfires', etc – which that theory will either take into account (thus perforce undermining its normative claims) or exclude by an act of unwarranted *de jure* stipulation (thus proving inadequate to the task). In the above passage – from his second-round response to Searle – Derrida puts the case in explicitly Kantian (constative or transcendental-deductive) terms, since he is concerned to counter Searle's idea of deconstruction as just a kind of sophistical wordplay, a textualist ploy for evading the requirements of genuine (honestly-argued) philosophical debate. The approach is very different in

Limited Inc, his previous rejoinder, where Derrida notoriously has great fun at Searle's expense by exploiting all manner of performative ('literary') tricks and devices in order to problematise Searle's confidently orthodox assumptions. But even here – despite all the textual high jinks – there is a cogent deconstructive critique of those assumptions conducted through a reading of Austin and Searle (more precisely: of Austin *contra* Searle) that brings out the latter's manifest failure to grasp the more challenging implications of Austin's thought.

III BORDER-CROSSINGS: DERRIDA, AUSTIN, RYLE

Such is the 'logic of supplementarity' – the questioning of preconceived truth-claims, values and priorities – that Derrida discovers everywhere at work in the texts of Western logocentric tradition. But he does so always as the upshot of a reading that respects both the intricate detail of the text (including those details that would appear 'deviant' or 'marginal' from an orthodox interpretive standpoint), and also the need for argumentative rigour in the strictest philosophical sense of that term. For it is an error – albeit a deeply-rooted error, one that goes back to the inaugural moment of Western philosophy in Plato's quarrel with the poets – to think that these are mutually exclusive activities, opposed along an axis that runs (roughly speaking) between logic and rhetoric, philosophy and literature, or a discourse accountabale to reason and truth and a discourse of textual close-reading aware of its own rhetorical complications. This is why Derrida can claim Austin – outrageous though the claim must appear to a thinker like Searle – as a proto-deconstructionist *malgré lui*, one whose systematising ambitions (or whose desire to come up with a workable *theory* of speech-acts) are subject to a kind of involuntary questioning at so many crucial points in his text. Of course this is not the view taken by most commentators in the Anglo-American 'analytic' camp. For them (as for Searle) there is simply no question but that Derrida got Austin wrong, and that he did so either through sheer incompetence or out of a desire – a perverse, wrong-headed, typically 'French' desire – to obfuscate the issues and cock a snook at the protocols of reasoned argumentative debate. To which one can only respond that in his reading of Austin – as also in his readings of Plato, Kant, Husserl, Heidegger and (not least) John Searle – Derrida achieves an order of jointly exegetical and philosophical rigour that his critics would do well to emulate.

So why has his work encountered such a barrage of resistance, hostility and obdurate incomprehension? Adorno perhaps comes closest to the mark when he remarks how obsessional are the defences mounted by an unreflecting positivism when exposed to the kind of speculative thought that refuses to take language (or 'style') for granted, and which demands – like Derrida – a vigilant awareness of the non-identity between word and concept.[47] Not that such awareness has been altogether lacking in the wider analytic tradition. I have already mentioned Wittgenstein and Ryle – together with Austin – as thinkers who maintained a lively awareness of the potential within language for creating problems with any simplified – non-self-reflexive – account of meaning, reference, intentions, speech-act implicature and so forth. But in each case, especially with Wittgenstein and Austin, their texts underwent the kind of mainstream-orthodox appropriative reading which obscured those problems from view and produced on the one hand a consensus-based doctrine of 'language-games' or cultural 'forms of life', and on the other a wholesale systematic 'theory' of performative utterance. And so it has come about that the cardinal texts of 'ordinary language' philosophy have found their most subtle, intelligent, responsive and (yes) *rigorous* readers among those – not only Derrida but literary theorists like Shoshana Felman – whose powers of observation are not thus constrained by a pre-set philosophical agenda.[48]

This is (I repeat) very far from suggesting that deconstruction has no use for the 'traditional' philosophic virtues of reasoned argument, careful exposition, and fidelity to the text in hand. For, as Derrida remarks, such thinking, 'if it troubles all exclusion or simple opposition, should not capitulate to confusion, to vague approxi- mations, to indistinction: it leads instead to an extreme complication, multiplication, explication of "precise and rigorous distinctions" '.[49] That his reading of Austin is dismissed out of hand by adherents to the orthodox (Searlean) view is not so much a genuine conflict of interpretations as a comment on the current boundary-dispute between philosophy and literary theory, or – as this quarrel is often represented – between genuine (analytic) philosophy and the 'continental' sort that mostly finds a home in departments of comparative literature. Here it is worth recalling Derrida's observations, in *Limited Inc*, on the complex network of debts,

resistances and unwitting affinities that has marked the development of
these two (supposedly quite distinct) lines of thought from Kant to the
present day. Thus he asks at one point (with reference to the issue of
intentionality in speech-act theory): 'Isn't Searle ultimately more
continental and Parisian than I am?'.[50] And again, it strikes Derrida that
this curious exchange 'seems to be occurring – to take geographical
bearings – in an area that disrupts all cartography, midway between
California and Europe, a bit like the Channel, midway between Oxford
and Paris'.[51] To which he might have added Germany (or Frankfurt,
Freiburg and Heidelberg), since the main point at issue is the complex
relation that exists between linguistic philosophy in its Anglo-American
(analytical) mode and the tradition of phenomenological thought whose
chief exemplars are Husserl and Heidegger.

Gilbert Ryle is perhaps the most interesting figure for anyone
attempting to figure out this tangled genealogy of influence. For it is a
fact overlooked by most commentators that Ryle's early work included
some lengthy and detailed (albeit highly critical) essays on Husserl and
Heidegger, published at a time – the late 1930s – when as yet the lines of
battle were not so clearly drawn up.[52] Indeed one could date that parting
of the ways with some precision, at the point when Ryle concluded
(wrongly as regards Husserl) that phenomenology was just a form of
naive or uncritical 'psychologism' dressed up in false (pseudo-
transcendental) colours. All the same there is an interesting parallel to be
remarked between Ryle's later work – in books like *Dilemmas* and *The
Concept of Mind* – and Derrida's deconstructive reading of Husserl.[53]
Both thinkers start out from a principled suspicion of the appeal to
self-presence, to primordial intuitions or mentalist predicates as a means
of securing indubitable truths. Moreover, both arrive at this position
through a critique of certain deep-grained 'metaphysical' ideas (for
Ryle, the Cartesian mind/body dualism; for Derrida, the priority of
speech over writing, presence over absence, 'expressive' as opposed to
'indicative' signs, etc) which are shown to produce insoluble antinomies
when exposed to a rigorous conceptual exegesis. For Ryle and Derrida
alike this involves a negative version of the Kantian argument from
'conditions of possibility', i.e. a demonstration that it is *strictly
impossible* to maintain such dualist or logocentric principles insofar as
their logical grammar gives rise to inconsistent, aporetic or contradictory entailments.

Thus Ryle takes issue with the folk-psychology – the 'commonsense'
variant of Cartesian dualism – whose philosophic upshot is that notion

of the 'ghost in the machine' which thinkers since Descartes have vainly striven to exorcise. And he does so by invoking other, less systematically misleading instances and expressions from 'ordinary language' which enable him – in Wittgensteinian fashion – to talk philosophy down from its heights of self-imposed metaphysical delusion. Such idioms suggest (for example) that we can manage without dualist or essentialist notions like 'mind', 'intelligence', disembodied 'thought', etc, by replacing them with various adverbial modifiers, phrases on the pattern of 'doing this or that thoughtfully, carefully, attentively, skilfully, with adequate concentration' and so forth.[54] Of course there is a difference – which I should not wish to minimise – between Ryle's very 'Oxford' manner of appealing to the wisdom of ordinary language, as against the high gyrations of speculative thought, and Derrida's willingness (as commonly perceived) to pursue those gyrations to the giddy limit. But the commonplace perception is also prone to exaggerate this difference in keeping with the standard ('analytic' *versus* 'continental') typology. For on the one hand Ryle – like Austin – could just as well be called an '*extraordinary* language' philosopher in so far as he discovers all kinds of problem with our estabalished (commonsense) ways of talking and thinking. Such are the dilemmas or category-mistakes – the 'aporias', in Derridean parlance – which may indeed follow with strict necessity from the dualist conception, but whose removal would require quite a mind-wrenching effort of linguistic reform. And on the other hand Derrida is *not* just concerned – as the received wisdom would have it – to deconstruct all our taken-for-granted beliefs about mind, language, expression, self-presence, speech-act commitment, and so forth. What he does seek to question (in company with Ryle and also, be it noted, with Husserl) is the philosophers' habit of erecting those *de facto* commonsense-intuitive notions – natural and indeed indispensable in the conduct of our everyday lives – to a high point of *de jure* principle whereby they serve to exclude (to render 'perverse' or illegitimate) any dealing with marginal or problematic cases. Such a gesture of exclusion indeed returns philosophy to the stage of a dogmatic (pre-critical) adherence to truths whose very questioning is taken to constitute an affront to reason and commonsense alike.

This is what enables Searle to construct his systematic theory of speech-acts supposedly derived from – and faithful to – Austin's way of treating these issues, but in fact ignoring all the counter-evidence that surfaces in Austin's texts. For it is precisely by considering such 'deviant' or 'anomalous' instances that philosophy can enable us to see (in Wittgenstein's phrase) how a certain language-game has hitherto 'held us captive', whether through some piece of specialised (but obdurate) philosophic jargon or – just as often – some everyday, commonsense habit of talk. These are the cases that chiefly concern Derrida in *Limited Inc*, that typify the various 'dilemmas' examined by Ryle, and which crop up constantly in Austin's writing (not least in his footnotes, mock-casual parentheses, passing anecdotes, etc). To view them as lacking philosophical pertinence – or as offering no hold for rigorous analytic treatment – is an attitude complicit with the worst sorts of ingrained cultural prejudice, those that emerged with depressing regularity in the recent Cambridge 'debate'. Such counter-instances should at least give pause to anyone who thinks, like Searle, that the business of genuine (serious) philosophy is to beat the bounds between 'normal' and 'deviant' cases, between 'ordinary' and 'extraordinary' language, 'analytic' and 'continental' schools of thought, or again – as with Derrida – conceptual exegesis of the highest order and textual close-reading in the 'literary' mode. For there is simply no reason – professional motives aside – to regard this rigid demarcation of realms as anything more than a curious fact of present-day intellectual life.

Derrida makes the point with admirable precision in the course of his 'Afterword' to the exchange with Searle. The logic of deconstruction, he writes,

> can be 'other' to the point of overturning a good many habits and comforts. It can lead us to complicate – distinctly – the logic of binary oppositions and a *certain use* of the value of distinction attached to it. The latter has indeed certain limits and a history, which I have precisely tried to question. But that leads neither to 'illogic' nor to 'indistinction' nor to 'indeterminacy'. This other logic does not authorise, in theoretical discourse *as such*, any kind of approximate statement. It never renounces, as Searle in the haste of a polemic seems to do and to advocate, clear and rigorous distinction.[55]

This is not to deny that some 'literary' readers – for instance, a poet-critic-theorist like Paul Valéry – may approach the source-texts of philosophy with a different kind of analytic rigour, one more keenly attuned to their tonal or stylistic qualities, their formal attributes and (very often) their blind-spots of 'logocentric' prejudice. Even so,

Derrida writes, 'this elaboration would pass through the re-reading of all those texts ... It demands that one become engaged in it without endlessly circling around the form of those texts, that one decipher the law of their internal conflicts, of their heterogeneity, of their contradictions, and that one not simply cast an aesthete's glance over philosophical discourse'.[56] One could cite many passages to similar effect, each of them cautioning against the idea – the facile or vulgar-deconstructionist idea – that 'philosophy' can somehow be played off the field by a 'literary' reading that blithely disregards the requirements of logic and truth. This is where deconstruction parts company with New Criticism, post-structuralism and other such movements which elevate the rhetoric of multiple meaning (paradox, irony, intertextuality, etc) to a touchstone of literary value, an aesthetic ontology that finds no place for logic and its merely quotidian constraints. That the point was wholly lost upon Derrida's Cambridge antagonists – both philosophers and literary critics – says a good deal about what counts as 'serious', 'competent' debate among those whose voices were most loudly raised in defence of precisely such values.

Their petition chalked up more than ninety signatories, among them (according to a *Sunday Times* report) 'Sir John Plumb, the eminent historian, Elizabeth Anscombe, the philosopher, and Derek Brewer, the distinguished Chaucer scholar'.[57] It included the charge – unsupported (as usual) by any show of evidence or argument – that the main effect of Derrida's work had been 'to deny and dissolve those standards of evidence and argument on which all academic disciplines are based'. To which one can only respond that the charge comes back like a boomerang, whether upon those (like Miss Anscombe) who should have known better by professional avocation or those others (like Plumb and Brewer) whose knowledge of that work one may reasonably doubt. For as Derrida remarks in his 'Afterword' there is an ethical as well as a 'technical' aspect to this matter of simply *getting things right* – putting in the necessary homework – as regards deconstruction and its supposed 'irrationalist' or 'nihilist' character. What are we to think when so many (doubtless eminent and distinguished) authorities go on record with opinions that demonstrate only their ignorance of Derrida's work?

If one effect of Derrida's deconstructive readings – as likewise of Paul de Man's late essays – is to complicate the logic/rhetoric distinction, this is not for want of rigorous argument on their part, or out of some bother-headed 'literary' desire to have done with reason, logic, and truth. 'To empty rhetoric of its epistemological impact', de Man writes, 'is possible only because its tropological, figural functions are being bypassed. It is as if rhetoric could be isolated from the generality that grammar and logic have in common and considered as a mere correlative of an illocutionary power'.[58] Which is also to say that those commentators err who suppose deconstruction to be just a 'rhetorical' bag of tricks on account of its extreme – and to their minds perverse – attentiveness to matters of textual detail. Thus deconstruction's 'final insight may well concern rhetoric itself, the discovery that what is called "rhetoric" is precisely the gap that becomes apparent in the pedagogical and philosophical history of the term. Considered as persuasion, rhetoric is performative but when considered as a system of tropes, it deconstructs its own performance'.[59] Such statements would carry little weight – would indeed amount to so much empty rhetoric – were they not backed up by that level of sustained conceptual exegesis that one finds most impressively (if disconcertingly) displayed in de Man's essays on Pascal, Locke and Kant.[60] And the debate is likely to become yet more heated as deconstruction approaches the source-texts of modern analytic philosophy, pointing out some of the unresolved problems – 'aporias' in the strictest sense of that term – which accompanied Frege's strenuous attempt to demarcate the realm of logical truth from those of rhetoric, metaphor, ambiguity, and other such ills to which natural language was all too frequently prone.[61]

To be sure it is the case – as neither Derrida nor de Man would for a moment deny – that such claims are open to argued and cogent refutation; that they involve determinate values of truth and falsehood (as well as protocols of right reading) which set deconstruction firmly apart from its pseudo-deconstructive offshoots in literary criticism. But in order to demonstrate the falsity (or innacuracy) of Derrida's or de Man's readings, one would need at least to match – and at certain points to surpass – the standards of interpretive rigour and probity established in their own best work. In some few cases the adversary discourse has achieved something like this level of sustained interrogative critique. Elsewhere – as in Gasché's exemplary essay on de Man – it has started out from a position of principled resistance, and then come around, as the argument proceeded, to a standpoint of grudging but compelled respect for the force and validity of his claims.[62] (Thus de Man: '[w]hat makes a reading more or less true is the necessity of its occurrence, regardless of the reader's or of the author's wishes ... It depends, in other words, on the rigour of the reading as an argument ... Reading is an argument ... because it has to go against the grain of what one would want to happen in the name of what has to happen'.[63]) But for the most part the whole 'debate' has been characterised by the mixture of ignorance, prejudice and downright *failure to read* which stood plain to view in the Cambridge petition. No doubt it will provide fascinating material for some future cultural historian or latterday Flaubert with a relish for such catalogues of pompous fatuity and clichéd common-room wisdom. Meanwhile Derrida's writings are there – well served in English translation – for those puzzled by the Cambridge charade and willing to read for themselves.

NOTES

1. Sufficient to recount that Derrida was nominated for an Honorary Doctorate at Cambridge; the proposal challenged by (among others) two members of the University who arose to declare *non placet* at the preliminary hearing; and the award eventually confirmed – after much agitated canvassing on both sides – by a sizable (nearly two-thirds) majority when the matter was put to the vote in May 1992.
2. See for instance the extraordinary episode that Derrida narrates in his footnote to *Limited Inc* (2nd edn., Evanston, Ill.: Northwestern University Press, 1988), pp158-9.
3. Jacques Derrida, *Edmund Husserl's 'Origin of Geometry': an introduction*, trans. John P. Leavey (Pittsburgh: Duquesne University Press, 1978); *Speech and Phenomena and Other Essays on Husserl's Theory of Signs*, trans. David B. Allison (Evanston, Ill.: Northwestern University Press, 1973); 'Plato's Pharmacy', in *Dissemination*, trans. Barbara Johnson (London: Athlone Press, 1981), pp61-171; *Of Grammatology*, trans. Gayatri C. Spivak (Baltimore: John Hopkins University Press, 1975).
4. Derrida, *Of Grammatology* (*op cit*) p158.
5. *Ibid*, p158.
6. Richard Rorty, 'Philosophy as a Kind of Writing', in *Consequences of Pragmatism* (Minneapolis: University of Minnesota Press, 1982), pp89-109.
7. See Stanley Fish, *Is There a Text in This Class? The authority of interpretive communities* (Cambridge, Mass.: Harvard University Press, 1980).
8. Derrida, *Writing and Difference*, trans. Alan Bass (London: Routledge, 1978) and 'Parergon', in *The Truth in Painting*, trans. Geoff Bennington and Ian McLeod (Chicago: University of Chicago Press, 1987), pp15-147.
9. See especially Derrida, *Margins of Philosophy*, trans. Alan Bass (Chicago: University of Chicago Press, 1982).
10. *Ibid*, pp207-71.

11. Derrida, *Limited Inc* (*op cit*), pp29-107.
12. Derrida, 'Plato's Pharmacy' (*op cit*); 'The Double Session', in *Dissemination* (*op cit*), pp173-286; 'The Law of Genre', trans. Avital Ronell, *Critical Inquiry*, Vol. VII, No. 1 (1980), pp55-81; 'Coming Into One's Own', in Geoffrey Hartman (ed), *Psychoanalysis and the Question of the Text* (Baltimore: Johns Hopkins University Press, 1978), pp114-48 and 'To Speculate: on "Freud" ', in *The Post Card: from Socrates to Freud and beyond*, trans. Alan Bass (Chicago: University of Chicago Press, 1987), pp292-409.
13. See for instance Jürgen Habermas, *The Philosophical Discourse of Modernity*, trans. Frederick Lawrence (Cambridge: Polity Press, 1987) and John R. Searle, 'Reiterating the Differences: a reply to Derrida', *Glyph*, Vol. I (1977), pp198-208; also John M. Ellis, *Against Deconstruction* (Princeton, New Jersey: Princeton University Press, 1989).
14. See Derrida, 'Signature Event Context', *Glyph*, Vol. I (1977), pp172-97 and *Limited Inc* (*op cit*).
15. Christopher Norris, *Jacques Derrida* (London: Fontana, 1987).
16. J.L. Austin, *How to Do Things with Words* (London: Oxford University Press, 1963).
17. Geoffrey Galt Harpham, *The Ascetic Imperative in Culture and Criticism* (Chicago: University of Chicago Press, 1987); Simon Critchley, *The Ethics of Deconstruction: Derrida and Levinas* (Oxford: Basil Blackwell, 1992); J. Hillis Miller, *The Ethics of Reading* (New York: Columbia University Press, 1987).
18. Derrida, 'Structure, Sign and Play in the Discourse of the Human Sciences', *Writing and Difference* (*op cit*), pp278-93; p292.
19. Derrida, *Of Grammatology* (*op cit*), p55.
20. Rodolphe Gasché, *The Tain of the Mirror: Derrida and the philosophy of reflection* (Cambridge, Mass.: Harvard University Press, 1986).
21. See Paul Ricoeur, *The Conflict of Interpretations: essays in hermeneutics*, D. Ihde (ed) (Evanston, Ill.: Northwestern University Press, 1974).
22. See especially Rorty, 'Nineteenth-Century Idealism and Twentieth-Century Textualism', in *Consequences of Pragmatism* (*op cit*), pp139-59.
23. Derrida, 'Parergon', in *The Truth in Painting* (*op cit*), pp15-147.
24. P.F. Strawson, *The Bounds of Sense* (London: Methuen, 1958) and *Individuals* (London: Methuen, 1963).
25. For an interesting variant on this cross-channel exchange of stereotypes, see Jacques Bouveresse, 'Why I Am So Very UnFrench', in Alan Montefiore (ed), *Philosophy in France Today* (Cambridge: Cambridge University Press, 1983), pp9-33.
26. Paul de Man, 'Phenomenality and Materiality in Kant', in Gary Shapiro and Alan Sica (eds), *Hermeneutics: questions and prospects* (Amherst: University of Massachusetts Press, 1984), pp121-44. See also Derrida, 'Economimesis', trans. Richard Klein, *Diacritics*, Vol. XI, No. 2 (1981), pp3-25 and '*Mochlos*, ou le conflit des facultés', *Philosophie*, No. 2 (1984), pp21-53.
27. Jürgen Habermas, *The Philosophical Discourse of Modernity* (*op cit*).

28. Roland Barthes, *S/Z*, trans. Richard Miller (London: Jonathan Cape, 1975).
29. See for instance Derrida's 'Afterword' to *Limited Inc* (*op cit*), pp111-54.
30. See Rorty, 'Philosophy as a Kind of Writing' (*op cit*) and Geoffrey Hartman, *Saving the Text: literature/Derrida/philosophy* (Baltimore: Johns Hopkins University Press, 1981).
31. Derrida, 'Plato's Pharmacy' (*op cit*).
32. Derrida, *Of Grammatology* (*op cit*), p243.
33. *Ibid*, p229.
34. See Derrida, *Speech and Phenomena* (*op cit*).
35. Derrida, 'Force and Signification', in *Writing and Difference* (*op cit*), pp3-30; p8.
36. Derrida, *Edmund Husserl's 'Origin of Geometry': an introduction* (*op cit*), p46.
37. See for instance Roland Barthes, *S/Z* (*op cit*) and Colin MacCabe, *James Joyce and the 'Revolution of the Word'* (London: Macmillan, 1978).
38. See Derrida, 'The Time of a Thesis', in Alan Montefiore (ed), *Philosophy in France Today* (*op cit*), pp34-50.
39. Paul de Man, *Allegories of Reading: figural language in Rousseau, Nietzsche, Rilke, and Proust* (New Haven: Yale University Press, 1979).
40. Derrida, 'The Principle of Reason: the university in the eyes of its pupils', *Diacritics*, Vol. XIX (1983), pp3-20; p9.
41. Derrida, 'Of An Apocalyptic Tone Recently Adopted In Philosophy', trans. John P. Leavey, *The Oxford Literary Review*, Vol. VI (1984), pp3-37.
42. Derrida, 'The Principle of Reason' (*op cit*), p17.
43. See especially Derrida, *Of Spirit: Heidegger and the question*, trans. Geoff Bennington and Rachel Bowlby (Chicago: University of Chicago Press, 1989).
44. Derrida, 'The Principle of Reason' (*op cit*), p16.
45. See Derrida, *The Post Card* (*op cit*), p98.
46. Derrida, 'Afterword' to *Limited Inc* (*op cit*), pp118-9.
47. See for instance Theodor W. Adorno, *Against Epistemology: a meta-critique*, trans. Willis Domingo (Oxford: Basil Blackwell, 1982) and *Negative Dialectics*, trans. E.B. Ashton (London: Routledge & Kegan Paul, 1973).
48. See Shoshana Felman, *The Literary Speech-Act: Don Juan with J.L. Austin, or seduction in two languages*, trans. Catherine Porter (Ithaca, N.Y.: Cornell University Press, 1983) and Henry Staten, *Wittgenstein and Derrida* (Lincoln, Nebr. & London: University of Nebraska Press, 1984).
49. Derrida, *Limited Inc* (*op cit*), p128.
50. *Ibid*, p38.
51. *Ibid*, p38.
52. See Gilbert Ryle, 'Heidegger's *Sein und Zeit*' and 'Review of Martin Farber's *The Foundations of Phenomenology*', in Ryle, *Collected Papers*, Vol. 1 (London: Hutchinson, 1971), pp197-214 and 215-24.
53. Ryle, *The Concept of Mind* (London: Hutchinson, 1949) and *Dilemmas* (Cambridge: Cambridge University Press, 1953).

54. See also Ryle, *On Thinking* (Oxford: Basil Blackwell, 1979).
55. Derrida, *Limited Inc* (*op cit*), p127.
56. 'Qual Quelle: Valery's sources', in *Margins of Philosophy* (*op cit*), pp273-306, p305.
57. 'Cambridge Dons Declare War over Philosopher's Honorary Degree', *The Sunday Times*, 10 May 1992, p5.
58. Paul de Man, *The Resistance to Theory* (Minneapolis: University of Minnesota Press, 1986), pp18-9.
59. de Man, *Allegories of Reading* (*op cit*), p131.
60. de Man, 'Pascal's Allegory of Persuasion', in Stephen J. Greenblatt (ed), *Allegory and Representation* (Baltimore: Johns Hopkins University Press, 1981); 'The Epistemology of Metaphor', *Critical Inquiry*, Vol. V, No. 1 (Autumn 1978), pp13-30; 'Phenomenality and Materiality in Kant' (*op cit*).
61. See for instance Ora Avni, *The Resistance to Reference: linguistics, philosophy, and the literary text* (Baltimore: Johns Hopkins University Press, 1990); Andrea Nye, *Words of Power: a feminist reading of the history of logic* (London: Routledge, 1990); also Nye, 'Frege's Metaphors', *Hypatia*, Vol. VII, No. 2 (Spring 1992), pp18-39.
62. Rodolphe Gasché, 'Indifference to Philosophy', in Lindsay Waters (ed), *Reading de Man Reading* (Minneapolis: University of Minnesota Press, 1989).
63. de Man, Foreword to Carol Jacobs, *The Dissimulating Harmony* (Baltimore: Johns Hopkins University Press, 1978), ppvii-xiii; pxii.

INDEX OF NAMES

INDEX